ALL NEW 100 LITERACY HOURS

- Differentiated lesson plans
- Photocopiable extracts
- Covers the Early Learning Goals and NLS objectives

YEAR 6

Chris Webster

CREDITS

Author
Chris Webster

Illustrations
Mary Hall

Editor
Jane Bishop

Series Designer
Joy Monkhouse

Assistant Editors
Catherine Gilhooly

Designers
Erik Ivens &
Catherine Mason

Text © Chris Webster
© 2005 Scholastic Ltd

Designed using Adobe InDesign

Published by Scholastic Ltd
Villiers House
Clarendon Avenue
Leamington Spa
Warwickshire CV32 5PR

www.scholastic.co.uk

Printed by Bell and Bain Ltd, Glasgow.

2 3 4 5 6 7 8 9   5 6 7 8 9 0 1 2 3 4

ACKNOWLEDGEMENTS

The publishers gratefully acknowledge permission to reproduce the following copyright material:
Carcanet Press Ltd for the use of 'The Lesson' by Edward Lucie-Smith from *A Tropical Childhood* by Edward Lucie-Smith © 1961, Edward Lucie-Smith (1961, Oxford University Press). **Carlton Books Limited** for the use of 'Away from it All' by Ogden Nash from *Candy is Dandy: The Best of Ogden Nash* with an introduction by Anthony Burgess © 1994, Odgen Nash (1994, Andre Deutsch). **Jonathan Clowes Ltd** for the non-exclusive right to adapt 'Sherlock Holmes and the Green Paint' and making use of the trademarked characters Sherlock Holmes™ and Dr.Watson.™ Printed with kind permission of Jonathan Clowes Ltd., London on behalf of Andrea Plunket, the Administrator of the Sir Arthur Conan Doyle Copyrights. **David Higham Associates** for the use of 'Little Spider' by Mervyn Peake from *A Book of Nonsense* by Mervyn Peake © 1972, Mervyn Peake (1972, Peter Owen). **Houghton Mifflin** for the use of an excerpt from *A Wizard of Earthsea* by Ursula K Le Guin © 1968, 1996 The Inter-Vivos Trust for the Le Guin Children (1968, Houghton Mifflin). **Mrs. Anne Longepe** for the use of an extract from 'The Shooting of Dan McGrew' by Robert Service originally from *The Spell of the Yukon and Other Verses* published in the UK as *Songs of a Sourdough* © 1916, Robert Service (1916, Barse and Co., New York; A. & C. Black). **The Peters Fraser and Dunlop Group** (www.pfd.co.uk) on behalf of Roger McGough for the use of 'Nooligan' and 'The Lesson' by Roger McGough from *In the Glassroom* by Roger McGough © 1976, Roger McGough (1976, Jonathan Cape). **Plain English Campaign** for the use of two extracts 'Words to avoid' and 'Stop and think…' from their website www.plainenglish.co.uk and the use of the Plain English Campaign logo © 2005, Plain English Campaign. **Caroline Sheldon Literary Agency** on behalf of John Agard for the use of 'Half-caste' by John Agard from *Get Back Pimple* by John Agard © 1996, John Agard (1996, Viking). **A P Watt Limited** on behalf of The Literary Executors of the Estate of H G Wells for the use of an extract from *War of the Worlds* by H G Wells © 1897, The Literary Executors of the Estate of H G Wells (originally serialised in 1897 in Cosmopolitan magazine).

Every effort has been made to trace copyright holders for the works reproduced in this book, and the publishers apologise for any inadvertent omissions.

British Library Cataloguing-in-Publication Data
A catalogue record for this book is available from the British Library.

ISBN 0-439-971-705
ISBN 978-0439-97170-6

The right of Chris Webster to be identified as the author of this work has been asserted by him in accordance with the Copyright, Designs and Patents Act 1988.

Extracts from The National Literacy Strategy © Crown copyright. Reproduced under the terms of HMSO Guidance Note 8.

Contents

ALL NEW 100 LITERACY HOURS: YEAR 6

About the series

The books in the updated *All New 100 Literacy Hours* series offer a set of completely new term-by-term lesson plans, complete with objectives and organisation grids and accompanied, where relevant, with photocopiable texts and activity sheets. The series offers a core of material for the teaching of the English curriculum within the structure of the Literacy Hour, but now perfectly matches the recent NLS *Medium-Term Plans, Grammar for Writing*, and *Speaking, Listening and Learning* guidelines. The series also builds on current teaching ideas including providing activities to match children's preferred learning styles.

Using this book

The units of work

This book provides 100 literacy hours for Year 6 based on the *National Literacy Strategy Medium-Term Plans*, which either form a core scheme of work or can be used to supplement your existing planning. This core should be extended in several ways. For example:

● Repeating the sequence of lessons, but with different texts. For example, the first unit on narrative in Term 2, could usefully be followed by a further scary story or parody novel that you are already reading or plan to read as your class book.

● Adding additional texts. Unit 1 in Term 1 is based on two poems by John Clare and one by John Agard, and it is recommended that more of their poems are read to appreciate the range of subjects, forms and styles.

● Giving extra time for the drafting and redrafting process. This is essential if it is to be done with the thoroughness recommended in NLS exemplification, particularly the unit on extended writing in Term 3.

● It is also well worth allowing more time for final presentation. An example is Term 1, Media/plays, where the unit culminates in a performance of screenplays and an evaluation of the performances.

In addition to the above, tried-and-tested resources from previous schemes of work, other publications, or the original 100 Literacy Hours series, can be used to supplement the new materials.

The lesson plans

The lesson plans should be seen as a source of ideas, not as a straitjacket, and should therefore be used flexibly. Most lessons plans can easily be adapted for rotational use by rotating the independent and guided activities. The number of guided activities that are possible in one week will depend on the number of available adults. When planning rotation, it is important to ensure that all children experience the key activities throughout the week. If following the linear model, guided activities will usually need to involve a guided version of the independent activity, otherwise children may miss out on key experiences.

INTRODUCTION

Organisation of teaching units

Each term is divided into teaching units comprising between 5 and 10 hours. Each of the units cluster the NLS text-, sentence- and word-level objectives. The units are organised as follows:

Links to the NLS Medium-term plans

The units provide clear links to the requirements of the NLS *Medium-Term Plans*. Genres are matched exactly with appropriate texts for the age group and the range of objectives covered, as shown on the grid for

---

Unit overview
Introduction
Overview of each unit including ideas for extending units.

Organisation grid
Outlines the key activities for each lesson.

Key assessment opportunities
A bulleted list of key assessment opportunities. These will help you to plan assessment opportunities throughout each unit.

Unit lesson plans
Each unit of lesson plans is written with the following headings:

Objectives
NLS objectives including Speaking and Listening emphases.

What you need
Provides a list of resources required for each lesson.

Shared work
Sets out the shared text-, sentence- and word-level work in each lesson. Some of these objectives are taught discretely, while others are integrated into the theme of the unit as the NLS recommends.

Guided work and Independent work
Every unit contains at least two suggestions for guided work to be used if the lessons plans are re-organised on a rotational basis. The lessons also include ideas for independent group, paired or individual activities. In some units, you may wish to re-organise these, along with the suggestions for guided work, on a rotational basis, for example, when a group set of books is being shared around the class.

Plenary
Sets out what to do in the whole-class plenary session.

Differentiation
Ideas for supporting more or less able children including ideas for peer and other adult support.

---

each term. Some of the word- and sentence-level objectives identified in the *Medium-Term Plans* have been relocated from the specified units to meet the needs of specific texts and the running order of the selected units.

Differentiation

In every lesson plan, suggestions for supporting the less able and stretching the more able are given. However, it is important to use these advisedly as a child may be 'less able' in some aspects of literacy, but 'more able' in others. These suggestions should be applied when appropriate to the individual child and not be automatically given to a predetermined group. Other important considerations are children's different learning styles, and the concept of 'multiple intelligences'. Children also need to experience working individually, in pairs, and in a range of larger groups, organised in different ways to meet different educational objectives. The number of groups will depend on class size, spread of ability and learning style. Try to ensure a balance of gender and personality type in each group, and don't hesitate to separate children who cannot work well together.

Assessment

Each unit includes a list of bullet points to help with ongoing assessment. These are not intended to replace National Curriculum assessment, but represent the 'bottom line' that all the children should have achieved by the end of the unit. If a number of children have failed to achieve satisfactory standards in any of the bulleted areas, then the unit may need to be revisited (with different resources).

Using the photocopiable resources

Where there is instruction to copy material from copyright texts, you must ensure that this is done within the limits of the copying licence of your school. If pupils are using their own exercise books or paper for answers, then all photocopiable resources are reuseable.

Usually, the best way to share a resource with the class is to make a display version for an overhead projector or data projector. However, try to avoid this becoming routine. An effective alternative is to sit with the children in a circle and to work with a hard copy of the text and where possible, engage the children with actual books.

Interactive whiteboard use

Permission is granted for those pages marked as photocopiable to be used in this way. Where third party material is used, permission for interactive whiteboard use must be obtained from the copyright holder or their licensor. This information can be found in the acknowledgements at the front of the book.

Annotations

The methodology of analysing texts by annotation is used in this book. Annotations to texts are given in one margin only, without lines pointing to the textual features they describe. This allows the resource to be used both as an exemplar of annotations and as a blank resource. To make blank resources, cover or fold back the annotations when photocopying. The annotations can be used in several ways:
● Write them 'live' on an enlarged version of the blank resource, adding lines from notes to text as appropriate, to demonstrate how to annotate a text.
● Read a text with the annotations covered, discuss key points, then reveal the annotations.
● Annotate the first part of a text for demonstration purposes then ask children to complete the annotations for the rest of the text in the independent session.
● In an independent reading session, give children a jumbled up version of the annotations and ask them to link them to the appropriate text features.
● In a plenary session, display the text and notes together, and add lines from notes to text as each point is raised in discussion.

Speaking and listening

When speaking and listening is one of the main focuses of the lessons, links are made to the Primary National Strategy's *Speaking, Listening and Learning* (DfES, 2003), and to the speaking and listening emphases within the *Medium-Term Planner*. These links are also highlighted in the objectives grid through the use of a logo.

Children will use speaking and listening as a process skill in every lesson. To encourage this, particular emphasis is given to children working with 'talk partners'. When a larger group is needed, 'talk partners' can join into fours. Groups of this size are ideal for discussion and collaborative work as they provide a range of opinion and yet are not too large to make full participation difficult. It is important to vary group organisation so that children experience working with different partners with different approaches or abilities.

Creativity

Recent reports have emphasised the importance of creativity and creativity is embedded within many of the lessons in this book. Also encourage creativity by using some of the following ideas:
● Children as Real Writers - encourage children to see themselves as real writers writing for real purposes. This means giving them a strong sense of audience and purpose, using redrafting techniques and finding a way of 'publishing' completed work.
● Writing Journals - encourage the children to write something in their journal every day. This can be anything they like - diary entry, story, poem, exploration of a problem, and so on. This is the one place where grammar, and punctuation do not matter. The aim is to develop writing fluency, as in a free flow between thought and written page.
● First-Hand Experiences - many NLS writing tasks are responses to texts. Balance this by using stimulating 'real-life' starting points such as visits, visitors, artefacts, and so forth.
● Experimentation - encourage the children to play with ideas, and explore alternatives. Positively encourage them to suggest alternative tasks.
● Writing Materials - provide inspiring media such as paper in various colours and sizes; a variety of pens and pencils (felt-tipped pens, calligraphic pens); rulers; scissors; glue; DTP and presentation software; a clip art library; a colour printer.

Learning styles

Researchers have identified three different learning styles: auditory, kinaesthetic and visual. Most children will use a mixture of all three styles, but in some children, one style will predominate. Many lessons in this book offer specific opportunities for different learning styles.

Media and ICT

There have been major advances in media and ICT. We need to give more emphasis to media education and ICT in the primary classroom. This can be done by showing film versions of books and documentaries on non-fiction topics, and by ensuring that, every time writing takes place, at least one group is writing on a word processor and that children take it in turns to do their research via the internet.

Unit	Text level	Sentence level	Word level	No of hours	Text(s)	Links to GfW, S&L	Outcomes
Poetry	3, 4, 10	1	7	5	To Anna, Three Years Old and 'First Love' by John Clare; 'Half-caste' by John Agard	GfW 44, S&L 60	Personification poems
Narrative writing	7	1, 4, 5	6	10	'Say Cheese' and 'Van Gogh's Ghost' by Chris Webster; *Short and Scary!* by Louise Cooper	GfW 45–47	Short story analysis; own short scary stories
Media/plays	1, 2, 3, 6, 8, 9	1, 6	7	5	Novel and film versions of *A Christmas Carol*	GfW 47, S&L 61	Screenplay; film review
Journalistic	8, 12, 15, 16, 18	6	10	5	Newspaper articles	S&L 50	Newspaper article; group front page
Biography/autobiography	3, 5, 8, 11, 14	1, 4, 5	5	5	Biography of John Clare	S&L 64, 65	Biography from research; autobiography
Reports	13, 17, 18	2, 3, 5	8	5	Report on Mars	GfW 45	Class booklet of reports

TERM 2

Unit	Text level	Sentence level	Word level	No of hours	Text(s)	Links to GfW, S&L	Outcomes
Poetry	3, 4, 5, 6, 14	3	6	5	'The Lesson' and 'Nooligan' by Roger McGough; 'Away From it All' by Odgen Nash; 'Little Spider' by Mervyn Peake; 'The Lesson' by Edward Lucie-Smith	S&L 65	Poetry analysis and critical commentary.
Narrative 1	1, 7, 11	3		5	*The Last Vampire* by Willis Hall		Textual analysis. Oral and written scary stories using stock characters, parody and flashback.
For and against	15, 16, 18, 19	5	1, 8	10	'Internet dangers and delights'; debate speech on internet use.	GfW 51. S&L, 56, 58, 62, 63	Balanced oral and written arguments. Group debate.
Narrative 2	2, 8, 9, 10, 12	3		5	*The War of the Worlds* by HG Wells; 'The Shooting of Dan McGrew' by Robert Service; *A Wizard of Earthsea* by Ursula le Guin; 'Sherlock Holmes and the Green Paint' by Chris Webster		Genre story writing in different forms.
Formal	17, 20	2, 5	8	5	Product guarantee; complaint correspondence; guide to plain English	S&L 66	Role-play. Formal letter. Simplified guarantee.

Before the KS2 tests

Unit	Text level	Sentence level	Word level	Hours	Text(s)	Links to GfW, S&L	Outcomes
Reading and writing narrative	7, 12, 18, 21	1, 4		5	'Future School' by Chris Webster; mock test papers		Test practice in reading and writing narrative
Poetry	4, 6	1	1, 3, 4	5	'Haunted Hide and Seek' by Chris Webster		Test practice in reading poetry
Reading and writing non-fiction	15, 19	1, 3		5	Explanations and reports		Test practice in reading and writing non-fiction

After the KS2 tests

Unit	Text level	Sentence level	Word level	Hours	Text(s)	Links to GfW, S&L	Outcomes
Poetry	2, 3, 4, 7	2, 4	6, 7	5	Four 'Lucy' poems by William Wordsworth	S&L 63, 65	Essay on sequence of poems. Own sequence of short poems
Authors and texts	1, 5, 6, 7, 8, 9, 12	1, 2, 3		5	*Mrs Frisby and the Rats of NIMH* by Robert C O'Brien; *Greyfriars Bobby* by Eleanor Atkinson	GfW 54	Reading journal. Comparison essay
Extended narrative	10, 14	1, 4	6, 7	5	Story cubes	S&L 60, 67	Extended animal story
Impersonal writing	16, 17, 20	3, 4	5, 6, 7	5	Explanation, magazine report, magazine review	S&L 65	Product report and review

UNIT 1

Poetry

This unit is based on the work of two very different poets, John Clare (1793–1864) and John Agard (b1949). It is recommended that children read several poems by these poets and the unit is extended over two weeks. The poems of John Clare are available in collections and on the internet (www.poemhunter.com), and John Agard has several collections of children's poetry in print, such as *Half-Caste* (Hodder) and *We Animals Would Like a Word with You* (Red Fox). Guided work on personification in Hour 1 meets a key objective and is also essential to the independent work in Hour 5. It is therefore important to rotate it throughout the week. If this is difficult to organise, teach it to the whole class in one of the shared sessions. Hours 4 and 5 link to Unit 44 in *Grammar for Writing*.

Hour	Shared text-level work	Shared word-/ sentence-level work	Guided and independent work	Plenary
1 To Anna	Reading and analysing poem.	Revising and experimenting with personification.	Analysing the poem in detail.	Noting themes and ideas in the poem.
2 First Love	Reading a love poem; noting poetic language.	.	Analysing the poem in detail.	Noting themes, patterns and language style.
3 A modern poet	Reading 'Half-Caste'; sharing first impressions.	Examining dialect and punctuation and how this affects reading and understanding.	Analysing this poem in detail.	Discussing themes.
4 Analysis print-out	Beginning to construct a full analysis of one of the poems.	Revising parts of speech and word classes and noting the effect of particular examples in the poems.	Writing a full analysis of their chosen poem.	Checking fluency of writing; comparing responses.
5 Personification	Revising personification; shared writing of personification poem.	Consolidating understanding of parts of speech.	Writing poems; checking them with response/criticism partners.	Sharing poems, noting successful personification.

Key assessment opportunities
● Are the children familiar with the work of two established poets?
● Can they respond to literature considering mood, expression, verse form, figures of speech, personification and themes?
● Can they write their own poems inspired by those read?

To Anna

Objectives

NLS

T4: To be familiar with the work of some established authors, to know what is special about their work, and to explain their preferences in terms of authors, styles and themes.

W7: To understand how words and expressions have changed over time, eg old verb endings -*st* and -*th* and how some words have fallen out of use, eg *yonder, thither.*

What you need

● Photocopiable pages 17 and 18.

Shared text-level work

● Display photocopiable page 17 and ask the children to imagine it is a hi-tech device for analysing poems. First, they need a poem to analyse.

● Display the first poem on photocopiable page 18. Explain that John Clare was a farm worker who lived over 150 years ago, best known for his poems about nature.

● Read the poem a couple of times. Explain any difficult words and sentence patterns. When the children understand the poem, ask them to talk in pairs for a few minutes about their first impressions, and to jot down any questions they have. Share first impressions.

● Now go through the PoetryPod section by section up to Data entry 4. Revise/teach each term as necessary.

Shared word-level work

● Explain that, in older literature, we come across words that have changed or fallen out of use, such as the pronouns *thou* and *ye* and verb endings -*est* and -*eth*. Look for examples of archaic words in the poem.

● Revise or teach the term personification: a form of metaphor in which language relating to human action, motivation and emotion refers to non-human things: *the weather is smiling on us today; love is blind.*

● Help the children to understand personification by exploring some traditional examples:

Idea, quality, object...	...is given human qualities as:	...with the effect:
love	Cupid – a blindfolded young boy with a bow and arrow	describes how anyone can suddenly fall in love

● Next, ask the children to see the personification of the willow tree in the poem (in verse 2, it is an ancient invalid daring to lean over the deepest water). What other examples of personification are there?
'brook that leaps'
'walls that stride'

Differentiation

Less able

● Remove 'figure of speech' from the PoetryPod, but let children work on figures of speech in guided work at some point during the week.

More able

● Enhance the PoetryPod to make PoetryPod+, which includes data entry boxes for effects of sound (alliteration, onomatopoeia and assonance) and patterns (repetition).

Guided and independent work

● Ask the children to work in pairs to use the PoetryPod (entries 1 to 4 only for now) to analyse the poem.

Plenary

● Draw attention to Data entry 6. Explain that every poem expresses an idea (or ideas) and that this is the theme of the poem.

● What is the underlying theme of this poem? (The poet's joy in his daughter's delight in nature.) Work together to fill in Data entry 6.

● Conclude the lesson by discussing questions jotted down earlier – how far have they been answered?

First Love

<table>
<tr><td valign="top">

Objectives

NLS
T3: To articulate personal responses to literature, identifying why and how a text affects the reader.
T4: To be familiar with the work of some established authors, to know what is special about their work, and to explain their preferences in terms of authors, styles and themes.

What you need
● Photocopiable pages 17 and 18.

</td><td valign="top">

Shared text-level work

● Explain to the children that when John Clare was at school, he fell in love with a beautiful blue-eyed blonde girl called Mary Joyce. But later on, her father, who thought Clare was too poor, stopped them getting married. This poem is about John Clare's love for Mary.

● Read 'First Love'. Again, go over difficult words and sentence constructions and ask the children to talk in pairs for a few minutes about the poem and to note any questions. Share first impressions and questions.

● Revise the terms simile and metaphor and ask the children if they can find any similes in the poem. If necessary, give the children the clue to look for the word '*like*' then find what is being compared to what. For example, '*Her face it bloomed like a sweet flower*'.

● Then ask the children if they can find any metaphors in the poem. Tell them to look for statements that are not literally true. For example, '*Words from my eyes did start*'.

● Finally, look for examples of personification in the poem: '*They spoke as chords do from the string.*'

● Demonstrate how to fill in Data entry 5, taking prompts from the children where possible. Explain each entry as you make it, and emphasise that explaining the effect, though not always easy, is the most important thing.

Figure of speech		Things compared	Effect
Simile	√	her face and a flower	it emphasises her beauty
Metaphor	√	the way he looked at her is compared to speaking	it describes a very expressive look
Personification	√	words and the strings of a musical instrument	he wants to say something beautiful and harmonious to her

● NB. Ask the children to copy out the table on the back of the sheet to record any other similes and metaphors, for example, '*blood burnt round my heart.*'

Guided and independent work

● Ask the children to work in pairs to use the PoetryPod (all six entries) to analyse 'First Love'.

Plenary

● As Hour 1 for a five day unit.
● For a ten day unit, analyse at least two more poems by John Clare. Discuss recurring patterns in his poems, for example the verse forms he uses most (traditional rhyming poetry), how he uses language (archaic language with some local dialect), and common themes (nature, love).
● Also, ask the children to talk about their personal responses: What did the poem make you think and feel?

</td></tr>
</table>

Differentiation

Less able
● Remove 'figure of speech' from the PoetryPod, but let children work on figures of speech in guided work at some point during the week.

More able
● Enhance the PoetryPod to make PoetryPod+, which includes data entry boxes for effects of sound (alliteration, onomatopoeia and assonance) and patterns (repetition).

A modern poet

Objectives

NLS
T4: To be familiar with the work of some established authors, to know what is special about their work, and to explain their preferences in terms of authors, styles and themes.
S1: To revise from Y5: the conventions of standard English; adapting texts for particular readers and purposes.
Year 5 Term 3 W9: To understand how words vary across dialects.

What you need
● Photocopiable pages 17 and 19.

Shared text-level work

● Explain that this lesson introduces a poem by a poet very different from John Clare. John Agard was born in British Guyana and came to Britain in 1977. In 1998 he became the first Poet in Residence at the BBC. His poetry is full of fun, but he also writes about the issues involved as a black person living in a mainly white country.
● Read 'Half-caste' aloud to the children.
● Then read it again with the children and use the first few lines of the second verse to explain the spellings used to represent West Indian dialect.
● Explain the title and discuss any difficult vocabulary or unfamiliar names such as Picasso and Tchaikovsky, and encourage the children to interpret metaphorical imagery such as standing on one leg.
● Ask them what the poem is about. What is the poet saying at the end of the poem?
● When you are sure that the children have understood the poem, ask them to talk in pairs for a few minutes to note responses and questions. Share these first impressions and read the poem again.

Shared word- and sentence-level work

● Ask the children to point out the dialect words and highlight them on the text (for example, *wha, yu, an*, and so on). Prompted by the children, write the meanings or conventional spellings as near as possible to each word (they are all easy to deduce).
● Note how Agard's punctuation differs from standard English. How is this apt for his purpose? (He is writing dialect poetry and wishes to emphasise its difference from Standard English.)
● Discuss why John Agard uses West Indian dialect. (It emphasises his identity; it is particularly effective when writing about racial issues. It also affects the way the poem is read aloud.)

Differentiation

Less able
● Remove 'figure of speech' from the PoetryPod, but let children work on figures of speech in guided work at some point during the week.

More able
● Enhance the PoetryPod to make PoetryPod+, which includes data entry boxes for effects of sound (alliteration, onomatopoeia and assonance) and patterns (repetition).

Guided and independent work

● Ask the children to work in pairs to use the PoetryPod to analyse 'Half-caste', leaving Data entry 6 until after discussion in the plenary session.

Plenary

● For a five-day unit, discuss how Agard handles the theme of discrimination (see Shared word- and sentence-level work) before asking the children to complete Data entry 6.
● For a ten-day unit, analyse at least two more poems by John Agard, then discuss recurring patterns in his poems, such as his verse form (mainly free verse), how he uses language (often writes in West Indian dialect) and common themes (humour, relationships, the issues affecting black people).

Objectives

NLS
T3: To articulate personal responses to literature, identifying why and how a text affects the reader.
S1: To revise from Y5 the different word classes, eg prepositions.

What you need

● Display version of one of the children's PoetryPods
● the children's completed PoetryPods
● photocopiable pages 17 and 19.

Differentiation

Less able
● Remove 'figure of speech' from the PoetryPod, but let children work on figures of speech in guided work at some point during the week.

More able
● Ask children to compare the work of the two Johns. Either:
● compare each section at a time, for example verse forms, or:
● write about one poet first, then the other, referring back to the first poet where there are interesting comparisons to make.

Analysis print-out

Shared text-level work

● Explain to the children that, if the PoetryPod was real, all they would have to do now is press a button and a full analysis of each poem would be compiled and printed out. However, it is not real, so they will have to write the analysis themselves! Explain that the PoetryPod can be used as a writing frame because each data entry section will become one paragraph.
● Display the child's PoetryPod and demonstrate how to turn the entries into sentences and paragraphs. Give a commentary as you write. For example, write:

'First Love', by John Clare, is a poem which describes what it feels like when you suddenly fall in love.

My first impression of the poem was that it was very true to life, especially the way it described how he turned pale and was embarrassed...

While you are saying something like:

I am putting the information in boxes 1a and 1b together to form one paragraph. I am starting a new paragraph for Data entry 2, and am making a short paragraph out of the notes.

Shared word- and sentence-level work

● Quickly revise the following word classes as a better understanding of them will help the children with Data entry 3b: adjective, adverb, verb. Use the definitions in the NLS Glossary as a starting point, then look for effective examples in one of the poems.
● Ask the children to try to explain why each example is effective. For example, the verb '*struck*' emphasises how John Clare suddenly fell in love. The adjective '*sweet*' tells us that, though love came like a sudden blow, it was beautiful, not painful.

Guided and independent work

● Visual learning: ask each child to choose one of the poems they have analysed during the unit and to write an analysis print-out as demonstrated in whole class work. Encourage them to use ICT to maintain the technological feel.

Plenary

● Choose children to read out one or two paragraphs from their poetry analysis print-outs. Briefly discuss what they have said about the particular section of the poem and give advice, where appropriate, about turning the data into more fluent sentences and paragraphs.
● Compare different responses to the same section of poem. Discuss that there can be several different responses to the same piece of writing. Are the children surprised that this is so? Can they think of any reasons for this?

Personification

Objectives

NLS
T10: To write own poems experimenting with active verbs and personification; produce revised poems for reading aloud individually.
S1: To revise from Y5 the different word classes, eg prepositions.
S&L
60 Group discussion and interaction: To understand and use a variety of ways to criticise constructively and respond to criticism.

What you need
● The children's notes on personification.

Shared text-level work
● Remind the children of the work they have been doing on personification throughout the week. Explain that they are going to write their own personification poems using the following pattern:
● First word – personified quality or thing.
● Verse form – free verse, no more than ten syllables per line, four lines per stanza.
● Active verbs to begin most lines.
● Demonstrate this by scribing an example like the following, commentating as you write:

Verse	Commentary
Love sneaks up craftily from behind mugs you in the street robs you of your peace leaves you sobbing on your pillow	The first word is the quality I am personifying – but notice that this is not Cupid – I am personifying love in my own way. The next three lines begin with active verbs.
Love takes over your life monopolises your mobile phone fills it with soppy text messages like I luv u do u luv me 2?	I am starting a new stanza with the quality I am personifying. I am trying to give a modern personification of love so I am referring to mobile phones. The last line is in txt msg style.

● Ask the children for ideas for a third stanza and continue scribing.

Shared sentence-level work
● Consolidate recognition of parts of speech by asking the children to find in the above examples nouns, verbs, adverbs, adjectives, prepositions. (Pronouns, conjunctions and connectives will be covered in Unit 2.)

Guided and independent work
● Ask the children to work in pairs for discussion as they come up with ideas and create their poem, but to produce individual personification poems.
● Tell the children to try out their first drafts by reading aloud to their partners and to redraft on the basis of the partner's advice.
● Advise response partners to check that the first word is the quality or thing that is personified and to check that the personification actually works.

Differentiation

Less able
● Ask children to write poems with one stanza only in the first instance.

More able
● Ask children to develop their poems by using rhyming verse, and/or including similes and metaphors.

Plenary
● Ask some of the children to read their poems aloud. Tell the rest of the class to listen carefully for the effect of the personification.
● Discuss how vividly the personification helped to express the quality or thing that it represented.

PoetryPod

INPUT   MIC

ON/OFF   Data entry 1a

Title of poem and
name of poet

Data entry 1b

Basic information about the poem. Perhaps state the subject of the
poem in one sentence

Data entry 2

Your first impressions of the poem

Enjoyment LED (shade)

Difficulty LED (shade)

MAX

Data entry 3a

Words and phrases from the poem that create a mood or effect on the reader

Data entry 3b

Expressive adjectives, adverbs and verbs

MAX

MIN

Data entry 4	Data entry 5
Free verse	Figure of speech
Blank verse	Simile
Rhyming verse (and form, if known)	Metaphor
No of syllables in first line	Personification
No of stresses in first line	Things compared
Rhyme scheme	Effect

MIN

DATA

READ   Data entry 6

Explain the ideas that the poet is writing about.

OK

PRINT

Analysis print-out slot

USB

TERM 1

To Anna, Three Years Old

My Anna, summer laughs in mirth,
  And we will of the party be,
And leave the crickets in the hearth
  For green fields' merry minstrelsy.

joy

beetles

fireplace

music

The old pond with its water weed
  And danger-daring willow tree,
Who leans, an ancient invalid,
  O'er spots where deepest waters be.

over

The ivy-covered walls that stride
  O'er where the meadow water falls
Will turn thee from thy path aside
  To gaze upon the mossy walls.

you

your

And limpid brook that leaps along,
  Gilt with the summer's burnished gleam
Stoppeth thy little tale or song
  To gaze upon the crimping stream.

clear stream

golden

polished

stops

'rippling'

I see thee now with little hand
  Catch at each object passing by,
The happiest thing in all the land
  Except the bee and butterfly.

First Love

I ne'er was struck before that hour
With love so sudden and so sweet.
Her face it bloomed like a sweet flower
And stole my heart away complete.
My face turned pale as deadly pale,
My legs refused to walk away,
And when she looked, what could I ail?
My life and all seemed turned to clay.

never

And then my blood rushed to my face
And took my sight away.
The trees and bushes round the place
Seemed midnight at noonday.
I could not see a single thing,
Words from my eyes did start;
They spoke as chords do from the string
And blood burnt round my heart...

*Two poems by
John Clare*

Half-caste

Excuse me
standing on one leg
I'm half-caste

Explain yuself
wha you mean
when yu say half-caste
yu mean when picasso
mix red an green
is a half-caste canvas/
explain yuself
wha yu mean
when yu say half-caste
yu mean when light an shadow
mix in de sky
is a half-caste weather/
well in dat case
england weather
nearly always half-caste
in fact some o dem cloud
half-caste till dem overcast
so spiteful dem dont want de sun pass
ah rass/
explain yuself
wha yu mean
when yu say half-caste
yu mean when tchaikovsky
sit down at dah piano
an mix a black key
wid a white key
is a half-caste symphony/

Explain yuself
wha yu mean
Ah listening to yu wid de keen
half of mih ear
Ah lookin yu wid de keen
half of mih eye
an when I'm introduced to you
I'm sure you'll understand
why I offer yu half-a-hand
an when I sleep at night
I close half-a-eye
consequently when I dream
I dream half-a-dream
an when moon begin to glow
I half-caste human being
cast half-a-shadow
but yu must come back tomorrow

wid de whole of yu eye
an de whole of yu ear
an de whole of yu mind

an I will tell yu
de other half
of my story

John Agard

UNIT 2

Narrative writing

This unit is based on two short stories: *Say Cheese!*, and *Van Gogh's Ghost*, both of which are included in the resources. However, a selection of other stories will be needed for further analysis. *Short and Scary!* by Louise Cooper (OUP) is particularly recommended. The advantage of this collection is that most stories are between 250 and 450 words in length – similar to the length of story that would be expected of a Year 6 child. Also, like the two stories mentioned above, they are stories in the horror genre, and thus contribute to the range of genres covered during the year. Each reading hour is followed by a writing hour in which the children are helped to apply what they have learned to writing their own story, step by step. Additional literacy hours should be allocated for the redrafting and presentation of their stories. Sentence-level objectives are addressed by a mini-course in sentence-building in the guided sessions. As sentence-building is the subject of several key objectives in Year 6, as well as the KS2 Test Marking Schemes, the guided sessions in the unit should be seen as essential, not optional, and every effort should be made to ensure that every child experiences them at some point. The unit matches the medium-term plans for Narrative writing 1 and 2. Hours 6, 8 and 9 make use of activities from Units 45, 46 and 47 of *Grammar for Writing*.

Hour	Shared text-level work	Shared word-/ sentence-level work	Guided and independent work	Plenary
1 Opening	Revising story structure; reading opening of short story.	Examining conjunctions that link clauses within a sentence.	Using conjunctions; analysing a short story opening.	Beginning a 'good short story' checklist.
2 Van Gogh's Ghost (opening)	Demonstrating writing the opening of a story.	Revising conjunctions.	Using opening conjunctions, discussing meanings; writing opening to own short scary story.	Checking good story openings.
3 Build-up	Examining a story's build-up.	Revising pronouns and relative pronouns.	Using pronouns; analysing a story's build-up.	Adding to the story checklist.
4 Van Gogh's Ghost (build-up)	Adding the build-up section to the class story.	Finding relative pronouns in the text.	Using relative pronouns; developing own stories.	Using the checklist to identify good build-ups.
5 Dilemma	Reading and analysing the next section of the story.	Revising dialogue punctuation.	Combining clauses; continuing their stories.	Adding 'dilemma' to the short story checklist.

UNIT 2

Hour	Shared text-level work	Shared word-/ sentence-level work	Guided and independent work	Plenary
6 Van Gogh's Ghost (dilemma)	Writing the dilemma/ problem in the class story.	Revising connectives, particularly temporal and causal.	Using connectives in sentences; continuing own stories.	Sharing and evaluating dilemma story sections.
7 Events	Reading a story to see introduction of significant events.	Examining different sentence structures and lengths.	Exploring sentences containing phrases in apposition; annotating a story for exciting events.	Adding 'events' to the story checklist.
8 Van Gogh's Ghost (events)	Adding events to the class story.	Finding participle phrases in the story.	Using participle phrases; adding events to their stories.	Sharing and evaluating this section of their stories.
9 Ending	Reading the ending of the story; discussing plot types.	Revising active and passive sentences.	Experimenting with active and passive sentences; evaluating the story ending and plot type.	Completing the checklist.
10 Van Gogh's Ghost (ending)	Ending of the class story.	Noting use of paragraphs and complex sentences.	Using different methods of sentence construction; ending their own stories.	Reading some of the complete stories.

Key assessment opportunities
● Can the children read and recite poems, paying attention to punctuation and rhyme?
● Have they used simple poetry structures to write their own poems?
● Do they use phonological and graphical knowledge to spell words?
● Do they understand that words with the same sounds may be spelled differently?
● Is their knowledge of long-vowel digraphs secure?

UNIT 2 HOUR 1 📖 Narrative writing

Opening

Objectives

Early Learning Goals
Reading p62–63

Stepping Stone
Begin to recognise some familiar words.

NLS
T7: To plan quickly and effectively the plot, characters and structure of their own narrative writing.
S5: To form complex sentences through, eg using different connecting devices.

What you need

● Photocopiable page 32
● selection of other short stories (such as *Short and Scary!*).

Shared text-level work

● Recap elements of story structure from Year 5. Write these headings on the board: Opening, Build-up, Dilemma, Events, Ending and briefly talk about each one. Also, talk about Characters and how they are central to a plot.
● Focus on the opening of stories. Ask the children what types of opening they know, for example dialogue, description of character, description of setting.
● Read the first two sections on photocopiable page 32, keeping *Say Cheese!* hidden. Use it to confirm and supplement the ideas suggested by the children.
● Next, reveal and read the opening of *Say Cheese!* Ask the children which of the features in the first two sections can be found in this story opening (*asking the reader a question; introducing something intriguing; relying on portraying character through action and dialogue*). Mark them with arrows.

Shared sentence-level work

● Begin by revising how conjunctions link clauses within sentences:

Co-ordinating conjunctions join two clauses of equal weight.	Subordinating conjunctions join a clause of lesser importance to a main clause.
and, but, or, so	after, although, because, before, if, since, though, until, when, where, while

● Ask the children to find examples in *Say Cheese!* (*and, but*).

Guided and independent work

● Start the mini-course in sentence building with one group, on conjunctions. Make up sentences like the following and help the children to complete them using conjunctions from the list above.
1. In the country of Romania is an ancient castle ___ the legendary Count Dracula used to live.
2. Jonathan Harker had just finished making plans for his journey ___ an unexpected problem arose.
● Ask other pairs to read and analyse the opening of another short story (refer to it as Story 2) using the points listed in the first two sections, and then to discuss and make notes about these questions:

● What grabs the reader in this opening?
● Who are the characters and how are they introduced?
● What do you think will happen next?

Differentiation

Less able
● Allocate suitably accessible stories – those in Short and Scary! are ideal.

More able
● Give children stories with more challenging vocabulary and sentence construction.

Plenary

● Tell the children that, during the week, they are going to draw up a class checklist entitled *How to write a good story*. The first section is *Opening*. Ask them what they would like to write in their checklist. Refer them to the main points of the lesson, particularly their responses to question one during independent work.

Van Gogh's Ghost (opening)

Objectives

NLS
T7: To plan quickly and effectively the plot, characters and structure of their own narrative writing.
S1: To revise from Y5: re-expressing sentences in a different order; the construction of complex sentences.
S5: To form complex sentences through, eg using different connecting devices.

What you need
● Photocopiable pages 32 and 37
● checklist from Hour 1.

Shared text-level work
● Explain to the children that you are going to write the opening of a story. You can write your own story, or use photocopiable page 37. Begin by introducing the story: it is about a modern artist who sees the ghost of the famous Impressionist painter, Vincent Van Gogh.
● As you write, give a commentary on what you are doing and why. For example: I am going to begin with a description. Look how effective it is to go straight into a description without any clichéd 'story-telling' language...
● Ask the children to look at the options for openings (see photocopiable page 32) to identify the techniques you are using (*introducing something intriguing*).

Shared sentence-level work
● Revise conjunctions from Hour 1, and ask the children if they can find in your text any examples used at the beginning of a sentence:
Although the picture was just paint and canvas, it felt as though a real vase of sunflowers had been brought into the room.

Guided and independent work
● Continue the work on conjunctions with a guided group. Explain that conjunctions can also be used at the beginning of a sentence. Use the two following clauses as examples:

● he tried to escape
● he found out the truth about Count Dracula
to give:
● *When* he found out the truth about Count Dracula, he tried to escape.
● Discuss how, if the clauses were swapped around, the meaning would be basically the same but the emphasis would be different. (*He tried to escape when he found out the truth about Count Dracula.*)

● Give the children several pairs of clauses to experiment with and encourage them to create their own to challenge each other.
● Remind the rest of the children that they have now looked at three different story openings. Ask them to decide which opening was most effective and use it as a model for the opening of their own scary story.
● Tell them to share ideas with a response partner, but to write individually.
● Ask some children to write on OHT in this and following sessions so that their work can be used in the plenary.

Plenary
● Discuss the story openings written on the OHTs. Ask the class to use the checklist to identify features of good openings.
● Also ask the children to identify any conjunctions that have been used to build complex sentences.

Differentiation

Less able
● Ask children to write an opening very similar to the one modelled in whole class work.

More able
● Encourage children to include at least one sentence with an initial conjunction.

Build-up

Objectives

NLS
T7: To plan quickly and effectively the plot, characters and structure of their own narrative writing.
S5: To form complex sentences through, eg using different connecting devices.

What you need
● Photocopiable pages 32 and 33
● selection of other short stories
● checklist from Hour 2.

Shared text-level work
● Tell the children that this lesson focuses on the next section in a story – build-up.
● Re-read the opening of *Say Cheese!* on photocopiable page 32, and ask the children what they think would be a good build-up.
● Display photocopiable page 33, keeping the story hidden, and read through the bullet points. Use it to confirm and supplement ideas about build-up suggested by the children.
● Next, reveal and read the build-up of *Say Cheese!*. Ask the children to help you to identify and mark with arrows the features from the bullet points that can be found in the story opening (*making the characters do something; lulling the reader into a false sense of security*).

Shared sentence-level work
● Revise or teach the following terms: pronouns replace nouns to avoid repetition. Relative pronouns do this and join clauses together. The most commonly used relative pronouns are who, whose, which and that.
● Ask the children if they can find an example in the story. (...near the rockery, which made the best background...)

Guided and independent work
● Continue the mini-course in sentence building with relative pronouns, such as, *which, that, who, whose, whom*. Make up pairs of clauses like the following and ask the children to link them using suitable relative pronouns:

> ● The count took me to a room
> ● I had never seen the room before
> to give:
> ● The count took me to a room *that* I had never seen before.

● Ask the rest of the children, in pairs, to re-read the opening of Story 2 and to read straight on into the next section, the build-up.
● Next, ask them to analyse the build-up of Story 2, annotating the relevant parts in the text from the bullet points on resource 33.
● If the build-up introduces a character, ask the children to annotate it using the appropriate bullet points from photocopiable page 32.
● Ask the children to discuss and make notes about the following questions:

> ● What new things kept your interest?
> ● How is the main character developing?
> ● What new characters have been introduced?
> ● What do you think will be the main dilemma or problem in this story?

Differentiation

Less able
● Allocate suitably accessible stories – those in Short and Scary! are ideal.

More able
● Give children stories with more challenging vocabulary and sentence construction.

Plenary
● Work with the children to write the second section, the build-up, of the class checklist.

Van Gogh's Ghost (build-up)

Objectives

NLS
T7: To plan quickly and effectively the plot, characters and structure of their own narrative writing.
S5: To form complex sentences through, eg using different connecting devices.

What you need
● Photocopiable pages 33 and 37
● children's copies of photocopiable page 33
● checklist from Hour 3.

Shared text-level work

● Demonstrate how to write the build-up of a story, using photocopiable page 37 if required. Encourage the children to contribute ideas if appropriate. As you write, give a commentary on what you are doing and why. For example, *I started the story with description, so now I am using dialogue to introduce the main character and get the story moving...*
● Ask the children to look at the checklist on photocopiable page 33 to see which techniques you are using. Encourage volunteers to mark these with arrows as before.

Shared sentence-level work

● Revise relative pronouns from Hour 3, and ask the children if they can find in your text any relative pronouns used to insert a clause between commas or between a comma and a full stop. For example:
...sighed Max, who had been hoping for more.

Guided and independent work

● Work with the guided group to revise the use of relative pronouns between two clauses (see Hour 2). Then explain that sometimes, the second clause has to be inserted into the first as close as possible to the noun it refers to, as in this example:

> the vampire smelled blood +
> the vampire was emerging from his tomb =
> The vampire, *who* was emerging from his tomb, smelled blood.

● Give the children similar pairs of clauses to experiment with and ask them to think up their own.
● Ask the other children to share ideas with their response partners about what their own stories could be building up to. Then, using these and ideas from the stories they have read as well as the checklist ask them to write the build-up in their own scary stories begun in Hour 2.

Differentiation

Less able
● Ask children to write a build-up very similar to that modelled in shared work – dialogue between the main character and another character.

More able
● Encourage children to include an example of a relative pronoun that introduces an inserted clause.

Plenary

● Discuss the story build-ups written on the OHTs, and use the checklist to identify the features of a good build-up.
● Ask the children to identify any conjunctions and relative pronouns that have been used in the building of sentences.

Dilemma

Objectives

NLS
T7: To plan quickly and effectively the plot, characters and structure of their own narrative writing.
S5: To form complex sentences through, eg using different connecting devices.

What you need
● Photocopiable pages 32–34
● selection of other short stories
● checklist from Hour 4.

Shared text-level work
● Tell the children that today they are going to focus on the next section in a story, the dilemma.
● Re-read the opening of *Say Cheese!* on photocopiable page 32 and the build-up on photocopiable page 33, and ask the children what they think would be an exciting dilemma or problem from this point.
● Display photocopiable page 34, keeping the story hidden. Use the bullet points to confirm and supplement the children's ideas.
● Next, reveal the story and read the problem in *Say Cheese!*: the 'ghost' in the photographs and what to do about it.
● Mark any of the features listed in the bullets that can be found in the story text (*introducing a problem; using 'empty' words, such as 'someone' to create suspense; varying sentence openings; drawing the reader in by asking a question*).

Shared sentence-level work
● Use the dialogue in 'Say Cheese!' on photocopiable page 34 to revise how to punctuate and set out dialogue. You could use a copy of the text with all punctuation removed, and work with the children to replace the punctuation. Note the new paragraphs too.

Guided and independent work
● Continue work on sentence building with the guided group, this time consolidating what has been learned so far. Help the children to combine the following clauses into sentences in different ways, using conjunctions and relative pronouns as appropriate:

● Dracula gave Jonathan something to eat
● he ate nothing himself
● he could not eat human food
● Jonathan sliced his bread
● he cut himself
● Dracula licked his lips
● Dracula was thirsting for blood
● he dared not attack Jonathan just yet.

● Discuss differences in rhythm, style and emphasis. Which sentence flowed best? Which sounded clumsy? Which focused on Jonathan?
● Ask the other children to continue working on their stories in pairs. Tell them to re-read Story 2 from the beginning all the way through to the next section, the dilemma.
● Next, ask them to analyse the dilemma of Story 2, annotating relevant points from resource 34.
● Ask the children to discuss and make notes on what is exciting about the dilemma or problem and what they think will happen next.

Differentiation

Less able
● Allocate suitably accessible stories – those in Short and Scary! are ideal.

More able
● Give children stories with more challenging vocabulary and sentence construction.

Plenary
● Use the learning from the lesson to write the third section of the class short story checklist – the dilemma.

Van Gogh's Ghost (Dilemma)

Objectives

NLS
T7: To plan quickly and effectively the plot, characters and structure of their own narrative writing.
S4: To investigate connecting words and phrases.
S5: To form complex sentences through, eg using different connecting devices.
W6: To investigate meanings and spellings of connectives: *therefore, notwithstanding, furthermore,* etc.

What you need
● Photocopiable pages 34 and 37.

Shared text-level work
● Model writing the dilemma or problem of a story. Use photocopiable page 37 if appropriate. As you write, give a commentary on what you are doing and why: I am showing how Max is desperately trying to develop his own style but can only paint in Van Gogh's style. His dilemma is what to do next – he even thinks of suicide.
● Ask the children to look at the bullet points on photocopiable page 34 to see the techniques you are using: *employing suspense* (will Max give up art – or even kill himself?); *using short sentences to be dramatic* (*Then he spotted the ideal thing. His computer*); *varying sentence openings* (initial conjunction, *when*; adverb, *finally*, and so on.)

Shared word- and sentence-level work
● Revise the term connective: a connective is a word or phrase that links sentences. A connective is often followed by a comma.
● Ask the children to suggest some of the most common connectives. (After all, anyway, besides, finally, first, for example, however, later, meanwhile, next, on the other hand, therefore.)
● Ask the children if they can find examples of connectives in your text (next, however, finally).
● Next, ask them to look at the function of the connectives, how they connect the ideas in the text. (Usually by linking sentences by time sequence or cause and effect.)

Guided and independent work
● Continue the mini-course in sentence building with the guided group. Ideally, begin work on connectives with the cloze exercise on page 130 of *Grammar for Writing*.
● Guide the children in writing another version of the task from Hour 3 in which they join clauses with connectives. Note that using a connective causes a sentence break, whereas a conjunction joins clauses into one sentence.

Using conjunctions	Using conjunctions and connectives
Dracula gave Jonathan something to eat *but* he ate nothing himself *because* he could not eat human food.	Dracula gave Jonathan something to eat. *However,* he ate nothing himself because he could not eat human food.

● Remind the rest of the children that they have now analysed three examples of dilemmas. Ask them to use these analyses, along with the list of points on photocopiable page 34, as a basis for writing the dilemma in their own story.

Differentiation

Less able
● Ask children to write a similar dilemma to that modelled in shared work – the main character tries hard to do something, but fails.

More able
● Encourage children to include one or more connectives in their story sentences.

Plenary
● Discuss the children's dilemma story sections written on OHTs. Ask the class to evaluate how well the writers have formed complex sentences using the techniques taught so far (conjunctions, relative pronouns, connectives) and how interesting and exciting the dilemmas are.

UNIT 2 HOUR 7 ■ Narrative writing

Events

Objectives

NLS

T7: To plan quickly and effectively the plot, characters and structure of their own narrative writing.
S5: To form complex sentences through, eg using different connecting devices.

What you need
● Photocopiable pages 32-35
● selection of other short stories
● checklist from Hour 5.

Shared text-level work
● Tell the children that the focus of this lesson is on the next section of a story, events. Explain that this is the part of the story that can most easily be expanded to turn a short story into a long one. Also, there may have been events in the build-up, but these, following the problem/dilemma, are more significant or dynamic.
● Re-read Story 1 on photocopiable pages 32 to 34, and ask the children what events they think will come next.
● Display photocopiable page 35, keeping the story hidden, and read the bullet points, using it to confirm and supplement the ideas suggested by the children. Next, reveal the story and read the events of *Say Cheese!* Ask children which of the bullet point features can be found in the events in the story and mark them with arrows.

Shared sentence-level work
● Examine the different sentences structures (bullet two in the checklist) in *Say Cheese!* on photocopiable page 35. Ask the children to look for:

● short sentences (such as *What a performance that was!*)
● a sentence beginning with a participle (*Draining the well...*)
● a sentence with a phrase in apposition between two dashes (the last sentence).

Guided and independent work
● Introduce 'phrase in apposition' as part of the course on constructing sentences. A phrase in apposition is a short explanatory phrase inserted into a sentence between two commas (or between a comma and a full stop if at the end of the sentence). For example, Dracula hired a ship, a three-masted merchantman, to carry his coffin to Whitby.
● Give the children some sentences like the following to experiment with. Help them to put the phrase in apposition into each sentence.

Sentence	Phrase in apposition
Mina waited anxiously for a letter. The ship was commanded by Captain Smith.	Jonathan's fiancée a highly experienced navigator

● Ask the rest of the children, in their pairs, to re-read Story 2 from the beginning, continuing straight into the next section, events.
● Next, ask them to analyse the events in Story 2, annotating the text with relevant points from resource 35.
● Ask the children to discuss and make notes about the following:

● What was exciting or interesting about the events in the story?
● How did they keep your interest?
● How do you think the story will end?

Differentiation

Less able
● Allocate suitably accessible stories – those in Short and Scary! are ideal.

More able
● Give children stories with more challenging vocabulary and sentence construction.

Plenary
● Complete the events section of the class checklist.

Van Gogh's Ghost (events)

Objectives

NLS
T7: To plan quickly and effectively the plot, characters and structure of their own narrative writing.
S5: To form complex sentences through, eg using different connecting devices.

What you need
● Photocopiable pages 35 and 37
● children's copies of photocopiable page 35
● checklist from Hour 7.

Shared text-level work
● Demonstrate how to write the events section of the story you have been writing throughout these lessons. Again, give a commentary as you write on what you are doing and why. For example, *I am using a simile here to evoke the sound made by a paintbrush on canvas...* Involve the children's ideas and questions as much as possible.
● Ask the children to look at the bullet points on photocopiable page 35 to see your techniques: *using metaphors and similes to help paint the scene* (*like someone vigorously brushing a coat*); *introducing further possible complications* (he sees a ghost).

Shared sentence-level work
● Explain the term participle phrase. A participle phrase is one that begins with a participle (the present participle is the *-ing* part of the verb) for example: *Hoping to find some ice cream, Tim opened the fridge.*
● Ask the children if they can find examples in your story text. (Using photocopiable page 37, *Thinking that it might be a burglar, he went cautiously downstairs...* and *Laughing bitterly, Max said...*)

Guided and independent work
● Continue the mini-course in sentence building, on participle phrases. Give the children pairs of clauses like the following to experiment with in constructing sentences:

> ● Jonathan grasped the stake firmly in his hand
> ● Jonathan walked towards the tomb
> to give:
> ● *Grasping* the stake firmly in his hand, Jonathan walked towards the tomb.

● Help the children to work through the Construct exercises in Unit 47 of *Grammar for Writing.*
● Remind the children working independently that they have now analysed three examples of the presentation of significant events in stories. Ask them to use ideas from the stories they have read and those on the checklist as a basis for writing the events in their own story.

Differentiation

Less able
● Ask children to write an event similar to that modelled in the shared session: the character has a dream, sees a ghost, receives a message...

More able
● Encourage children to include a participle phrase in their writing.

Plenary
● Read and discuss the children's story events written on the OHTs.
● Ask the rest of the children to evaluate how well the writers have formed complex sentences using the techniques taught so far (conjunctions, relative pronouns, connectives, phrase in apposition, participle phrase).
● Discuss how exciting and believable the events in the children's stories are.

Ending

Objectives

NLS

T7: To plan quickly and effectively the plot, characters and structure of their own narrative writing.
S5: To form complex sentences through, eg using different connecting devices.

What you need

● Photocopiable pages 32-36
● the children's resources used so far
● class checklist from Hour 8
● selection of other short stories.

Shared text-level work

● Re-read *Say Cheese!* from the beginning, and ask the children how they think it will end.
● Display photocopiable page 36, keeping the story hidden, and read through the bullet points, relating them to the ideas suggested in class.
● Next, reveal the story and read the ending of *Say Cheese!*.
● Find and mark the features from the bullet points. For example, *allowing help to arrive in an unexpected form* (the photographs taken by the old camera help the girl); *allowing the main character to think aloud*.
● Now ask the children how they would classify the plot. Consider these: anti-climax, circular, flashback, problem solved, quest, subplot, suspense, timeshift, twist-in-the tale, warning, whodunnit. (*Say Cheese!* has a 'problem solved' plot.)

Shared sentence-level work

● Revise the terms active and passive. Demonstrate the difference with the first sentence of the ending of the story:

> Active: A little girl had lived in that house.
> Passive: The house had been lived in by a little girl.

● Note that the subject and object change place, and the verb is modified to fit. What is the difference in emphasis? The active sentence emphasises the girl – which is appropriate for this story. The passive sentence emphasises the house, appropriate for a haunted-house story.

Guided and independent work

● Revise the use of active and passive forms of verb as part of the mini-course in sentence building. Give the children sentences like the following and help them to change them into the passive voice. Discuss the difference in emphasis that this change makes, particularly to the point of view (see the above example).

> ● The old woman hung the crucifix around Jonathan's neck.
> ● Jonathan thrust the stake into Dracula's heart.

● Play the 'Who-did-what-and-to-whom?' game in Unit 45 of *Grammar for Writing*.
● Ask the children working independently to read the ending of Story 2 and to annotate it as appropriate with points from photocopiable page 36.
● Tell them to discuss and make notes about the following:

> ● Did you think the story had a good ending? What was good about it?
> ● Can you think of a better ending?
> ● Can you classify the plot type?

Differentiation

Less able

● Allocate suitably accessible stories - those in Short and Scary! are ideal.

More able

● Give children stories with more challenging vocabulary and sentence construction.

Plenary

● Complete the final section of the class checklist on how to write a good story and display it prominently to support redrafting.

UNIT 2 HOUR 10 📄 Narrative writing

Van Gogh's Ghost (ending)

Objectives

NLS
T7: To plan quickly and effectively the plot, characters and structure of their own narrative writing.
S5: To form complex sentences through, eg using different connecting devices.

What you need

● Photocopiable pages 36 and 37
● children's copies of photocopiable page 36.

Shared text-level work

● Model writing the ending of the story you have been writing throughout the week. Encourage the children to contribute, and comment on what you are doing and why:
I am using the passive voice here to make it sound mysterious – at this point, Max doesn't know who put the painting on the easel.
● Ask the children to identify your techniques from the bullet points on photocopiable page 36.

Shared sentence-level work

● Remind the children how to use paragraphs in their narrative writing. A new paragraph marks a change: of focus, time, place or speaker in a passage of dialogue. The usual convention for narrative fiction is to indicate each new paragraph with an indentation.
● Explain to the children that they can use the five part story plan (Opening, Build-up, Dilemma, Events, Ending) as the basis of a paragraph plan for their stories. Some sections, particularly Events, may be expanded to two or more paragraphs. Occasionally a single sentence paragraph may be used for dramatic effect.

Guided and independent work

● Complete the mini-course in sentence building. Help group members to practise the different methods of sentence building by making the following group of clauses into one well-structured sentence. Let them make slight alterations or leave out words where necessary.

they went downstairs +
there they found Jonathan talking to a strange-looking person +
he sat by the fire +
he was warming a pair of extremely dirty hands = (for example)
They went downstairs where they found Jonathan talking to a strange-looking person who was sitting by the fire, warming a pair of extremely dirty hands.
● Ask the rest of the children to use the checklist and ideas from the stories they have analysed to inspire the ending of their own scary stories.

Differentiation

Less able
● Ask children to write an ending similar to that modelled in shared work: the character succeeds, but in an unexpected way.

More able
● Encourage children to include a passive sentence to alter the point of view where appropriate.

Plenary

● Read one complete story written on OHTs and use it as an example of what to look for when redrafting, as they will be doing this next week.
● Give particular attention to the points raised in the checklist and the techniques taught in the course on sentence building (conjunctions, relative pronouns, connectives, phrase in apposition, participle phrase, active and passive).
● Remember to discuss whether it is an enjoyable, exciting, scary, consistently written and easy-to-follow story!

TERM 1

Openings

1. Opening/setting scene or introducing characters

Some options for opening a story to grab the reader:

- Dialogue, for example, a warning given by one character to another.
- Asking the reader a question.
- Describing a character's strange behaviour.
- Using a dramatic exclamation ('Help!') or dramatic event.
- Introducing something intriguing.

Techniques for introducing characters:

- Using an interesting name.
- Limiting description on how the character feels or what they are.
- Relying on portraying character through action and dialogue.
- Using powerful verbs to show how a character feels and behaves.
- Giving the thoughts and reactions of other characters.
- Revealing the characters' thoughts and ideas.

Say Cheese!

Has anything strange ever happened to you? I mean, really strange, spooky strange? Something like that happened to me once.

It all began when I found an old camera in the attic.

"It's not what you would call portable, is it?" said Ben. Ben is my best friend, and a bit of a joker. "You want to get one of these." He took out a silver box the size of a pack of cards. "It's a digital camera," he said proudly. "I got it for my birthday."

"But this one's an antique. Look." I showed him the brass plate which said, in tiny copperplate writing, 'Rochester Optical Commodore, 5 x 4 Dry Plate Camera. 1886.'

"Does it work?"

"I suppose so. It doesn't look broken – but I haven't a clue how to work it."

"We can look it up on the internet," suggested Ben. "Come on..."

SCHOLASTIC

Build-up

2. Build-up and creating setting

- Making the characters do something.
- Using detail based on sense impressions – what can be seen, heard, smelt, touched or tasted.
- Basing settings on known places plus some invented detail.
- Using real or invented names to bring places alive and make them real and believable.
- Creating atmosphere, for example, what is hidden, what is dangerous, what looks unusual, what is out of place.
- Using the weather, time of day and season as well as place.
- Lulling the reader into a false sense of security.

...We had to take the photographs outside because the camera had no flash. I slid the ground glass screen into the back of the camera and put the dark cloth over my head.

"Let me look!" said Ben, pushing me away and putting his head under the cloth. "What do I do now?"

I slid the ground glass screen out and put a dark slide in its place. "It's ready," I said. "All you have to do is press the bulb."

"Go over there," said Ben. "Back a bit... Say Cheese!" He took the picture, and then we swapped. We tried a few different angles in different parts of the garden, ending near the rockery, which made the best background of all.

"That's it," I said. "I only had six plates."

"What! My camera can take hundreds on one memory card!"

Dilemma

3. Dilemma

- Introducing a problem.
- Using 'empty' words, for example, 'someone' to create suspense.
- Using short sentences for drama.
- Strengthening nouns and verbs rather than adding adjectives and adverbs.
- Employing suspense words such as 'suddenly', 'without warning'.
- Drawing the reader in by asking a question.
- Occasionally breaking the sentence rule by using a fragment to emphasise a point.
- Varying sentence openings by sometimes starting with an adverb, for example, 'Carefully'; a prepositional phrase, such as, 'At the end of the street'; a subordinate clause, for example, 'Although she was tired, Vanya...' or 'Swinging his stick in the air, he...'
- Delaying the revealing of the 'monster'.
- Using ominous sounds, darkness or cold to build tension.

...Ben was at my house when the photographs came back from the developer. Eagerly, I opened the package and spread the photographs out on the table.

"Wow!" Ben said, "Look at the detail! I'd get one of those cameras myself if it would fit in my pocket!"

But something was not right. "There's someone else in the picture," I said, pointing to a faint, cloudy image standing next to Ben. "It's hard to make out, but it looks like a girl dressed in Victorian clothes."

"Thought so," joked Ben. "Stupid old camera doesn't work properly after all!"

We looked more closely. The girl was in every photograph, but the last one was the strangest. In that picture, behind a grinning image of Ben, she was pointing down at something.

Although I wasn't sure, I couldn't help saying, "I think it's a... ghost!" Well, what other explanation was there?

"Weird!" said Ben with a shudder.

Events

4. Reaction/events

- Building on techniques used earlier.
- Using some longer sentences to get a rhythm going to describe the increasing tension as events unfold.
- Using alliteration and short sentences to portray sounds within the action.
- Using metaphors and similes to help paint the scene and describe the feelings of the characters.
- Introducing further possible complications, using connecting words and phrases.

...We identified the place, but there it was, just the rockery. Ben suggested digging it up to see what was underneath. We found a circular stone like a giant draughts piece.

"It could be a well cover," he said.

"It's cracked – dangerous," I said. "I'd better tell Dad."

Dad phoned the local authority and asked them to check its safety. What a performance that was! Draining the well was bad enough, what with all the workmen and pipes snaking all over the place, but when they found the body, all hell broke loose! We had yellow police tape round the house.

But the worst thing was being questioned by the police. They made me feel like a murderer! Luckily, forensic experts soon established that the body – well, the bones – had been there for over 100 years.

Ending

5. Resolution and ending

Techniques for resolving the dilemma:

- Allowing help to arrive in an unexpected form and suddenly.
- Making the character(s) do something unexpected.
- Showing that the problem/dilemma was only in the characters' minds.
- Allowing the character some extra effort to overcome the problem.
- Only resolving a part of the dilemma so the characters learn a lesson.

Some options for closing a story:

- Commenting on the resolution.
- Dialogue – a comment from a character.
- A question.
- Making a mysterious remark.
- Telling the reader to remember or do something.
- Showing how a character has changed.
- Using one word or an exclamation.
- Avoiding clichés.
- Reflecting on events and perhaps providing a moral.
- Allowing the main character to think aloud.
- Maintaining an element of mystery, for example, 'Vanya would never know how lucky she was that...'
- Looking to the future.
- Revisiting where the story began.

...It turned out that a little girl had lived in that house many years ago. One day she had gone missing, and though they searched everywhere, no one could find her. There was even an article in the local newspaper offering a reward, but she never turned up. It looks as though she must have fallen down the well, and nobody ever knew about it – until now.

So why the ghostly photographs? Ben reckons that her ghost was trying to communicate with the living, so that her remains could be given a proper burial. Or perhaps it was a camera fault, or a double-exposure on the old plates – I'll never know for sure.

I know one thing though, I'm selling that camera as soon as I can. It should fetch a good price. And do you know what I'm going to do with the money? I'm going to get a shiny new digital camera, just like Ben's.

Van Gogh's Ghost

[Opening]

The sunflowers looked almost real. The paint had been applied so thickly that it looked as though real petals had been stuck to the canvas. It was not that the sunflowers were realistic in the way that a photograph is realistic, but that they somehow expressed the essence of the real thing. Although the picture was just paint and canvas, it felt as though a real vase of sunflowers had been brought into the room.

[Build-up]

"I can only give you £100 for it," said the dealer, matter-of-factly.

"But it's the best painting I've ever done," sighed Max, who had been hoping for more.

"Yes, I can see that," said the dealer, "but it's just a copy. Now, if this were a real Van Gogh, you could add another four noughts to the figure I just mentioned."

Max could hardly imagine such a sum.

"On the other hand," continued the dealer, "if you developed your own style, your work would be worth more – perhaps as much as £1000 per painting."

[Dilemma]

When Max got back to the studio, he threw the sunflower painting onto the floor and placed a blank canvas on his easel. Next, he looked around for a subject. It must be something that Van Gogh had never painted, something that would inspire him to develop his own original style. Then he spotted the ideal thing. His computer.

He painted quickly and confidently for about an hour, and then stood back to get an overall impression. However, he saw at once that he was wasting his time and was doomed to scratching a living by painting copies of Van Goghs. He threw the painting in the bin, feeling that his dreams went with it. What should he do now? Give up? Get a job in a factory? End it all? Finally, he went upstairs where he threw himself onto his bed in deep despair.

[Events]

He was woken up at about midnight by a noise that sounded like someone vigorously brushing a coat. Thinking that it might be a burglar, he went cautiously downstairs to investigate. In the dim light he saw a shadowy figure working at his easel.

"Er, who are you?" said Max nervously.

"I am the ghost of Vincent Van Gogh," replied the figure.

"What do you want?"

"To help you, of course."

Laughing bitterly, Max said, "I already know how to paint like you – and it has done me little good!"

[Ending]

When Max opened his eyes, he was back in bed. "So it was just a dream after all," he thought, "but what a strange dream!" He went downstairs, and sure enough, everything was just as he had left it – or was it? The sunflower painting had been put on the easel. It was somehow brighter, fresher, livelier. But best of all, in the bottom right hand corner was something much more valuable – the authentic signature of Vincent Van Gogh.

UNIT 3

Media/plays

This unit is based on *A Christmas Carol* by Charles Dickens (of the film versions, *Scrooge*, starring Alastair Sim, is highly recommended). As photocopiable pages 44 and 46 are generic, the unit can easily be adapted to other book–film combinations. If possible, provide the books for close study and for reading at home. Read the whole story before the unit starts, and then focus on key sections during the week. The first two lessons involve close textual study and creative responses to key scenes. If time allows, a further three lessons on the same pattern could be added. Additional time will also be needed for a complete viewing of the film before the children write their film reviews in Hour 5. Hour 2 links with Unit 47 in *Grammar for Writing*.

Hour	Shared text-level work	Shared word-/ sentence-level work	Guided and independent work	Plenary
1 Scrooge	Reading beginning of the story, noting characterisation and viewpoint.		Rewriting the scene from another viewpoint.	Comparing film and book versions.
2 Christmas Past	Reading next extract.	Examining uses of unusual punctuation; looking at words that have changed over time.	Describing their own Christmases Past.	Sharing and evaluating descriptions.
3 Film language	Introducing film structure and language.		Identifying camera shots.	Checking camera shots and discussing effects of the director's choices.
4 Screenplay	Examining screenplay conventions and text changes.		Adapting a scene as a screenplay.	Performing and evaluating the screenplays.
5 Film review	Demonstrating how to analyse/review the film.		Reading film reviews before writing their own.	Discussing reviews; comparing different versions.

Key assessment opportunities
● Can the children identify the viewpoint in a novel?
● Can they prepare a short section of story as a screenplay?
● Can they compare and evaluate a novel in print and a film version?

Scrooge

Objectives

NLS
T2: To take account of viewpoint in a novel through, eg identifying the narrator; explaining how this influences the reader's view of events; explaining how events might look from a different point of view.
S1: To revise from Y5 the different word classes eg personal pronouns.

What you need
● Display version of the story, from the beginning to 'Bah!' said Scrooge, 'Humbug!'.

Shared text- and sentence-level work
● Display and read the extract.
● Discuss how Dickens builds up the character of Scrooge, and what Scrooge's counting-house shows about his character. For example, through particular adjectives (*tight-fisted*), similes (*hard and sharp as flint*) and metaphors (*a frosty rime was on his head*). Scrooge's small fire (and Bob's which is even smaller) shows how mean he is.
● Explain that viewpoint (or point of view or narrative perspective) is created mainly by the person in which the text is written.
● Show the following table of personal pronouns. (Quickly write the first three columns on the board, taking prompts from the children; use the fourth as a basis for your explanations.)

Person	Singular	Plural	Comment
first person	I	we	The best way to show what the main character thinks or feels. However, it limits the author as s/he can only present what the main character knows.
econd person	you	you	Rarely used, but is found in some adventure stories.
third person	he/she/it	they	The most common way of telling a story. The fullest version of this is an omniscient narrator, where the writer knows everything that all the characters think and feel, and sometimes comments on what is happening.

● Ask the children to identify the viewpoint of the story by examining which personal pronouns are used (The story is written in the third person, omniscient narrator.)
● Re-read from *Old Marley was as dead as a door-nail...* to *...emphatically, that Marley was as dead as a door-nail.* Ask the children: Who is speaking here and to whom? What is the effect? (Dickens is speaking to the reader. The effect is to make us feel that Dickens is telling the story to us personally. It also exemplifies Dickens as an omniscient narrator who comments on the action.)
● Discuss how the story would be different if Dickens narrated it in the first person through the character of Scrooge. (Scrooge would portray himself in a more positive light.)

Differentiation

Less able
● Give children this starter to help them establish Scrooge's viewpoint: *I was just about to open my front door when I saw Jacob Marley's face in the door knocker. When I looked more closely, it had gone, so I just muttered 'Pooh!' and went in.*

More able
● Encourage children to imitate Dickens' style and vocabulary.

Guided and independent work
● Ask the children to rewrite a scene from the story in the first person from another character's viewpoint, for example:

● The opening of the story from Scrooge's viewpoint.
● The episode of Marley's ghost from the ghost's viewpoint.
● The Cratchet family Christmas from Tiny Tim's viewpoint.

Plenary
● Show the same scene in the film and discuss similarities and differences. For example, ask the children: What visual techniques does the director use to introduce the character of Scrooge?

UNIT 3 HOUR 2 🔲 Media/plays

Christmas Past

Objectives

NLS
T6: To manipulate narrative perspective by: writing in the voice and style of a text; producing a modern retelling; writing a story with two different narrators.
S6: To secure knowledge and understanding of more sophisticated punctuation marks: colon; semicolon; parenthetic commas, dashes, brackets.
W7: To understand that the meanings of words change over time, eg through investigating words such as *presently* and *without*.

What you need
● Display version of the story, from '*Why, it's old Fezziwig'...* to *... a counter in the back-shop*.

Differentiation

Less able
● Help children to understand how to write about themselves in the third person by giving them an example: Instead of: *Two years ago, I got a mountain bike for Christmas...* write: *The Spirit of Christmas Past took John back to the Christmas when he got a mountain bike...*

More able
● Encourage children to imitate Dickens' style and vocabulary.

Shared text-level work
● Display and read the extract.
● Ask the children: What does the Spirit of Christmas Past want Scrooge to learn from this scene? (How easy it is to give happiness to people, by reminding him how happy Fezziwig made him that Christmas.)

Shared sentence-level work
● Revise the terms and uses of colons, semicolons, parenthetic commas and dashes. Go through the extract, and with help from the children, highlight examples of these punctuation marks.
● Discuss how Dickens uses them. For example, note the mix of commas and semicolons in the complex list beginning: *Old Fezziwig laid down his pen...* and the creative use of dashes in the paragraph beginning: *You wouldn't believe...* Discuss the effect of these dashes, which is to give a sense of breathless excitement.

Shared word-level work
● Help the children to find words that have changed over time. For example, *followers* here means boyfriends, but has lost that meaning in the present day. Also discuss *porter* and *four-and-twenty*.
● Briefly create a modern retelling of this scene. How would it be different in modern times and in modern language? The office party would have different music and dances; sentences would be shorter; and words like *waistcoat* and *'prentice* wouldn't be used.

Guided and independent work
● Ask the children to describe what happens when the Spirit of Christmas Past takes them back to one of their own Christmases. Tell them that they should:

● write about themselves in the third person
● imagine that they are taken back to that Christmas by the Spirit of Christmas Past to learn a lesson; perhaps not to be selfish, to share toys, to be nice to grandparents, to be grateful for gifts and so on.

Plenary
● Share examples of children's visits to Christmases past.
● Ask the rest of the class to evaluate how effectively each text fulfils the brief given in the bullet points above.

Film language

Objectives

NLS
T1: To compare and evaluate a novel or play in print and the film/TV version, eg treatment of the plot and characters, the differences in the two forms, eg in seeing the setting, in losing the narrator.

What you need
● Copies of *A Christmas Carol* by Charles Dickens
● photocopiable page 44
● storyboards (these can be made by blanking out text and images on photocopiable page 44 but keeping the framework and headings)
● film version of *A Christmas Carol.*

Shared text-level work
● Give out photocopiable page 44. Tell the children that it includes some of the particular language used in the film industry.
● Explain that, just as a story in a book is narrated with a sequence of words making up sentences, paragraphs and chapters, so a film is narrated with a series of camera shots making up scenes. Of course, photocopiable page 44 gives only a very basic vocabulary; film makers use a much wider range of shots and techniques, and more able children could undertake further research if there is time.
● Discuss a few story adaptations that the children know and see if they can relate particular sections of the book to the film.
● Briefly explain some of the terminology of camera shots as the children look at the illustrations on photocopiable page 44:

> long shot – from distance, used to established where the action is taking place
> mid/medium shot – used for most scenes in which characters interact
> close up – used to show the emotions or reactions of characters, or a detail
> pan – used to follow movement from side to side
> zoom – used to move smoothly between mid shot and close up
> cut – the normal way of ending a scene (scenes can also end with a fade to black or another technique).

Guided and independent work
● Visual learning: show a short extract from the film, for example, when Scrooge wakes up at the end of the story and finds out that it is still Christmas.
● Ask the children to identify the camera shots and to note them down in column two of photocopiable page 44. Show the extract several times.
● Ask some children to write on OHTs of photocopiable page 44 for use in the plenary session.

Plenary
● Display the OHTs of photocopiable page 44 and check that the main shots have been identified correctly.
● Next, ask the children to discuss the effect of each shot. For example, the close up of Scrooge's face shows how happy he is.

Differentiation

Less able
● Check that comments describe the shot and do not simply retell the story.

More able
● As a follow-up, ask children to find out about a wider range of camera shots, by visiting www.mediacollege.com/video/shots or a similar site.

Screenplay

Objectives

NLS
T9: To prepare a short section of story as a script, eg using stage directions, location/setting.

What you need
● Photocopiable page 45
● copies of *A Christmas Carol* or copies of an extract from *Then up rose Mrs Cratchit* to *'God bless us every one!' said Tiny Tim, the last of all*
● *A Christmas Carol* screenplay, eg from http://geocities.com/emruf/xmas.html
● internet access.

Shared text-level work
● Read the extract with the children.
● Display photocopiable page 45 and tell the children that it is a screenplay version of part of the same scene. Explain, if necessary, that a screenplay is a special kind of script written for film or television.
● Briefly discuss the changes that have been made to the story. (A great deal of description has been left out and the dialogue has been abridged and simplified, perhaps because the film is intended for a modern audience; details of camera shots have been inserted.)
● Go through photocopiable page 45 again, pointing out the conventions used to set out a screenplay:

> ● Each scene begins with a line in capitals giving the information about interior or exterior, location and time (day or night) - the setting.
> ● Directions often include suggestions for camera shot (these are not underlined in real screenplays, but underlining is recommended to pick them out and help the children to think carefully about them).
> ● Character names are in capital letters for easy identification.
> ● Dialogue is tabbed to distinguish it from directions.

Guided and independent work
● Ask the children to work in pairs to adapt any scene from the story into a screenplay. Try to organise the work so that all the key scenes in the story are covered.
● Explain to the children that it is important to imagine how each scene will look in a film and to write suggestions for camera shots and angles and even for how long to hold particular shots (takes).
● Remind the children to follow the conventions as shown on photocopiable page 45.

Plenary
● Select some children to perform a short section of their screenplay. (If any groups have finished their writing early, allow them a little rehearsal time for this if possible.)
● Ask the rest of the class to evaluate the effectiveness of their scene. For example, does it tell the story clearly? Has extra dialogue or action effectively replaced narrative?

Differentiation
Less able
● Ask children to finish off the screenplay of the scene on photocopiable page 45.

More able
● Encourage children to refer to the wider range of camera shots that were researched as a follow-up to Hour 3.

Film review

Objectives

NLS
T1: To compare and evaluate a novel or play in print and the film/TV version, eg treatment of the plot and characters, the differences in the two forms, eg in seeing the setting, in losing the narrator.
T3: To articulate personal responses to literature, identifying why and how a text affects the reader.
T8: To summarise a passage, chapter or text in a specified number of words.
S&L
61 Drama: To consider the overall impact of a live or recorded performance, identifying dramatic ways of conveying characters' ideas and building tension.

What you need
● Chosen film version of *A Christmas Carol* and time to see the whole film before this lesson!
● other film/TV versions of the story
● photocopiable page 46
● internet access.

Differentiation

Less able
● Omit section 3 and concentrate on the synopsis and evaluation.

More able
● Encourage children to use the headings on photocopiable page 46 as a basis only and to write a fuller, more analytical review and a more detailed personal response.

Shared text-level work
● Display photocopiable page 46, and talk the children through how to use it. Begin by giving them the details of the film version you have been using, for example *Scrooge*, 1951, starring Alastair Sim, directed by Brian Desmond Hurst.
● For section 2, explain that a very brief outline of the story is required. Challenge them to come up with (orally) the shortest outline that includes the main points of the story. Write down the best example, and demonstrate how to cut it down even further, and then make it more stylish by experimenting with different ways of joining the ideas.
● Briefly discuss each of the points in section 3, relating them to examples in the film.
● Explain to the children that, for section 4, they can write a paragraph based on their work in Hour 3.
● To help them with section 5, tell them your own personal response to a scene by saying something like: I was moved by the scene with Tiny Tim. It made me realise how important every human life is, and I suppose it had the same effect on Scrooge.
● Finally, discuss the children's overall evaluation of the film and the success of the adaptation.

Guided and independent work
● Work with the children to analyse some real examples of suitable film reviews on the internet. They will find that these range from very short recommendations, to extended works of film criticism; and that opinions vary widely, which is a good thing!
● Ask the children to jot down useful terminology and descriptive phraseology to use in their own film reviews.
● Then ask the children to write a review of the film version of *A Christmas Carol*. Allow them to work in pairs to exchange ideas, but ask each child to produce an individual film review.

Plenary
● Select a number of reviews in which different opinions are expressed about the same film and use them as a basis for discussion. Remind them that all views are valid, if backed up by reference to the film.
● If time allows, compare the extracts of your chosen film with those in different versions of the story, for example *The Muppet Christmas Carol* or *Blackadder's Christmas Carol*.

TERM 1

Film language

	long shot
	medium shot
	close up
	pan
	zoom
	cut

SCHOLASTIC

Screenplay

INT. BOB CRATCHIT'S HOUSE – DAY

<u>Medium shot</u> showing Mrs Cratchit and her daughter, Belinda, laying the table for Christmas dinner. Behind them, cooking pots can be seen on an old-fashioned range. <u>Cut</u> to the parlour door which opens suddenly as the other children, Peter, Bob and a younger boy and girl rush excitedly into the room.

> MRS CRATCHIT
> I wonder where your father is? And your brother, Tiny Tim, and Martha?
> BELINDA
> Here's Martha, mother!
> TWO YOUNG CRATCHITS
> She's brought the goose!

<u>Close-up</u> of goose to emphasise how small it is to feed such a large family.

> TWO YOUNG CRATCHITS
> There's father coming – Hide, Martha, hide!

<u>Pan shot</u> to show Martha hiding behind a cupboard. <u>Cut</u> to Bob Cratchit coming in with Tiny Tim, upon his shoulder. <u>Close up</u> to show Tiny Tim's crutch and his weak legs supported by an iron frame.

> BOB
> Why, where's our Martha?
> MRS CRATCHIT
> Not coming.
> BOB
> Not coming upon Christmas Hour?

<u>Zoom in</u> on his face to show his disappointment. <u>Cut</u> to Martha's face. She is upset to see how disappointed he is. <u>Pan shot</u> to show her jumping out from behind the cupboard and running into his arms.

> MRS CRATCHIT
> And how did little Tim behave?
> BOB
> As good as gold. He told me, coming home, that he hoped the people saw him in the church, because he was a cripple, and it might be pleasant to remember on Christmas day who made lame beggars walk, and blind men see.

<u>Zoom in</u> very close to Bob's face to show his emotion and a tear in his eye.

> BOB
> But I think that Tiny Tim is growing strong and hearty.

Film review

1. Film details

2. Synopsis
- Write a brief outline of the plot.

3. Analysis
- Write brief notes on the following (as appropriate):

Adaptation   (If adapted from a novel, what changes were made?)

Casting   (How well the actors fit the parts they have been chosen for.)

Costume   (How authentic are the costumes?)

Direction   (How successful is the director's overall idea for the film?)

Music   (What does the music add to the effect of the film?)

Script   (Is the dialogue, for example, realistic and effective?)

Settings   (Which are on location, which in the studio? Are they realistic?)

Special effects (What do they add to the film?)

4. One scene in detail
- Analyse one scene in detail using film language (see Hour 3).

5. Personal response
- Give a personal response to the above scene and the film as a whole. Explain what it made you think and feel, if you liked it, and how it relates to your own experiences.

6. Evaluation
- Say what you think were the main good and bad points in the film and whether you would recommend it. If the film was adapted from a novel, assess how well you think this has been done. End with a star rating (5 = excellent, 1 = poor).

Journalistic

This unit is based on two different versions of an article on global warming, one for a broadsheet and one for a tabloid newspaper. In comparing the two articles, children learn about some differences between the two types of newspapers, key features of journalistic style and balanced ethical reporting. The articles are used as examples for sentence-level work on sophisticated punctuation. In Hour 5, the children are asked to research and write their own newspaper articles in broadsheet or tabloid style. They should do the research and interviewing for homework, and the writing, redrafting and presentation (preferably using ICT) in two or more follow-up literacy hours.

Hour	Shared text-level work	Shared word-/ sentence-level work	Guided and independent work	Plenary
1 Global warming fears	Reading and annotating a news article, analysing the structure.	Identifying colons and semicolons.	Writing own news article.	Discussing news style and headlines; noting punctuation.
2 What? When? Where? Who? Why? 💬	Identifying the form of a news article; watching an interview.	Learning more complex punctuation marks.	Interviewing in pairs for a short article.	Reading out the articles; noting parenthetical information.
3 Journalese	Identifying typical journalistic style features.		Finding and classifying newspaper headlines and jargon.	Collecting jargon words and phrases.
4 The tabloid version	Writing a tabloid news article.	Using etymological dictionaries.	Continuing the tabloid news article.	Noting further differences between tabloid and broadsheet styles.
5 Own article	Identifying and learning terminology for front page features.		Organising group work to research and write articles for a front page.	Discussing plans; later, share articles and identify techniques used.

Key assessment opportunities
● Do the children understand the difference between broadsheet and tabloid newspapers?
● Do they know how to use more sophisticated punctuation?
● Do they recognise 'journalese' and newspaper layout features?
● Can they write and publish their own newspaper articles?

Global warming fears

Objectives

NLS

T12: To comment critically on the language, style, success of examples of non-fiction such as reports.
S6: To secure knowledge and understanding of more sophisticated punctuation marks: colon; semicolon.

What you need
● Photocopiable page 53.

Shared text-level work

● Tell the children that they are going to read an article (or news story) of the type found in broadsheet newspapers. Explain that broadsheet is often used as a synonym for 'quality' or 'serious' newspapers. Similarly, tabloid refers to 'popular' newspapers. These terms originated when quality newspapers were printed on larger paper.
● Display and read photocopiable page 53 (without the annotations box). Go through it again, and annotate it with the children. Use the notes in box 1a as a starting point.
● Work to analyse the paragraph structure and write a subtitle for each paragraph. Help the children to see the structure: an introduction, a series of paragraphs and a conclusion. Help them to see the balance in the article. The main thrust is the human causes of global warming and their effects, but it also includes two paragraphs about a different explanation of the causes of global warming.

Shared sentence-level work

● Go through the article again, highlighting and explaining the following punctuation marks (using box 1b):

Colon – used to introduce something, such as a list, a quotation, or related information. (Point out the example in paragraph three.) Semicolon – used to separate items in a list if these items consist of longer phrases. (Point out the example in paragraph three and compare it with the commas used to separate the list of short items in paragraph two.) A semicolon can also work in a similar way to a full stop when the following sentence is closely related in meaning. (Point out the example in paragraph four and demonstrate that, if the semicolon is replaced by a full stop the result is two grammatically correct sentences.)

Guided and independent work

● Ask pairs of children to annotate photocopiable page 53 by drawing lines from the notes in boxes 1a and 1b to the features in the text.
● Then ask them to write their own short news articles about home or school, including: an attention-grabbing headline, key information, sentences with colons and semicolons.
● Ask some of the pairs to write on OHT for use in the plenary.

Plenary

● Share the children's news articles. Discuss the effectiveness of the headlines and the completeness of the information. Is the style suitably journalistic? Display the work on OHTs. Note uses of colons and semicolons.

Assessment

● Do the children understand the difference between broadsheet and tabloid newspapers?
● Do they know how to use more sophisticated punctuation?
● Do they recognise 'journalese' and newspaper layout features?
● Can they write and publish their own newspaper articles?

Differentiation

Less able
● Help children to use colons and semicolons in a list.

More able
● Encourage children to attempt the more sophisticated uses of colons and semicolons.

What? When? Where? Who? Why?

Objectives

NLS
T8: To summarise a passage, chapter or text in a specified number of words.
S6: To secure knowledge and understanding of more sophisticated punctuation marks: colon; semicolon; parenthetic commas, dashes, brackets.
Speaking and listening emphasis: summarise and present succinctly the main points of a report for a known audience in the style of a radio or television journalist.

What you need

● Photocopiable page 53
● the children's annotated copies of photocopiable page 53
● excerpt from a TV news interview.

Shared text-level work

● Explain that every newspaper article aims to answer five key questions: What? When? Where? Who? and Why?
● Ask the children to listen out for these as you re-read the article. Annotate the text according to the children's suggestions.
● Tell the children that they will be conducting an interview to find out answers to the five key questions. Show them a brief extract from a television news interview and ask them to note carefully how the interviewer tries to get answers from the interviewee.

Shared sentence-level work

● Highlight and explain the following punctuation marks in the article (see box 2b):
Dash – often used to emphasise the point that follows. (Point out the example in paragraph two.)
Hyphen – used to join two words that act as one (compound words). Compare with the dash. (Point out examples in paragraphs two and five.)
● Next, examine the three different methods of presenting parenthetical information ('extra' information slotted into a sentence):
Between brackets – generally, brackets give parenthetical information in low-key way. Information in brackets can often be left out with no great loss. (Point out the example in paragraph one.)
Between commas – generally commas give parenthetical information at almost the same level of importance as the rest of the sentence. (Point out the examples in paragraphs one and five.)
Between dashes – generally, dashes emphasise the parenthetical information. (Point out the example in paragraphs five and six.)

Guided and independent work

● Ask the children to interview a partner about something that happened to them at home or school (a different event to the last lesson).
● Ensure that they elicit answers to the five key questions: What? When? Where? Who? Why?
● Ask the interviewers to take notes during the interview. Set a time limit.
● Ask the pairs to swap roles.
● Then ask them to work individually to write up the information as a short news article to include:

● an attention-grabbing headline
● key information to answer What? When? Where? Who? Why?
● two different ways of presenting parenthetical information.

Differentiation

Less able
● Ask children to include at least one method of presenting parenthetical information.

More able
● Ask children to write a longer article and to include all three methods of presenting parenthetical information.

Plenary

● Ask some children to read out their articles. Evaluate how well each article answers the five key questions.
● Display some of the OHTs to consolidate understanding of the different ways of presenting parenthetical information.

Journalese

Objectives

NLS

T12: To comment critically on the language, style, success of examples of non-fiction such as reports.

What you need

● Photocopiable pages 53 and 54
● range of newspapers (Ask the children to bring them in; tear out inappropriate images or stories.)
● computer access.

Shared text-level work

● Read through the first part of photocopiable page 54. Then, with the children's help, pick out the headline-writing techniques and compile a table with headings like the following:

Straightforward information	Alliteration	Shock	Humour or wordplay	Quotation

● Read through the second part, then, using this and the range of newspapers, draw up another table:

Jargon words	Jargon phrases

● Revise the term alliteration (a phrase where adjacent or close words begin with the same phoneme: one wet wellington; free phone; several silent, slithering snakes).
● Encourage the children to suggest a few alliterative phrases off the top of their heads.
● Ask the children to try to explain why it is effective; for example, why is one wet wellington, more powerful than a wet boot? (For example, it is like rhyme at the front of a word; the words with alliteration are emphasised; it is memorable.)
● Ask the children to make up more examples that can be used as headlines or subheadings for their own articles.

Guided and independent work

● Visual and kinaesthetic learning: give two or three newspaper pages to each pair of children. Ask them to find and classify headlines (not just the front page, but the headlines for articles throughout the paper) by copying them out into the appropriate box on their headlines table. Kinaesthetic learners may appreciate doing this by cut-and-paste.
● Ask the children to find examples of jargon words and phrases – not just the ones referred to on photocopiable page 54, but any words and phrases that are used to exaggerate the effect of a news story. Add these to the other table.

Differentiation

Less able
● Less able children may also benefit from using a cut-and-paste approach.

More able
● Give children tabloid and broadsheet articles and ask them to indicate with T or B the sources in their tables. Ask them to look for patterns.

Plenary

● Briefly share examples of each type of headline, but make the main focus of this plenary the collection of jargon words and phrases as these will be needed in Hour 4.
● Ask the children to call out their examples, write them on the board, then ask everyone to add them to their tables.

UNIT 4 HOUR 4 Journalistic

The tabloid version

Objectives

NLS
T12: To comment critically on the language, style, success of examples of non-fiction such as reports.
T15: To develop a journalistic style through considering: balanced and ethical reporting; the interest of the reader; selection and presentation of information.
W10: To understand the function of the etymological dictionary, and to use it to study words of interest and significance.

What you need

● Photocopiable page 55
● the children's annotated copies of photocopiable page 53
● etymological dictionaries.

Shared text-level work

● Demonstrate how to use the jargon words and phrases collected in Hour 3 to write a tabloid-style newspaper article.
● Scribe the first two paragraphs of *Global Warning!* from photocopiable page 55 (or something similar) while you make comments such as the examples in the bottom half of the page. Encourage the children to contribute ideas and structural/grammatical comments as you write.
● Ask the children to compare what you are writing with the broadsheet version in photocopiable page 53 with particular reference to the following:

● language
● style
● balance
● reading level
● treatment of subject (for example, serious or humorous; important or trivial/minor).

Shared word-level work

● Discuss etymology – the study of the origin and history of words. Most dictionaries contain some etymological information. The abbreviations used in different dictionaries may differ slightly, but they will be similar to the following. Revise or explain them to the children making use of the example below:

L Latin, Gk Greek, F French, G German, It Italian, ME Middle English (c1200–1500), OE Old English (c700–1200). For example, *Shock 1565 (F. choc, choquer) a sudden impression on the mind or feelings.*

From this entry we learn that the first recorded example of the word *shock* was in 1565 and the word comes from French.
● Hand out dictionaries and ask the children to find out quickly about the etymology of more of the key words in the first paragraph of the article on the board.

Guided and independent work

● Organise the children into pairs to discuss and write a tabloid version of the article on photocopiable page 53, continuing from the beginning that was written in shared work if appropriate.
● Advise the children to make use of their annotations from Hour 1.

Differentiation

Less able
● Ask children to write their own version of the two opening paragraphs on the board.

More able
● Give children the opening paragraphs of a real broadsheet article to rewrite.

Plenary

● Ask the children to read out their tabloid-style articles.
● Then display the second half of the article on photocopiable page 55 to note other differences between broadsheet and tabloid articles. Use paragraph three, and the notes, to reinforce points about journalese; use paragraph four, and the notes, to highlight problems with a lack of balance and over-simplification of political information.

Own article

Objectives

NLS

T16: To use the styles and conventions of journalism to report on eg real or imagined events.
T18: To use IT to plan, revise, edit writing to improve accuracy and conciseness and to bring it to publication standard, eg through compiling a class newspaper, paying attention to accuracy, layout and presentation.

S&L

50 Group discussion and interaction: To plan and manage a group task over time by using different levels of planning.

What you need
● Any suitable newspaper front page
● computer access, with desktop publishing or word-processing software.

Shared text-level work
● Display the newspaper front page. Don't read the text; focus on layout features, such as: headline, columns, captioned photographs, subheadings, typeface, particularly sizes and changes in weight. Discuss the impact of each layout feature.
● Explain in detail the terminology of typefaces, and look for examples:

Typeface/font – typeface is the traditional term used to describe the style of the letters; IT uses the term font.
Bold – a heavy version of a typeface, used for emphasis.
Italic – a sloping version of a typeface, used for contrast or emphasis.
Upper-case, lower-case. In the days of hand printing, the capital letters were kept in a case positioned above the case for small letters. Upper-case/capital letters are sometimes used in headlines to stand out and grab attention.

Guided and independent work
● Organise groups of four to research and write their own newspaper articles in broadsheet or tabloid style. Good articles will need research, interviewing, or both, so this should be a planning session. The children should do the research and interviewing for homework, and the writing, redrafting and presentation (preferably using ICT) in two or more follow-up Literacy Hours. Ask them to choose from the following topics:
1. School or local news (research school documentation, interview participants)
2. Own version of a national news item (research newspapers, TV and radio)
3. A newspaper article to explore literature or history, for example 'Rocket' wins Rainhill Trails (1829).
● Tell the children that, during the session, they should agree on the following: choice of overall topic, four subtopics and who will write them, style – tabloid or broadsheet?
● In the follow-up literacy hours they will:

● help each other to proofread and edit their articles
● arrange them as a newspaper front page (deciding on the order of the stories, editing stories for length, deciding where to place text and illustrations)
● desktop-publish the newspaper page (kinaesthetic learners will benefit from assembling a front page by physical cut and paste).

Differentiation

Less able
● Allocate a specific news item for research, such as the school sports day.

More able
● Encourage the group to reproduce details of newspapers, including logo, date, price, advertisements.

Plenary
● Discuss the plans so that children are prepared for their homework.
● After the follow-up lessons, when the newspaper pages are complete, share one or two articles, asking the class to look for the techniques covered throughout the week, such as:
● an attention-grabbing headline
● full information (answering the five questions)
● sophisticated punctuation
● language appropriate to the intended audience
● effective layout.

Global warming fears

A recent jump in greenhouse gases might be the start of faster global warming, scientists said on Monday. Carbon dioxide, the main greenhouse gas, has risen by more than two parts per million (ppm) in the past two years.

Scientists believe that emissions from cars, homes, factories and power stations are making things worse. If this continues, they predict serious problems: alpine glaciers will melt by 2050; European winters will disappear by 2080; and sea levels will rise – a particular concern for low-lying countries such as the Netherlands.

The earth is already experiencing unusual weather conditions, for example, the floods of 2001 that killed about 80 people; the heatwave of 2003 that led to more than 20,000 deaths; and the three large hurricanes: Frances, Ivan and Jeanne which hit the Caribbean and Florida in 2004.

However, there is another point of view: a study by Swiss and German scientists says that global warming is caused by the Sun burning more brightly than at any time during the past 1000 years. Their evidence is based on the number of sunspots; the more there are, the hotter the sun shines.

The research was welcomed by some leading conservationists who describe global warming as a modern-day myth. A growing number of scientists also agree, but are concerned that the world's politicians and policy-makers are convinced otherwise.

Whatever the main cause of global warming, it is probable that human emissions do have some impact. It was for this reason that 123 countries signed the 1997 Kyoto Protocol to reduce emissions of greenhouse gases by 5 per cent by 2012. Unfortunately, the biggest emitter of greenhouse gases – the USA – refused to sign.

1a: text	1b: punctuation	2a: text	2b: punctuation
headline	colon to introduce a list	key information – what? when? where? who? why?	dash to emphasise the point that follows
connective to introduce a different point of view	colon to introduce a quotation		hyphen to join two words which act as one (compound words)
different point of view = balanced reporting	colon to introduce related information		hyphens to bracket information with extra emphasis
quotation	commas to separate short items in a list		phrase in apposition between commas
	semi colons to separate phrases in a list		extra information in brackets
	semi-colon to show that what follows is related in meaning		

Headlines

Headlines differ from everyday language by using a telegraphic style which leaves out less important words. For example, a headline like **Fatty food fears** is a shortened way of saying "There are fears about the effects of too much fatty food".

Headlines of broadsheet (quality) newspapers usually give straightforward information, for example, **Pressure on Government to halt 10p petrol rise**. Tabloid (popular) newspapers like to pep up their headlines, for example: **Petrol price protest!** This headline also demonstrates another common technique, alliteration, which adds to the "punch" of a headline.

Another attention-grabbing technique is to use shock, as in this example: **Bomb hits British Embassy**.

Humour and wordplay are also commonly used, for example, **Snow joke!** This headline, which plays on the double meaning of "snow" and "'s no" (short for "it's no") appeared after winter snow brought most of England to a halt.

Another technique is to use quotations. This example introduces an article on obesity: **'I nearly ate myself to death'**.

Jargon

Journalists, especially those writing for tabloid newspapers, have developed a stock of jargon words which they use to make even the most ordinary event sound exciting. For example, a fire, however small, is always a 'blaze'. A scientific discovery, however minor, is a 'breakthrough'. Even a simple problem, such as blocked drains, can be made newsworthy by calling it a 'crisis' or 'drama' (**Council in blocked drains crisis**). Things like prices or temperatures, never just go up or down, they 'soar', 'plunge' or 'plummet'.

As a last resort, journalists can always tack on the word 'horror' or 'shock' or even both! (**Obese toddlers horror shock!**)

There is also a stock of jargon phrases that add to the hype. Anyone who makes some effort is 'bending over backwards'. Someone who keeps a check on something is 'keeping a finger on the pulse'. If there is a situation that could go either way it is 'balanced on a knife edge', and new laws or scientific facts can be announced with the 'official' tag (**Salt is bad for you – official**).

Finally, it is surprising how many heatwaves, hurricanes, floods, droughts and millimetres of rainfall are 'the worst since records began'.

Global warming – the tabloid version

GL BAL WARNING!

In a shock news release yesterday, scientists predicted that global temperatures will soar. The in-depth study shows that the hike in greenhouse gases was the worse since records began.

"We shouldn't get alarmist about this," said top boffin Richard Betts as he painted a nightmare scenario of the Europe of the future. The ice will melt – great if you want to cross the Atlantic in the Titanic – but not so good if you enjoy skiing. Water levels will rise – so if you live in Holland, or any other low-lying bits, you'd better start building your ark.

The planet is already experiencing freak weather conditions, for example, the floods of 2001 that killed about 80 people; the heatwave of 2003 that led to more than 20,000 deaths; and the three devastating hurricanes which hit the Caribbean and Florida in 2004.

And while we in Britain are bending over backwards to slash harmful emissions, for the world's biggest polluter – the USA – it's business as usual.

Example comments

My headline is a play on words – which two words am I playing on?

I am using jargon to make the article more exciting – which are the jargon words and phrases?

When I use quotation marks I have to give Richard Betts exact words – but they're a bit low-key, so I've stopped quoting and am giving the information in my own way.

Notice how I am using humour to make it more interesting – and though the flippant tone is hardly appropriate for such serious information, it is typical of some tabloid newspapers.

This paragraph is very similar to the paragraph in *Global warming fears*, but a few jargon words and phrases have been used to pep it up – what are they?

To keep things simple, some important information has been left out. What is it? How does this affect the balance of the article?

Biography/ autobiography

This unit is based on a biography of John Clare which links with Unit 1, 'Poetry'. You could organise this unit rotationally by using the five creative responses suggested in Hour 3 as independent work rotated throughout the week; or in a linear way by working through each unit as given. The former method explores a wide range of creative responses to a biography, the latter places a greater emphasis on the reading and writing of biography and autobiography. Clare's life provides an interesting insight into the life of ordinary people at the beginning of the 19th century, and thus could be used as source material in a history investigation.

Hour	Shared text-level work	Shared word-/sentence-level work	Guided and independent work	Plenary
1 The life of John Clare	Distinguishing biography and autobiography, fact and opinion.	Finding words within words; relating biography and autobiography to first and third person writing.	Researching a biography; constructing a timeline.	Adding dates to a timeline, identifying the most important dates.
2 Drama response	Dramatising key scenes from Clare's life.		Processing research; improvising drama.	Performing; exploring other drama techniques.
3 Written response	Re-reading the biography.	Identifying and classifying connectives.	Drafting a biography; writing a creative response to Clare's biography.	Discussing the biographies and any interesting new information.
4 Oral autobiography	Deciding fact and fiction in a biographical anecdote.		Summarising a biography; planning a group anecdote.	Presenting anecdotes and identifying the truth.
5 Written autobiography	Modelling a structure for writing an autobiography.	Revising the use of connectives.	Writing autobiographies.	Reading and evaluating the autobiographies.

Key assessment opportunities
● Can the children distinguish between biography and autobiography?
● Can they respond creatively to biography?
● Have they developed the skills of biographical and autobiographical writing?
● Do they write complex sentences?

Objectives

NLS
T11: To distinguish
between biography and
autobiography: recognising
the effect on the reader of
the choice between first
and third person;
distinguishing between
fact, opinion and fiction.
S1: To revise from Y5: the
different word classes.
W5: To use word roots,
prefixes and suffixes as a
support for spelling.

What you need
● Photocopiable pages 62
and 63.

The life of John Clare

Shared text-level work
● Tell the children that they are going to read a biography of the poet
John Clare. Encourage them to tell you what they remember about his
poems if they have studied them.
● Then ask if they can define the term biography (a life story of an
individual written by another author; generally written in the third
person). Compare this with autobiography (a life story of an individual
written by that person; generally written in the first person).
● Read photocopiable pages 62 and 63 and explain to the children that
most of this biography is factual. Ask them: How could you check the
facts? (Parish records of births and deaths, records from the lunatic
asylum, original text of Clare's poems.)
● Establish the difference between fact and opinion. A fact is
something that can be proved to be true; an opinion is a point of view
about something. Re-read the biography and look for anything that is
not fact, but opinion. (It is opinion that Clare was not really insane; that
he is our finest nature poet; that Gray and Wordsworth spoil their work
with artificial language.)

Shared sentence- and word-level work
● Show the children how to break the words biography and
autobiography to reinforce understanding and spelling: graph – writing,
bio – person; auto – self.
● Relate the definitions of biography and autobiography to third person
and first person writing and revise personal pronouns.
● Ask the class to find examples of personal pronouns in the text,
stating whether they are first, second or third person and singular or plural.

Guided and independent work
● Help one group to develop their information retrieval skills by
researching a biography, for example of John Agard, using library books,
CD-ROMs and the internet, as available.
● Ask the other children to work in pairs to construct a timeline of John
Clare's life using the following format:

Date	Event
1793	John Clare is born in Helpston, Northamptonshire

● Explain that they will sometimes have to work out the dates when
Clare's age is given instead, or when phrases like four years later are used.

Plenary
● Draw a timeline on the board and ask the children to suggest dates
and events to complete it.
● Then ask the children to pick out the three most important events in
his life. (Probably: falling in love with poetry, falling in love with Mary,
being committed to a lunatic asylum.)

Differentiation

Less able
● Give children a prepared
timeline with all the dates,
but no events.

More able
● Ask children to write a
200-word summary of the
biography including all the
main events.

Drama response

Objectives

NLS
T14: To develop the skills of biographical and autobiographical writing in role, adopting distinctive voices, eg of historical characters through, eg: preparing a CV; composing a biographical account based on research.
S&L
64 Drama: To improvise using a range of drama strategies.

What you need
● Photocopiable pages 62 and 63.

Shared text-level work
● Tell the children that they are going to use photocopiable pages 62 and 63 as the basis for an improvised drama about the life of John Clare, entitled Nature, Poetry and Love.
● Explain that the first step is to explore how to dramatise key scenes in the poet's life. Ask the children to re-read the biography and suggest which scenes would be most effective, for example:

> ● Clare's mother finds out that her son writes poetry
> ● Clare asks Mary's father if they can have his permission to get married
> ● Clare escapes from High Beech Asylum.

● Discuss with the children how these scenes could be dramatised. For example, Clare would be very nervous before asking Mary's father for his permission to marry Mary. The scene might begin with him pacing up and down rehearsing lines to himself. The next scene might show him with Mary's father. He is so nervous that he stammers and makes himself seem stupid. Mary's father is angry and dismissive. While this happens, Mary is listening outside the door.

Guided and independent work
● Ask the research group from the previous lesson to 'process' the information retrieved during the research by:

> ● highlighting useful information on photocopies and printouts
> ● jotting down useful phrases and quotes from their notes, photocopies and printouts
> ● making a timeline.

● Organise the other children into groups of two to four. Ask them to choose a scene from Clare's biography for dramatic interpretation.
● Encourage them to work through ideas and roles as a group and improvise appropriate dialogue, positions and movements.
● Spend a few minutes helping each group to choose and discuss a scene, aiming to cover all the important episodes in Clare's life.

Plenary
● Ask some of the groups to perform their improvised scene.
● The following drama techniques could be used to explore the characters and situations further: hot-seating (questioning any of the characters in role); freeze-frame (asking the actors to freeze during improvisation and having the audience question them).

Differentiation

Less able
● Ask children to choose a scene that was discussed in the shared session.

More able
● Ask children to include some short readings from Clare's poetry (see Unit 1), either as a voice-over or read out by the child playing the character of Clare.

Written response

Objectives

NLS

T3: To articulate personal responses to literature.
T5: To contribute constructively to shared discussion about literature, responding to and building on the views of others.
T14: To develop the skills of biographical and autobiographical writing in role, adopting distinctive voices, through, eg composing a biographical account based on research.
S4: To investigate connecting words and phrases.

What you need
● Photocopiable pages 62 and 63.

Shared text-level work
● Re-read photocopiable pages 62 and 63 and explain to the children that they are going to write a creative response to Clare's biography.
● Select a creative response from below and discuss and demonstrate it in detail. Alternatively, display the list of responses, briefly talk about each one, and allow the children to make their own choices.

> ● Autobiography (Use imagination to add personal touches, but make sure they are appropriate.)
> ● Biography rewritten to include extracts from his poems
> ● A series of letters or diary entries (Add suitable personal touches.)
> ● A report from Clare's teacher or from a doctor at the asylum
> ● Screenplay, based on the improvised scenes from Hour 2.

Shared sentence-level work
● Remind children of the meaning of the term connective: a word or phrase that links clauses or sentences. Connectives can be conjunctions (but, when, because) or connecting adverbs (however, then, therefore). Temporal connectives are to do with time.
● Draw two columns on the board and ask the children to sort the following list of connectives into temporal connectives and other connectives (there are eight of each type):

after, also, as a result, as soon as, before, consequently, despite, due to, finally, first, however, later, nevertheless, next, then, therefore

● Ask the children to find examples of connectives in photocopiable page 62. Use different-coloured markers or highlighters to colour-code temporal connectives and other connectives, and relate their sequential use to the logical chronological ordering of the biography.

Guided and independent work
● Ask the research group to write the first draft of a biography from the information processed in Hour 2. Advise them to:

> ● use the timeline as a scaffold
> ● piece together the jotted phrases using sentence-building techniques (Unit 2)
> ● reword any phrases that are different from their own style.

● Ask the others to work on their chosen creative response.
● Tell them that it is fine to include extra details and personal touches as long as they fit in with the key facts of Clare's life.

Differentiation

Less able
● Direct children to the shorter, simpler tasks: the two reports or the diary or letters.

More able
● Ask a group to write a biography of Clare illustrated with extracts from his poems. Suggest they begin by re-reading the poems studied in Unit 1, and to look for other poems.

Plenary
● Share some examples of the children's work and ask the class to discuss how successful the writers have been in bringing the character of John Clare to life.
● Discuss any extra interesting facts that the children have found out.
● Also, discuss how his poems might be related to his life.

UNIT 5 HOUR 4 ◻ Biography/autobiography

Oral autobiography

Objectives

NLS
T8: To summarise a passage in a specified number of words.
T11: To distinguish between biography and autobiography: distinguishing between fact, opinion and fiction.
S&L
65 Speaking: To use techniques of dialogic talk to explore ideas, topics or issues.

What you need
● Short biography or autobiography (about 450 words)
● computer access.

Shared text-level work
● Tell the children that they are going to play the 'Autobiographical anecdote game'.
● Narrate an autobiographical anecdote and then invite questions to find out if it was fact or fiction. You could do this three times to demonstrate different possibilities. For example:

> ● Fact – something that happened when you were at school.
> ● Fiction, but like fact – can they find out if it is fiction by asking a question you can't answer?
> ● Obviously fiction – 'When I was at school, we had to carry a gas mask all the time...'

Guided and independent work
● Give one group a short biography or autobiography and ask them to summarise it in about one third of its length by:

> ● highlighting the key points
> ● putting the key points together in new sentences
> ● rewording
> ● checking the number of words and editing/rewriting as necessary.

● If the children are using a word processor and it has an auto-summarise feature, experiment with this and see how well (or badly!) it can do the same task.
● Ask the other children to work in groups of four and begin by planning and making notes for a short autobiographical anecdote. This can be fact or fiction, but should be believable.
● Help the groups to organise themselves:

> ● Each child takes it in turn to tell his/her autobiographical anecdote.
> ● The rest of the group asks one question each to try to find out if it was fact or fiction.
> ● The rest of the group has a brief meeting after which they have to state if the anecdote was fact or fiction.
> ● The narrator confirms or denies, then they swap roles.

● While the groups are working, circulate to listen for the most interesting example of each type of autobiographical anecdote and ask children to prepare to repeat their narration during the plenary.

Differentiation

Less able
● Allocate the oral tasks to this group.

More able
● Give children the short biography or autobiography to summarise, ensuring that it is suitably challenging.

Plenary
● Ask selected children to repeat their anecdotes to the whole class. Allow three questions (but not from fellow group members) and identify whether the anecdote was true or made up.
● Discuss the 'human interest' in each anecdote and explain how this kind of detail can bring an autobiography to life.
● Point out that many stories are written in autobiographical style – they read like autobiographies, but are actually fiction.

Written autobiography

Objectives

NLS
T11: To distinguish between biography and autobiography: recognising the effect on the reader of the choice between first and third person; distinguishing between fact, opinion and fiction; distinguishing between implicit and explicit points of view and how these can differ.
S5: To form complex sentences through, eg: using different connecting devices; reading back complex sentences for clarity of meaning, and adjusting as necessary; evaluating which links work best.

What you need
● The children's notes from Hour 4
● computer access.

Shared text-level work
● Tell the children that they are going to write their own autobiographies. Suggest using the following procedure:
1. Write a short 'outline' autobiography. Model this on the board something like the following:

I was born in 1995 in Collingham in Yorkshire. My brother was born in 1997. My first day at school was a disaster because I got lost. However, it got better after that...

2. Write two or three detailed autobiographical anecdotes:

When I was nine, my best friend Tina and I were playing in our old garden shed. A terrible thunderstorm started and we decided to go in to the house. It was lucky we did, because...

3. Produce a final version of the autobiography by blending the two together.
● Read the final version with the children and compare it to other biographies they have read.

Shared sentence-level work
● As appropriate, remind the class of the sentence-building task they completed in Unit 2. Encourage them to use complex sentences in their autobiographies by trying different connecting devices. For example:

● My first day at school was a disaster but it soon got better.
● Although my first day at school was a disaster, it soon got better.
● My first day at school was a disaster. However, it soon got better.

● Point out that these three ways are equally good. The choice depends on which fits best in the particular context.

Guided and independent work
● Ask the children to write their autobiographies, following the procedure modelled in the shared session.
● Allow them to discuss and share memories first but to write individually. Remind them it is a work of personal history.
● Encourage them to include personal detail and anecdotes to bring the story to life and to add variety.

Differentiation

Less able
● Help children to manage the transition between the 'outline' and 'detailed' parts of the autobiography.

More able
● Experiment with two levels of anecdotal detail: brief details and full details. The final text could include several scenes with brief detail and one or two with full details.

Plenary
● Ask some of the children to read their biographies while the rest of the class evaluate the use of connecting devices and how the detailed anecdotes give life and interest to the autobiography.
● This lesson could be developed into an extended project in which the children produce long autobiographies with photographs, and with more time allowed for redrafting (focusing on developing complex sentences) and presentation.

TERM 1

The life of John Clare

John Clare was born in Helpston in Northamptonshire in 1793. He was the son of a cottage farmer who was so poor that his family often did not have enough to eat. As soon as he could walk, he went for long rambles in the countryside. Once, when still very young, he walked so far that he got lost. He was eventually found several miles away from home.

The next thing he fell in love with was poetry. He would scrape together his pennies and buy second-hand books of poetry whenever he could. Then he began to make up his own rhymes, but as paper was expensive, he had to write on any scrap of paper he could find such as old sugar bags. Writing poetry was a very unusual hobby for a cottage farmer's son, so he kept it secret, hiding his verses in a little hole in the chimney breast. However, when his mother found out about it, she encouraged him to keep writing. Despite the fact that he was a good poet, Clare was bad at spelling and didn't know how to use punctuation. Also, he spoke in a strong Northamptonshire dialect and many dialect words found their way into his poems.

The third love of his life was Mary Joyce. She was the daughter of a well-to-do farmer and was four years his junior. Clare met her at the village school which they both attended. She was a beautiful girl with blue eyes and blonde hair, and Clare soon fell in love with her. When Clare grew older, he dreamed that he might one day marry her. However, Mary's father would never have agreed to the marriage. Clare was far too poor and he had no prospects. He wasn't even a good farm labourer.

By the time he was 23, Clare had given up all hope of marrying Mary, but he continued to love her and write poems about her. Soon after, in 1820, he married Martha Turner, the daughter of a poor farmer.

At the age of 27, Clare's first book of poems was published in London. It was a great success and went through four editions in a year. This was partly because his publisher, Taylor, had described him as a "a peasant poet" to tap into a recent fashion. However, the fad for peasant poets soon passed and his next three books sold badly. Taylor edited Clare's poems by correcting the

spelling, adding punctuation, and removing many dialect words. The latter was considered an 'improvement' at the time, but is now seen as a great loss.

Clare couldn't do farm work and earned very little from his poetry. As a result Clare and Martha, and their seven children, lived in utter poverty. Sadly, what little he did earn was often mismanaged by his agents. Clare's worries about money and a feeling that he didn't belong in the world of farming-folk nor the London literary world led to periods of depression and strange behaviour. He fought against these problems for many years, but by the time he was 44, his friends felt that he would be better off in High Beech Private Asylum in Epping Forest. Unfortunately, this didn't really help because he still worried about his family. Four years later, he ran away and remained free for six months. Finally he was caught and put in Northampton General Lunatic Asylum where he stayed until he died in 1864. It was during this period that he wrote some of his finest poetry, including his most famous poem 'I Am'.

Was Clare really insane? Probably not. All he needed was a modest income to provide for his family and the stress that caused his insanity would have been removed.

John Clare is our finest nature poet. He writes about the nature that he knew and loved in a natural language unspoiled by the artificiality of many better-educated poets such as Gray or Wordsworth.

UNIT 6

Reports

In this unit, children write a series of non-chronological reports for a science topic. It begins with an analysis of a report on Mars, then takes children through the process of researching, planning and writing their own reports for a class book on the solar system. The unit ends by exploring how the reports can be presented using IT to produce reference book double-page spreads, CD-ROMs or web pages. Hour 4 links to Unit 45 in *Grammar for Writing*.

Hour	Shared text-level work	Shared word-/ sentence-level work	Guided and independent work	Plenary
1 Reading a report	Reading report on Mars; identifying genre features.	Examining the report's use of tenses.	Revising active and passive; reordering paragraphs.	Discussing paragraph order, noting non-chronological nature.
2 Researching a report	Planning research for class topic.	Researching origins of astronomical bodies.	Researching allocated topics.	Comparing notes.
3 Planning a report	Showing how to develop a plan from research.	Improving sentences and paragraphs.	Making plans from research files.	Checking plans for subheadings and paragraphs.
4 Writing a report	Writing a report from the plan.	Revising active and passive sentences.	Writing reports.	Evaluating reports; converting active to passive.
5 Publishing a report	Analysing features of published report in different media; showing how to publish week's work.		Designing and publishing their work.	Making displays of the work.

Key assessment opportunities
● Do the children recognise the features of non-chronological reports?
● Can they research, plan and write non-chronological reports?
● Can they use IT to present the visual features?

Reading a report

Objectives

NLS
T13: To secure understanding of the features of non-chronological reports: introductions to orientate reader; use of generalisations to categorise; language to describe and differentiate; impersonal language; mostly present tense.
S2: To revise earlier work on verbs and to understand the terms active and passive; being able to transform a sentence from active to passive, and vice versa.

What you need
● Photocopiable page 70.

Shared text-level work
● Read photocopiable page 70 and identify some of these key features of non-chronological reports:

> ● an introduction to orientate the reader
> ● a number of paragraphs about different aspects of the subject – these could be arranged in any order
> ● technical, subject-specific vocabulary
> ● formal and impersonal language style
> ● mostly present tense, except for historical information or future predictions
> ● some passive constructions
> ● conclusion – an ending comment.

● Ask the children questions like the following:

> ● How does the introduction orientate the reader? (It introduces the subject in a general way and gives key facts that prepare the reader for the details that follow.)
> ● What technical vocabulary did you notice? (*Asteroid, iron-oxide* and so on.)
> ● How is it formal and impersonal? (Formal – no slang, chatty language or contracted forms; impersonal – use of third person, we are not aware of the personality of the writer.)

Shared sentence-level work
● Explore the use of tenses as one of the key features. Ask the children to find examples of the present tense (subject and verb) in the second half of the text. For example, *the atmosphere... is; temperatures... range.*
● Then ask them to find examples of the past and futures tenses and explain why they have been used. For example, *the European Space Agency launched...* and *the first astronauts will.* Here, the past tense is used because Mars Express has already been launched, two years ago; the future tense in the second example indicates that this is a prediction about future developments in space exploration.

Guided and independent work
● Revise with one group the use of active and passive by playing the 'Who-did-what-and-to-whom?' game in Unit 45 of *Grammar for Writing.*
● Kinaesthetic learning: ask the other children, working in pairs, to number each paragraph on photocopiable page 70 and then cut the text into paragraphs. They should then explore the second bullet point in the list of key features by sequencing the paragraphs in different ways. Ask them to record the sequences of paragraphs which work the best.

Plenary
● Discuss the sequencing exercise: the introduction and conclusion (one and seven) need to be placed at the beginning and end. Other than that, any order of paragraphs works well because the report is non-chronological.

Differentiation

Less able
● Ask children to paste the introduction and the conclusion at the top and bottom of an A3 page. They can then shuffle the other paragraphs freely and the result will always work.

More able
● Give a group of more able children a more difficult text to work with in the same way. For example, the *Encarta Encyclopedia* entry for Mars.

Researching a report

Objectives

NLS
T17: To write non-chronological reports linked to other subjects.
W8: To research the origins of proper names.

What you need
● Photocopiable page 71
● access to library, CD-ROMs and internet and/or selection of reference books.

Shared text-level work
● Tell the children that they are going to work together to write a class booklet entitled 'The solar system', and that the first step is to research their allocated topic.
● To do this, they will need to create a research file to ensure that they draw information from several sources and reuse information without merely copying it out.
● Display photocopiable page 71 and explain that it is a research file for Neptune. Ask the children to look at the file and state what different sources and different kinds of information they can see:

● picture of Neptune
● a table giving key facts
● notes from a reference book
● notes from a CD-ROM
● notes from the internet.

Shared word-level work
● Ask the children what the research file tells us about the origin of the name Neptune. (The planet was named after the Roman god of the sea because of its deep blue colour.)
● Ask them to find out about the origins of the names of the planets and moons they will be researching, including names for geographical features. For example, What is the origin of the name Olympus Mons on Mars? (It is named after Mount Olympus, the legendary home of the Greek gods, because of its large size.)

Guided and independent work
● Allocate a different topic to each child, for example a moon (only the important ones), a planet, comets, space exploration, theories about the solar system.
● Ask the children to prepare a research file. This should be one A3 sheet only, to focus note-making. On this the children should sketch illustrations or diagrams, copy tables and lists, and make notes (not merely copy out) from at least two sources.
● Ask one or two children to write their notes on OHT for use in the plenary session.

Plenary
● Remind the children that, to be helpful, notes need to contain key information, be brief and easy to read.
● Display some examples of notes written for the research file and ask the rest of the class to evaluate whether the notes are helpful.
● Note that many of the planets and their moons are named after Greek or Roman gods.

Differentiation

Less able
● Allocate one of the easier topics, for example, Pluto where there is enough information to research, but not so much as to become confusing.

More able
● Allocate one of the more challenging topics, such as theories about the solar system, and allow two A3 sheets for the resource file.

Planning a report

Objectives

NLS
T17: To write non-chronological reports linked to other subjects.
S5: To form complex sentences through, eg using different connecting devices; reading back complex sentences for clarity of meaning, and adjusting as necessary; evaluating which links work best; exploring how meaning is affected by the sequence and structure of clauses.

What you need

● Photocopiable pages 70–72.

Shared text-level work

● Display photocopiable page 71 and demonstrate how to make a plan from the research file by drawing a spidergram on the board. (The final result should resemble that on photocopiable page 72 and should be kept for use in Hour 4.)

● Begin by drawing a circle and write Neptune inside it. Ask the children to look at the information in the resource file and suggest a subtopic. Draw a line to another circle and write the subtopic inside it. Some of the subtopics will have further subtopics, for example the information about the Voyager space probes and the discovery of six more moons.

● Finally, decide on the order in which the subtopics will be presented as text, and if any need to be grouped into the same paragraph. You could say: Explaining key facts makes a good introduction, so we will number this 1. What shall we put next? And later on: How shall we paragraph the information about moons? We haven't much to say about Neptune's first two known moons, so let's put it in the same paragraph as the other six.

Shared sentence-level work

● Demonstrate how to achieve better sentence cohesion within paragraphs. Write these two sentences on the board:
  Saturn is a gas giant.
  Saturn is surrounded by rings.

● Ask the children how this information could be better expressed. (For example, replace *Saturn* with the pronoun it in the second sentence. Join the sentences by replacing *Saturn* with the conjunction *and,* or (better), the relative pronoun *which* or *that.*)

● Analyse the paragraph structure of photocopiable page 70 by giving each paragraph a subtitle.

● Explain that paragraphing is a matter of style. For example, can they find any two paragraphs that could have been combined into one longer paragraph? (Paragraphs one and two both give basic information about Mars; paragraphs three and four are both about the surface features of Mars.)

Differentiation

Less able
● Make sure that research files are clear and helpful. If necessary, give out prepared notes similar to those on photocopiable page 71.

More able
● Encourage children to use more complex spidergrams with more levels of organisation.

Guided and independent work

● Ask the children to make plans from their research files using the spidergram method:

  ● Make a spidergram.
  ● Number the subtopics in the order in which you want to present them.
  ● Decide if any subtopics need to be grouped together in the same paragraph.

Plenary

● Display and discuss some of the spidergrams. Are they clear? Have the subtopics been numbered? Has thought been given to grouping subtopics into paragraphs?

Writing a report

Shared text-level work
● Display photocopiable page 71, and the spidergram from Hour 3.
● Model how to write a non-chronological report about Neptune using the resource file and the spidergram. Some suggestions are given on photocopiable page 72 of what to write and comments to give the children while you write.
● Involve the children where possible to add ideas, suggest sentences and advise you how to punctuate your text.

Shared sentence-level work
● Revise the active and passive forms of verbs. Ask the children to refer back to the example of a passive sentence that you commented on during writing the report, for instance, *Neptune was discovered by German astronomer Johann Gottfried Galle*.
● Now ask the children to put this into the active voice (*German astronomer Johann Gottfried Galle discovered Neptune*) and discuss the difference in emphasis. The sentence in the passive voice emphasises Neptune, the subject of the report. The active sentence emphasises the person who discovered Neptune, Galle, and thus would be the best form to use in a biography of Galle.

Guided and independent work
● Ask the children to write their reports using the notes from their research files and their spidergram plans.
● Encourage them to use the passive voice where appropriate, and remind them to include some of the other key features of non-chronological reports identified in Hour 1 (some of these will be dictated by their plans):

> ● an introduction to orientate the reader
> ● a number of paragraphs about different aspects of the subject
> ● technical, subject-specific vocabulary
> ● formal and impersonal language style
> ● mostly present tense, except for historical information or future predictions
> ● conclusion – an ending comment.

● If the children finish their reports, remind them to read through their work, checking for sense, grammar, spellings and punctuation as well as genre features.

Plenary
● Read out some examples of the children's reports and evaluate them against the list of key features of non-chronological reports.
● Give the children some fun phrases in the active voice and challenge them to be the fastest to change them to passive.

Publishing a report

Shared text-level work
● Choose either a double-page spread from a reference book that makes good use of different subheadings, boxes, diagrams and so on, a page from a CD-ROM or a page on a website as the basis for this lesson.
● At the most basic level, the children can produce effective double-page spreads entirely by hand. At the most advanced level, appropriate software can be used to design a simple web page.
● Display an example, such as **www.spacekids.com**, and point out the visual features, in this case, illustrations, subheadings, hyperlinks. Other examples might include: bullet points, photographs, movie and animation clips, lists, tables, text boxes, use of different colours and fonts.
● Next, demonstrate or work with the children to present the information researched earlier in the week in the chosen format. For example, many word processors and desktop publishers allow pages to be saved in HTML format and then to be viewed in an internet browser. Some even include 'wizards' to guide you through the process.
● Using the four facts in the first paragraph of the Neptune report on photocopiable page 72, explore how to re-present information in different forms, and to consider which forms are best suited to which medium.

Guided and independent work
● Visual learning: help the children, working in pairs, to use the information researched earlier in the week to design one of the following (encourage them to make their own choice of form where possible):

● a reference book double-page spread
● a CD-ROM page
● a web page.

● Advise them to begin by planning everything on paper. For example, they may find it helpful to produce sketches of the page or screen layout, make notes about where hyperlinks will lead to, and think about a balance of text and images.
● Where possible, let them use IT resources to produce final versions to achieve as professional a result as possible.

Plenary
● Display and discuss examples of web pages (or other media). How easy is it to access information, and how interesting and enjoyable are they to use?
● Pull the week's work together by collating and binding all the reports (in handwritten or word-processed format depending on available resources) into a booklet entitled 'The solar system'.
● If possible, produce duplicate copies of the book and make it available throughout the school.

Mars

Mars, the fourth planet from the sun, is named after the Roman god of war because of its red colour. Mars is about 228 million km from the sun. It is about half the size of Earth and about one tenth of Earth's mass. The Martian day is 39 minutes longer than an Earth day and the Martian year is 687 Earth days.

Mars has two moons, Phobos and Deimos, named after the attendants of the Roman god Mars. Phobos and Deimos are not round, like our moon, but are heavily-cratered lumps of rock that are probably captured asteroids.

Mars is covered with iron-oxide dust. In other words, Mars is a 'rusty' planet. The colour varies from light red to dark red. The light colour is the heavily-cratered highlands, and the dark colour is the smoother lowlands. Two white polar caps are visible even from Earth. The northern ice cap is made of water ice and is about 1000 km in diameter. The southern ice cap consists mainly of carbon dioxide ice.

Close to the equator there is a huge canyon named Valles Marineris. This canyon is about 4000 km long, 200 km wide and 7 km deep. For comparison, the Grand Canyon in the USA is only about 1.6 km deep. Mars also has the largest volcano in the solar system, Olympus Mons. It is 24 km high – almost three times as high as Mount Everest. Nearby are three other large volcanoes.

The atmosphere of Mars is very thin and is composed of carbon dioxide (95%), nitrogen (3%), argon (1.6%), oxygen and other rare gases. However, the atmosphere is dense enough for clouds, dust storms and hurricanes similar to those on Earth. Temperatures on Mars range from about –130° C to 30° C.

In 2003, the European Space Agency launched Mars Express. Unfortunately, something went wrong with the lander Beagle 2 and it was unable to send back information. However, NASA's two Mars Exploration Rovers, Spirit and Opportunity, launched in the same year, were successful, and sent back evidence that Mars had once been covered in liquid water – a basic requirement for life.

Mars still holds on to its biggest secret – but even if there never has been life on Mars, there will be soon. Scientists predict that, before the middle of this century, the first astronauts will plant their footprints in the red Martian dust.

Neptune resource file

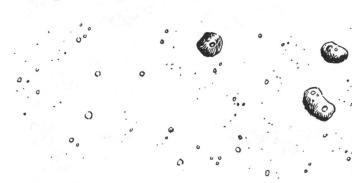

Illustration (from Source 1, internet)

Table (from Source 2, CD-ROM)

Neptune data

Distance from sun	4,500,000,000km
Distance from Earth	4,313,000,000km
Diameter	49,532km
Rotational period (day)	16 hrs
Period of orbit (year)	165 yrs
Temperature	–218°C
Number of satellites	8

Notes from Source 1 (CD-ROM)

1843 – British astronomer John Couch Adams notices irregularities in the orbit of Neptune

1846 – French astronomer Urbain Jean Joseph Leverrier calculates the position of a new planet

1846 – German astronomer Johann Gottfried Galle finds the planet in 1846 using Leverrier's calculations

Notes from Source 3 (reference book)

8th planet from the sun

4th largest in the solar system

named after Neptune, Roman god of the sea

gas giant – like Jupiter and Saturn

deep atmosphere around a liquid surface and a solid core

atmosphere consists of hydrogen, helium, and methane, which gives the planet its blue colour

has 5 thin rings and 8 moons

largest moon is Triton

2nd largest moon is Proteus

Notes from Source 2 (internet)

Voyagers 1 and 2 – NASA space probes launched in 1977

passed Neptune in 1989

discovered 6 new moons (only two known before)

discovered Neptune's rings

photographed huge storms in the atmosphere

measured wind speeds of 2000 km/h – highest on any planet

Neptune

Suggested text

Neptune is the eighth planet from the sun and the fourth largest in the solar system. It is 4.5 billion km from the sun and about 49,500 km in diameter.

Neptune was discovered by German astronomer Johann Gottfried Galle in 1846 after its approximate position had been worked out by mathematics.

Because it has a deep atmosphere, Neptune is described as a gas giant. The other gas giants in out solar system are Jupiter and Saturn.

Neptune's atmosphere consists of hydrogen, helium, and methane, which gives the planet its beautiful blue colour.

Eight moons orbit Neptune. The largest moon is Triton and the second largest is Proteus. However, it was not until Voyager 2 reached the planet in 1989 that scientists discovered that Neptune had six other moons and five thin rings.

Voyager also photographed huge storms in the atmosphere and measured wind speeds of 2000 km/h, which are the highest on any planet.

Suggested comments

I am giving the most important information in the introduction. I have picked out the four most important facts. These four facts are in two sentences, each containing two clauses linked by and.

Passive voice here to put the emphasis on Neptune.

I could add more details about how this was done.

This sentence starts with an initial conjunction to add variety.

So far, three of my paragraphs begin with Neptune, so I wanted to begin this one in a different way.

The connective, however, links the information from source 2.

The additional information five and thin comes from source 3.

The connective also links this paragraph to the previous paragraph.

The phrase *highest on any planet* rounds off the report effectively.

UNIT 1

Poetry

The unit begins with 'The Lesson', a humorous poem by Roger McGough, used to explore how poets play with meaning. Hour 3 introduces another poem of the same title by Edward Lucie-Smith, exploring powerful feelings. Hour 3, and the lessons that follow, offer a methodology that helps children to interpret poems with multi-layered meanings. The children begin by paraphrasing a poem, then focus on poetic techniques. In Hour 5, these two elements are blended to produce a commentary on the poem. Personal response is explored, and this is added to the commentary as a concluding paragraph. As personal response is an important component of the unit, try to ensure that all of the children experience it.

Hour	Shared text-level work	Shared word-/ sentence-level work	Guided and independent work	Plenary
1 Humorous verse	Reading 'The Lesson', noting style, form and language use.	Exploring proverbs.	Researching proverbs; annotating the poem, playing with words and meaning.	Sharing jokes that have come from poem analysis.
2 Nonsense!	Reading 'Nooligan'; finding nonsense words and pinpointing humour.		Analysing other poem, reporting to the class.	Listening to the reports.
3 Another lesson	Reading and analysing another 'The Lesson' poem.		Paraphrasing one verse of the poem.	Discussing the poem's meaning.
4 Analysis	Re-reading the poem, exploring feelings revealed in the poem.		Using annotations to build critical response to poem.	Sharing comments.
5 Commentary	Demonstrating how to write a critical commentary.	Editing the commentary.	Combining previous work to write a commentary on the poem.	Discussing views; comparing the two poems.

Key assessment opportunities
● Do the children understand how poets play with words and meaning to create humour?
● Do they recognise different verse forms?
● Can they explain main figures of speech, eg simile, metaphor, personification?
● Can they analyse how messages, moods, feelings and attitudes are conveyed in poetry?

Humorous verse

Objectives

NLS
T4: To investigate humorous verse: how poets play with meanings; nonsense words and how meaning can be made of them; where the appeal lies.
W6: To collect and explain the meanings and origins of proverbs.

What you need

● Photocopiable page 79
● reference books with proverbs or access to the internet
● table (see Guided and independent work) provided on A3 sheets.

Shared text-level work

● Display photocopiable page 79 and read the poem to the children.
● Ask: *Why do we find this poem funny when there is so much violence?* (It is the opposite of what we expect to happen, and it is comic-strip style violence.)
● Go through the poem again, and ask the children to look out for:

> play with words and meanings
> a simile
> an example of personification.

● Annotate these as the children find them.
● Demonstrate how to analyse the verse form by noting the rhyme scheme as ABCB.
● Discuss rhythm: the more or less regular alternation of light beats and heavy beats (stresses) in speech or music.
● Ask the children to count the beats in each line of the second stanza (they should find three in each line). Ask them to identify the stressed syllables in each line, and annotate them with stress marks, like this:

   /   /   /
The theme for today is violence…

Shared word-level work

● Discuss some examples of proverbs (sayings that state a belief about the world), for example, *a stitch in time saves nine*.
● Discuss how proverbs can be used as a basis for writing poems. For example, a poem could relate a short incident and end with the proverb.

Guided and independent work

● Ask one group of children to find other proverbs in the reference materials you have provided or the internet. Tell them to try to find about half a dozen unusual proverbs.
● Provide the following table at the top of an a A3 sheet and ask the other children to complete it using ideas from the annotations written in whole class work.
● Tell them to use their own words in the first column and not to copy from the poem.

Differentiation

Less able
● Check that children are using their own words in the first column of the table.

More able
● Ask children to add an extra column *Why this stanza is funny*.

What happens in the poem	What you expect to happen	Playing with words and meanings
There is chaos in the classroom, and when the teacher walks in, the children ignore him.	The children should stop misbehaving when the teacher comes in.	*'nooligans'* is a word made up by McGough from the word hooligans. It reflects a dialect that drops the 'h'.

Plenary

● Share some of the jokes and ideas from the tables, focusing particularly on where the appeal lies and where the humour is.

Nonsense!

Objectives

NLS
T3: To recognise how poets manipulate words: for their quality of sound; for their connotations; for multiple layers of meaning.
T4: To investigate humorous verse: how poets play with meanings; nonsense words and how meaning can be made of them; where the appeal lies.

S&L
65 Speaking: To use techniques of dialogue talk to explore ideas, topics or issues.

What you need
● Photocopiable page 80.

Shared text-level work

● Read 'Nooligan'. Then ask the children what a nooligan is (hooligan). How did Roger McGough make up the word? (From listening to the way people speak in some dialects. The '*h*' is dropped, and the '*n*' of '*an*' sounds as though it is the first letter of the next word.)
● Ask the children which other words in the poem have been formed in the same way. (Nard, nassassin, nired.)
● Ask what, apart from the nonsense words, makes the poem funny. As a clue, tell the children to look carefully at the line in brackets at the end of each stanza. This line gives an amusing anticlimax to each stanza:

> the boy is only one of the 'bosses'
> he would never actually kill anyone
> he is not good enough to play football, only to watch
> he is not going to be a hired gun, just a soldier.

● Tell the children to annotate their copies of the poem during the following discussion. Ask: *What other dialect or slang words and phrases can you find?* (*Give a toss, 'me' instead of 'my'*). *What spellings are used to represent the way the boy speaks?* ('*ead, bleedin, watchin, gonna.*)

Guided and independent work

● Ask the children to work in groups of four to discuss and analyse one of the poems on photocopiable page 80.
● Help the children to decide which poem to discuss (see differentiation notes below) and try to ensure that all of the poems are covered.
● Tell each group to be prepared to report back on how the poet may have got the idea for the nonsense words and why the poem is funny.

Plenary

● Ask one group to report back on each poem. Consider, for example:

> ● 'Limerick': the nonsense words are built on the form of the word hosiery. The poem is funny because of the nonsense words, the rhythm, and the idea that the ankle's connecting purpose is secondary to its fashion possibilities.
> ● 'Away from it all': if the word for a person/thing ends in *-onk/-unk* and the word for a place ends in *-astery* (as in *monk* and *monastery*), then a *trunk* goes in a *tronastery*. Additional humour comes from the examples.
> ● 'Little Spider': more difficult, but the humour is mostly in the sounds of the invented words. '*Sadly*' gives a word ending that is used to create nonsense words '*webly*', '*hebly*'; '*grieves*' comes from making '*grief*' rhyme with '*leaves*'.

Differentiation

Less able
● Ask the group to discuss 'Nooligan', using ideas from the shared session.

More able
● Ask this group to discuss 'Little Spider'.

Another lesson

Objectives

NLS
T6: To read and interpret poems in which meanings are implied or multi-layered; to discuss, interpret challenging poems with others.

What you need
● Photocopiable pages 81 and 82.

Shared text-level work
● Display the poem by Edward Lucie-Smith on photocopiable page 81 (without the annotations).
● Read the poem a few times, then ask the children if they can explain what it is about. What is the 'story' in the poem?
● Tell the children that you are going to work together to paraphrase the poem to help them to understand it. Explain that a paraphrase is an explanation of the poem in simple language.
● Scribe the suggested paraphrase from photocopiable page 82 (or write your own) while you explain what you are doing. For example, I am leaving out descriptive phrases and am not 'rewriting' line by line. (He burst into tears requires reading the second and third lines.)
● Analyse the verse form as in Hour 1. Ask the children to call out letters of the alphabet after each line to show the rhyme scheme (ABCBDADC).
● Revise the term half-rhyme and ask the children if they can find any examples (jar/bitterer; stilled/sculled).
● Ask the children to count the beats in each line (they should find five). Explain that lines of poetry with five stresses are called pentameters, from the Greek word for five. Ask them to identify the stressed syllables in the first stanza and annotate them with stress marks. Re-read the poem together, asking the children to notice the rhythm of stresses.
● Discuss personal responses to the poem. Ask: What did the poem make you think and feel? Have you had similar experiences of unexpected feelings? Did this poem describe them well?

Guided and independent work
● Ask the children to write a paraphrase of the second stanza of the poem. Explain that they should use the past tense here because the boy is now an adult and is remembering what happened.
● Emphasise the importance of using simple, clear language.

Plenary
● Ask some children to read out their paraphrases. Discuss differences, including between them and the suggestion on photocopiable page 82.
● Refer the children to what they learned about how poets play with meaning in Hour 1. Ask them what they make of the title of this poem. (It is a lesson, not because it is in school, but because the boy has learned something important about life.)

Differentiation

Less able
● Remove the paraphrase of the first stanza from display and ask children to write their own version of this.

More able
● Ask children to paraphrase the whole poem.

Objectives

NLS
T5: To analyse how messages, moods, feelings and attitudes are conveyed in poetry.

What you need

● Photocopiable pages 81 and 82.

Analysis

Shared text-level work

● Display photocopiable page 81, without the annotations.
● Read the poem again, then ask the children to point out any words to do with feelings. Annotate these as the children point them out: tears, grief, cried, shame, relief, indifferent, pride.
● Talk about the range of feelings experienced by the boy in the poem. Ask the children: What did the boy expect to feel about what happened? What did he feel instead? Why?
● Revise the term metaphor and ask the children to find examples (lines 2 to 3, 12 to 13, 16). Annotate the children's suggestions.
● Now ask the children how each metaphor helps to express a feeling more vividly. (Lines 2 to 3 describe the blinding effect of a sudden rush of tears; lines 12 to 13 give a visual comparison to describe the indifference of some of the pupils in assembly; line 16 helps us to imagine the suddenness with which the feeling of pride came and went.)
● Finally, ask the children to identify the poet's use of significant adjectives and powerful verbs. Annotate them as the children point them out and discuss the effect they have. In the line, *flashed a sudden fin*, for instance, the verb expresses vividly how quickly and strikingly the feeling came and the adjective reinforces this sense of speed.

Guided and independent work

● Leave your annotations on display. Ask the children to work in pairs to compose a sentence describing each one (and any others of their own), for example: A metaphor is used to describe the blinding effect of a sudden rush of tears. This will build into a critical response to the poem.

Plenary

● Share some of the children's sentences, then display photocopiable page 82 and read the examples in *Sentences from annotations*.
● Ask the children if they agree with all of the comments and to add anything they feel they have missed to their own lists.

Differentiation

Less able

● Help children to understand the comparative adjective bitterer by placing it in a table with headings Adjective, Comparative and Superlative and asking them to experiment with other adjectives.

More able

● After each sentence, encourage children to add another, giving a fuller analysis: A metaphor is used to describe the blinding effect of a sudden rush of tears. It emphasises the sudden and overwhelming feeling of grief felt by the boy.

UNIT 1 HOUR 5 🔲 Poetry

Commentary

Objectives

NLS
T14: To write commentaries or summaries crediting views expressed by using expressions such as 'The writer says that...'
S3: To revise work on complex sentences: identifying main clauses; ways of connecting clauses; constructing complex sentences; appropriate use of punctuation.

What you need

● Photocopiable page 82.
● the children's annotated photocopiable page 81, their paraphrases and sentences.

Shared text-level work

● Explain to the children that they are going to put together their paraphrase from Hour 3 with their sentences from Hour 4 to create a detailed commentary on Edward Lucie-Smith's 'The Lesson'.
● Demonstrate how to do this by displaying sections one and two of photocopiable page 82 and using section three as a basis for a scribed example of a commentary.
● As you write, explain what you are doing. For example:

> I am beginning with an introduction to orientate the reader. This is a good place to include the information about the poem being written in the first person...

● As you continue, help the children to understand how you are fitting the sentences into the paraphrase. For example, draw an arrow from section two, *A metaphor is used to describe the blinding effect of a sudden rush of tears*, to the place where you are going to put it, that is, after the first sentence in section one.

Shared sentence-level work

● Taking suggestions from the children, point out the places where you need to make changes to the wording to ensure that the commentary reads well. For example, the third paragraph begins with the phrase, *In the first stanza...*; the second sentence of this paragraph introduces the sentence about the metaphor and this is linked into the paraphrase by changing *makes it* to *making it*.

Guided and independent work

● Ask the children to combine their paraphrases from Hour 3 with their sentences from Hour 4 to produce a commentary on the poem, following guidance given in whole class work.
● Encourage them to make the last paragraph of the commentary their own personal responses.

Plenary

● Share some complete reviews of the poem. As each one is read out, ask the rest of the class to evaluate how well the different material (paraphrase, sentences and personal responses) have been blended together.
● Compare personal responses and make sure it is understood that all are valid if backed up by reference to and understanding of the poem.
● Ask the children to compare this '*lesson*' and that by Roger McGough.
● Which poem did they enjoy most and why?
● Which did they feel was the most true to life?
● Does either poem relate to their own experiences of school?

Differentiation

Less able

● Children may need help with the changes needed to the wording to ensure that the commentary reads well.

More able

● Remind children to incorporate the additional sentences they wrote in Hour 4.

The Lesson

A poem that raises the question:
Should there be capital punishment in schools?

Chaos ruled OK in the classroom
as bravely the teacher walked in
the nooligans ignored him
his voice was lost in the din

'The theme for today is violence
and homework will be set
I'm going to teach you a lesson
one that you'll never forget'

He picked on a boy who was shouting
and throttled him then and there
then garrotted the girl behind him
(the one with the grotty hair)

Then sword in hand he hacked his way
between the chattering rows
'First come, first severed,' he declared
'fingers, feet, or toes'

He threw the sword at a latecomer
it struck with deadly aim
then pulling out a shotgun
he continued with his game

The first blast cleared the backrow
(where those who skive hang out)
they collapsed like rubber dinghies
when the plug's pulled out

'Please may I leave the room sir?'
a trembling vandal enquired
'Of course you may' said teacher
put the gun to his temple and fired

The Head popped a head round the
      doorway
to see why a din was being made
nodded understandingly
then tossed in a grenade

And when the ammo was well spent
with blood on every chair
Silence shuffled forward
with its hands up in the air

The teacher surveyed the carnage
the dying and the dead
He waggled a finger severely
'Now let that be a lesson' he said

by Roger McGough

ZERO TOLERANCE POLICY!

Nooligan and other nonsense

Nooligan

I'm a nooligan
don't give a toss
in our class
I'm the boss
(well, one of them)

I'm a nooligan
got a nard 'ead
step out of line
and youre dead
(well, bleedin)

I'm a nooligan
I spray me name
all over town
footballs me game
(well, watchin)

I'm a nooligan
violence is fun
gonna be a nassassin
or a nired gun
(well, a soldier)

Roger McGough

Limerick

The ankle's is made for exposiery
Of the latest designs in silk hosiery;
Also, I suspect,
It's a means to connect
The part called the calf with the toesiery.

Anon

Away from it all

I wish I were a Tibetan monk
Living in a monastery.
I would unpack my trunk
And store it in a tronastery;
I would collect all my junk
And send it to a jonastery;
I would try to reform a drunk,
And pay his expenses at a dronastery.
If my income shrunk
I would send it to a shronastery.

Ogden Nash

Little Spider

Little spider
spider sadly
in the webly
light of leaves!
Why deride a
spide's mentadly
when it's hebly
full of grieves?
Little spider
legged and lonely
in the bony
way of thieves.
Where's the fly-da
on the phonebly?

Mervyn Peake

The Lesson by Edward Lucie-Smith

"Your father's gone," my bald headmaster said.
His shiny dome and brown tobacco jar
Splintered at once in tears. It wasn't grief.
I cried for knowledge which was bitterer
Than any grief. For there and then I knew
That grief has uses – that a father dead
Could bind the bully's fist a week or two;
And then I cried for shame, then for relief.

I was a month past ten when I learned this:
I still remember how the noise was stilled
In school-assembly when my grief came in.
Some goldfish in a bowl quietly sculled
Around their shining prison on its shelf,
They were indifferent. All other eyes
Were turned towards me. Somewhere in myself
Pride, like a goldfish, flashed a sudden fin.

Day 1
rhyme scheme
rhythm
first person

Day 2
words that describe feelings
metaphors
adjectives
comparative adjective
powerful verbs
What did the boy learn?

Commentary Paraphrase

The headmaster tells the boy that his father is dead. The boy bursts into tears and this makes it look like the headmaster's shiny bald head and his tobacco jar have broken into many pieces. The boy isn't crying for grief, he is crying because he realises that he can use his grief to stop the bullies for a few weeks. He cries with shame at this thought and then he cries with relief.

The boy was ten years and one month old when this happened. He still remembers how the noise in school assembly stopped when he came in. Everybody looked at him, except for a few who didn't care – like goldfish swimming around a bowl. Then the boy had another unexpected feeling – pride – which came suddenly, like the flash of a goldfish's fin.

Sentences from annotations

The poem is written in the first person. This might suggest that the boy is the author himself.

A metaphor is used to describe the blinding effect of a sudden rush of tears.

The comparative adjective 'bitterer' emphasises that he feels more grief about this feeling than about the death.

'Stilled' is a powerful verb which emphasises how suddenly the hall went quiet.

A metaphor is used to describe how some children showed no interest in him.

A metaphor is used to describe the feeling of pride.

The adjective 'sudden' describes how quickly the feeling came. It goes with the powerful verb 'flashed' in the metaphor.

Commentary

'The Lesson' is a poem by Edward Lucie-Smith which describes how a boy feels when he hears about the death of his father. The poem is written in the first person, which suggests that the boy is the author himself.

The poem is written in rhyming verse (ABCBDADC) and each line has five stressed syllables (pentameters).

In the first stanza, the headmaster tells the boy that his father is dead. A metaphor is used to describe the blinding effect of a sudden rush of tears, making it look like the headmaster's shiny bald head and his tobacco jar have broken into many pieces. The boy isn't crying for grief, he is crying because he realises that he can use his grief to stop the bullies for a few weeks. The comparative adjective 'bitterer' emphasises that he feels more grief about this feeling than about the death. He cries with shame at this thought and then he cries with relief.

In the second stanza...

UNIT 2

Narrative 1

This unit is based on **The Last Vampire** by Willis Hall (Heinemann, available through internet book shops). This fits key objectives closely in terms of literary features, particularly the use of parody. However, the teaching ideas in this unit can be adapted for use with any book. Other suitable texts include *Count Karlstein* by Philip Pullman (Corgi), *The Demon Headmaster* series by Gillian Cross (OUP), *Witch Week* by Diana Wynne Jones (Collins) and RL Stine's *Goosebumps* books (Scholastic). Hour 1 is really a series of lessons. The first part introduces character cards, which the children will use as a focus for note-taking while reading the book. Reading will take a few weeks and should be done partly in school and partly for homework. When the book is finished, the children write about the characters as described in the second part of Hour 1. Hour 5 may also need additional time, depending on the extent to which children edit and polish their stories.

Hour	Shared text-level work	Shared word-/ sentence-level work	Guided and independent work	Plenary
1 Stock characters	Talking about vampire stories and stock characters.	Writing sentences from notes.	Making notes on certain characters for discussion after reading.	Sharing character descriptions.
2 Parody	Talking about *Dracula*; introducing parody.		Playing a card game to explore characterisation and to make up a short story.	Retelling improvised stories; identifying parodies.
3 Linking paragraphs	Examining how writers use new paragraphs and link them together.	Revising nouns, pronouns and connectives.	Analysing paragraph use in class text.	Having a 'walkabout' to appreciate each other's work.
4 Linking chapters	Examining writers' use and linking of chapters.		Analysing a sequence of three chapters.	Holding another walkabout.
5 Flashback	Exploring how flashback is used in class text.		Writing a scary story that includes a flashback.	Sharing stories; revising work of the unit.

Key assessment opportunities
● Can the children describe characters from a literary text?
● Do they understand what stock characters and plots are?
● Can they recognise and explain parody?
● Can they analyse how paragraphs and chapters are linked?
● Can they write a story in which time is handled in a non-linear way?

UNIT 2 HOUR 1 🔲 Narrative

Stock characters

Objectives

NLS
T7: To identify the key features of different types of literary text, eg stock characters, plot structure, and how particular texts conform, develop or undermine the type.
S3: To revise work on complex sentences: identifying main clauses; ways of connecting clauses; constructing complex sentences; appropriate use of punctuation.

What you need

● *The Last Vampire* (or chosen text)
● character cards (see Shared text-level work).

Shared text-level work
● Make a photocopiable set of character cards for your chosen text. If using *The Last Vampire*, draw simple figures to represent Albert, Emily and Henry Hollins; Count Alucard; Sergeant Alphonse and Henri Rumboll.
● Introduce the book to the children. Talk about vampire stories and ask what typical, 'stock', characters, settings, objects and plots they would expect to find. (Vampire, wolves, bats, castle, tomb, stake, garlic; vampire sucks blood, is killed with stake...)
● Explain that stock characters are two-dimensional or stereotypical. By contrast, true-to-life characters are three-dimensional, well-rounded and individual.
● Discuss advantages and disadvantages of using stock characters, settings, objects and plots. For example:

Advantages	Disadvantages
They are a kind of 'shorthand' so readers recognise them straight away. Useful for minor roles because the author cannot give much space to description.	Because they are 'ready made', stock characters and plots can be boring. We know how characters will act and react. There are few surprises.

● Display the cards showing the main characters. Tell the children that they should make notes on each character as they read the story. Advise them to focus on basic information, stock elements, and parody (which you will explain more about in the next lesson). Use Albert Hollins as an example:
Basic information: wife Emily; son Henry; on a motoring holiday in Europe, though would have preferred Cockleton-on-Sea.
Stock elements: old-fashioned man; has typical tastes – a 'snooze' in a deck chair, a 'roast and three veg'.

Shared sentence-level work
● Explore constructing complex sentences. For example, *Albert Hollins, who has a wife called Emily and son called Henry, is on a motoring holiday in Europe, though he would have preferred Cockleton-on-Sea.*

Guided and independent work
● Before starting the book: ask the children to work in mixed-ability groups of six. Allocate a character card to each child to make notes on during reading. Use the headings *Basic information* and *Stock elements*.
● When the book is finished: ask the groups to discuss their characters, particularly the stock characteristics compared with things that make them different, for example Count Alucard is partly a stock vampire, but also unusual because he is vegetarian. Re-organise the groups so that the children discuss a range of characters. Help the children make their notes into a full description.

Differentiation

Less able
● Allocate Albert Hollins, as a framework for this character was provided in shared work.

More able
● Allocate Henri Rumboll or Sergeant Alphonse Kropotel as it is more difficult to collect all the information about these characters.

Plenary
● Share some of the descriptions and add any missing information.

Parody

NLS
T7: To identify the key features of different types of literary text, eg stock characters, plot structure, and how particular texts conform, develop or undermine the type, eg through parody.
S3: To revise work on complex sentences: identifying main clauses; ways of connecting clauses; constructing complex sentences; appropriate use of punctuation.

What you need
● *The Last Vampire*
● Character description from *Dracula*
● Character cards for class text and for *Dracula*.

Shared text-level work

● Spend some time sharing knowledge about the most famous vampire story of all time: *Dracula*.
● Summarise the story, illustrating it with the character cards (of Dracula, Harker, succubus, wolf, Mina and Lucy, Van Helsing):

Count Dracula (card 1) wants to buy a house in England. Jonathan Harker (card 2) an estate agent, visits him in his castle in Transylvania to give him the papers to sign. Jonathan finds he is a prisoner and is attacked by a succubus (card 3). He escapes, risking the wolves (card 4) and gets back to Whitby, but Dracula has also travelled there. Dracula attacks Jonathan's fiancée, Mina and her friend Lucy (card 5). Mina survives, but Lucy becomes a vampire. A Dutch professor, Van Helsing, (card 6) kills Dracula.

● Tell the children that *The Last Vampire* is a parody of *Dracula* and other 'straight' vampire stories based on it. Explain that a parody is a text that uses the form and features of another text to make fun of it.
● Explain how to use the cards:
1. Shuffle both packs and put them face down in the centre of the table.
2. The first player takes a card from the top of each pack.
3. He/she will now have a card from a serious vampire story, *Dracula*, and a parody, *The Last Vampire*.
4. He/she now has to make up a short oral story about what would happen if the two characters met. For example, what would happen if Emily Hollins had to face a real wolf?

Guided and independent work

● Ask one or two groups to examine how characters are described in *Dracula*.
● Discuss how true-to-life characters are built up. (They are much more complex and interesting than stock characters. Authors describe their appearance, thoughts and so on in more detail.)
● Ask the rest of the class to play the game in groups of four. When each player has had a turn, ask them to develop a presentation to explain how *The Last Vampire* parodies vampire stories. This template can support children where necessary:
1. Explain what happened in the game. For example, Emily Hollins met a real wolf, and it ate her.
2. Compare this to what happens in *The Last Vampire*. For example, Emily Hollins made friends with the wolves.
3. Explain the effect: it is funny, because it is not scary or gory and is the opposite of what we expect.

Plenary

● Ask some groups to retell an improvised story, and others to give their presentation about parody.
● Revise the term parody and recap on the funniest examples.

Differentiation

Less able
● Use the template opposite.

More able
● Refer to other aspects of parody in *The Last Vampire*. In a typical vampire story, the hero must kill the vampire; here Albert and his family end up helping the vampire.

Linking paragraphs

Objectives

NLS

T1: To understand aspects of narrative structure, eg how chapters in a book (or paragraphs in a short story or chapter) are linked together.
S3: To revise work on complex sentences: identifying main clauses; ways of connecting clauses; constructing complex sentences; appropriate use of punctuation.

What you need

- *The Last Vampire*
- photocopiable page 89
- blank analysis template (photocopiable page 89 with examples deleted, leaving just the headings)
- other sequences of paragraphs for the children to analyse.

Shared text-level work

- Explain that authors start new paragraphs for many reasons, for example a change of topic, a change of time, a change of place, or a change of speaker in a passage of dialogue. However, the paragraphs need to be linked in some way to preserve the coherence of the text, for example by using a subject name, noun or pronoun, conjunction or connective.
- Read the paragraphs to be analysed. (The example on photocopiable page 89 is based on the opening paragraphs of *The Last Vampire*.)
- Display photocopiable page 89 and read each paragraph again, using the ideas on the sheet to demonstrate how to make notes on the blank analysis template.

Shared sentence-level work

- Revise the terminology used to explain paragraph links:

> Subject name or noun - the name of the person, place or thing that the paragraph is about.
>
> Pronoun, personal pronoun - the pronoun or personal pronoun that stands in place of the name of the person, place or thing.
>
> Conjunction or connective - different types of joining words.

- Revise the punctuation as the examples crop up in the text.

Guided and independent work

- Give each pair of children a different sequence of three paragraphs from the text, trying to ensure that a wide sample of the book is covered. Ask them to make notes about how the paragraghs are linked together as demonstrated in shared work, for example by explaining why the author started a new paragraph, and what the link with the previous paragraph is.

Plenary

- Remind the children of the most common techniques for linking paragraphs (see shared work), and identify them in some of the examples the children have found.
- Ask the children to pin their extract and their paragraph analyses to a noticeboard. Then organise a class 'walkabout' in which children can read and appreciate each other's work.

Differentiation

Less able
- Remove the demonstration example from display and ask children to work on the same three paragraphs.

More able
- Ask more able pairs to give particular attention to the way punctuation is used to structure complex sentences.

Objectives

NLS
T1: To understand aspects of narrative structure, eg how chapters in a book are linked together.

What you need

● *The Last Vampire*
● photocopiable page 90
● blank analysis template (photocopiable page 90 with examples deleted)
● a sequence of chapters to be analysed.

Linking chapters

Shared text-level work

● Revise the work done on linking paragraphs and explain to the children that they are going to examine the use and linkage of chapters in a similar way.
● Explain to the children that authors start new chapters for many reasons, such as to present a different point of view, an important step forward in the plot, a change of character, a change of setting, a change of time.
● Chapters also need to be linked in some way to preserve the coherence of the narrative, perhaps by including the same characters, the same setting, the same situation but a different point of view.
● Explain to the children the content of the chapters they are going to analyse. (The example on photocopiable page 90 is based on chapters two to four of *The Last Vampire*.) This can be done by using the summaries in column one of photocopiable page 90.
● Demonstrate how to write notes in column two using the notes on photocopiable page 90 as an example. Encourage the children to contribute ideas as you talk through each reason and link.

Guided and independent work

● Organise the children into pairs and give each pair of children a different sequence of three chapters in the book. Ask them to make notes on how the story is broken up into chapters and how the chapters are linked, as demonstrated in shared work.
● If possible, try to organise the work so that the whole book is covered. (In the case of *The Last Vampire*, this is easy as it contains only 12 chapters.)

Plenary

● Discuss some of the most common techniques for linking chapters, using the notes on photocopiable page 90 as a starting point.
● Ask the children to add their chapter analyses to the noticeboard display begun in the previous lesson, then organise another walkabout session so that the children can look at each other's work.

Differentiation

Less able
● Remove the demonstration example from display and ask children to work on the same three chapters.

More able
● Ask more able pairs to analyse how time is managed. (In chapters two to four, three things are happening at more or less the same time - Albert goes to the village, Emily tames the wolves, Henry meets count Alucard.)

UNIT 2 HOUR 5 Narrative 1

Flashback

Objectives

NLS

T1: To understand aspects of narrative structure, eg how authors handle time, eg flashbacks, stories within stories, dreams; how the passing of time is conveyed to the reader.
T11: To write own story using, eg flashbacks or a story within a story to convey the passing of time.

What you need

● *The Last Vampire.*

Shared text-level work

● Re-read chapter one from the start to '*Emily thought hard. 'Germany,'* *she said at last*'. (If using another text, find a point where flashback is used.) Ask the children to listen carefully for the beginning and end of a flashback. (The flashback begins, fairly typically, *It had all started one muggy, overcast afternoon...* and ends *...sampling the delights of Europe*.)

● Ask the children if it would work if we placed the events of this flashback in 'real' chronological sequence, that is, at the beginning of the story. (It would, but the opening would not necessarily have grabbed the reader's attention. Purely linear stories sometimes lack the depth that the addition of flashback can add.)

● Discuss other techniques the author uses to handle time. For example, in chapters two to four of *The Last Vampire*, three things are happening at more or less the same time (*Albert goes to the village, Emily tames the wolves, Henry meets Count Alucard*). The author starts a new chapter to indicate a change of scene, and a different character, but we realise the events are happening at more or less the same time. Encourage the more able group to report on this.

● Ask the children to look for words and phrases that convey the passing of time to the reader, and write them on the board. For example, from chapter five: *it was well past mid-day*; *while*; *tea-time*.

Guided and independent work

● Ask the children to write a story in the horror genre that includes a flashback. Ask them to begin by discussing ideas in pairs, and then write individual first drafts.

● Recommend the following approach to planning; beginning with a linear plot, then converting it to a plot with a flashback:

Step 1: A linear plot
Beginning – Introduce characters and setting.
Middle – Describe an exciting event.
End – Explain how the characters escaped/survived/returned to normal.

Step 2: The same plot with flashback
Beginning – The exciting event.
Middle – A flashback explaining who the characters are and how they arrived in the setting.
End – As above.

Plenary

● Select some children to read out the first draft of their stories. Ask the rest of the class to listen carefully for the way in which the passing of time is conveyed.

● Round off the unit by recapping on what the children have learned by reading *The Last Vampire*: stock characters, parody, how paragraphs and chapters are linked and how authors handle time. Encourage them to give a verdict on it. Did they prefer it to other vampire stories they have read or seen?

Differentiation

Less able

● Ask children to use a flashback in the same way as Willis Hall: begin with an exciting event, then write a flashback to explain how the characters got into that situation, before continuing with the rest of the story.

More able

● Ask children to experiment with some of the techniques they found out about in Hour 4.

Linking paragraphs

Paragraph number 1 Length 4 lines **Topic** Albert is complaining that his wife, who is navigating, doesn't know where they are. **Punctuation** Speech marks and commas for dialogue. Dash and exclamation mark for emphasis.	**Reason for new paragraph** The beginning of the story. Albert Hollins and his wife Emily are introduced. **Link with previous paragraph** None.
Paragraph number 2 Length 5 lines **Topic** Description of their car and the danger of the mountain road. **Punctuation** Commas to mark off phrase in apposition. Hyphen to join compound words. Commas to separate items in list.	**Reason for new paragraph** Describes the setting and situation. **Link with previous paragraph** Personal pronoun 'their' refers back to Albert and Emily in previous paragraph.
Paragraph number 3 Length 5 lines **Topic** Emily explains that it is difficult to navigate in Europe. **Punctuation** Participle phrase between two commas. Speech marks and commas for dialogue. Dash for emphasis.	**Reason for new paragraph** Emily's response to Albert's complaint. **Link with previous paragraph** Paragraph begins with the name, Emily Hollins, so we know we are going to read about her reaction to Albert's complaint.

Linking chapters

Number of chapter 2 **Title** (if any) **Summary** The Hollins family pitch their tent in the grounds of Castle Alucard. They see the castle and wonder if they are trespassing. Henry goes to the castle for water. The castle is deserted. As he falls asleep to the sound of wolves howling, he works out that Alucard is Dracula spelled backwards.	**Reason for new chapter** Step forward in time. Change of setting – their campsite in the grounds of Castle Alucard. **Link with previous chapter** Same characters. The Hollins have been looking for somewhere to pitch their tent. The beginning describes them pitching it, or trying to!
Number of chapter 3 **Title** (if any) **Summary** Next day, Albert sets off for provisions. He finds a village and tries out bits of three different languages on the villagers which raises their suspicions. Meanwhile Emily has made friends with the wolves. When Sergeant Krotopel finds out that Albert is camping in the castle grounds, he suspects he is also a vampire.	**Reason for new chapter** Step forward in time – next day. Change of setting – the village. New characters – villagers, particularly Sergeant Krotopel. **Link with previous chapter** Same setting, different time. First sentence tells us it is the following morning.
Number of chapter 4 **Title** (if any) **Summary** Henry goes to the castle again and meets Count Alucard. He finds out that he is very different to his ancestors. He doesn't suck blood, indeed he is a vegetarian with a particular fondness for bananas and oranges. He explains that he is afraid of the villagers because they believe he is a blood-sucking vampire and want to kill him.	**Reason for new chapter** Change of setting – Castle Alucard. **Link with previous chapter** Albert sets out to the village (new setting) to find provisions (referred to in previous chapter). Emily's adventure takes place in the same setting. Henry visits the castle again (links to his first visit).

UNIT 3

For and against

This unit begins with a basic formula for constructing an argument: argument = point of view + reasons. From this, the children learn how to build up a balanced written argument. They then develop this further into a persuasive article. The second week shifts the focus to using argument orally in debates. The resources for this week can be used in two ways. The full version, using all the lesson plans and photocopiable sheets, explores how to develop argument and counter-argument in great depth and detail, for example, by examining five common fallacies. The sequence of lessons builds up to a full debate that includes main speeches, rebuttal speeches and supporting speeches. However, depending on the ability range in your class, you may prefer to repeat the simpler mini debate described in the plan for Hour 2 with either the whole class or a group of less able children. Hour 2 links to Unit 51 in *Grammar for Writing*.

Hour	Shared text-level work	Shared word-/ sentence-level work	Guided and independent work	Plenary
1 What is an argument?	Discussing an argument as a point of view.	Collecting and categorising useful connectives.	Playing an argument game to choose topics for debate.	Reporting on topics and connectives that came up in discussion.
2 Argument and counter-argument	Exploring structure for written argument.	Generating conditional sentences.	Expanding arguments or counter-arguments.	Giving detail about structure.
3 Introduction and conclusion	Establishing balance; focusing on ways to introduce and conclude argument.	Rewording conditional sentences.	Agreeing group opinion to be offered; writing introduction and conclusion and adding them to rest of text.	Sharing complete balanced arguments, checking structure.
4 A persuasive article	Reading a persuasive magazine article on an important issue.	Noting use of connectives and emotive language.	Writing a group article on their preferred topic.	Reading out draft articles.
5 Redrafting and presenting the article	Examining layout features and language of articles; considering editorial tasks.	Checking new and difficult spellings as part of editing.	Editing and presenting their articles.	Displaying and admiring articles.

UNIT 3

Hour	Shared text-level work	Shared word-/sentence-level work	Guided and independent work	Plenary
6 A debate speech	Introducing speech writing.	Brainstorming connectives and other useful speech words and phrases.	Writing debate speeches for and against their topics.	Writing prompt notes from the speech.
7 Mini debate	Going through procedure for group debate.		Holding the mini debate and vote.	Discuss how well the speeches went and how useful notes were.
8 Fallacies	Introducing the concept of fallacies in arguments.	Identifying generalisations and questionable statements.	Writing a debate speech free from fallacies; identifying fallacies in another speech text.	Annotating the fallacies; recapping on features of debate speaking.
9 Debate preparation	Organising the debate and allocating roles.		Preparing debate speeches.	Addressing problems and making final preparations.
10 The debate	Revising and commenting on debate procedure.		Holding the group debates.	Discussing debate process.

Key assessment opportunities
● Do the children understand how to construct an argument using the formula: argument = point of view + reasons
● Can they produce a balanced written argument?
● Can they develop an argument into a persuasive article?
● Do they recognise and use conditional forms?
● Can they write speech notes and take part in a debate?

UNIT 3 HOUR 1 📖 For and against

What is an argument?

Objectives

NLS

T15: To recognise how arguments are constructed to be effective, through, eg the expression, sequence and linking of points; the provision of persuasive examples, illustrations and evidence; pre-empting or answering potential objections; appealing to the known views and feelings of the audience.

W8: To build a bank of useful terms and phrases for argument.

S&L

58 Speaking: To use a range of oral techniques to present persuasive argument.

What you need

- Photocopiable page 103
- sets of two dice, one of each colour per set.

Shared text-level work

- Ask the children what an argument is. Sum up their contributions by explaining that an argument, as well as a verbal 'fight', is a point of view supported by reasons. Write this formula on the board:

  Argument = point of view + reasons.

- Next, discuss the following example (in tabular form for clarity):

Point of view	Reasons
Animal testing should be banned.	1. Animals suffer during testing. 2. The majority of testing is not for life-saving drugs, but cosmetics. 3. A range of alternative tests have been developed, eg computer simulations.

Shared word-level work

- Demonstrate how to rewrite the tabular information in a paragraph using connectives to join the ideas:

  Many people believe that animal testing should be banned *because* animals suffer during testing. *Furthermore*, the majority of testing is not for life-saving drugs, but cosmetics. *Another point is that* a range of alternative tests have been developed, such as computer simulations.

- Underline the connectives and ask the children to suggest more examples.
- Sort the connectives according to their function. Use a table like this:

Addition	Contrast/comparison	Consequence	Reason	Condition	Summary
also as well as	although however	as a result consequently	because due to	if so that	finally in

Guided and independent work

- Organise the children into groups of four to play the argument game:

  1. Players take it in turns to roll a pair of dice for the vertical axis and the horizontal axis of photocopiable page 103. This will select at random one of the 36 topics.

  2. The player reads out the topic. S/he then has to give two reasons for the topic.

  3. If the topic has already been used, s/he must give two reasons against the topic.

  4. If the topic has already been used for and against, the player should roll the dice again.

  5. If a player cannot think of two reasons, takes too long, or gives a 'bad' reason, s/he is out (but see Differentiation).

- After playing, ask each group to select the topic which most interested them and to discuss it in more detail, noting key points.

Plenary

- Let each group report on the topic they chose to discuss. What were the best reasons to support it? Add any new connectives to the list begun in shared work.

Differentiation

Less able

- Allow children to give just one reason to support/counter each topic.

More able

- Challenge children to give three reasons to support/counter each topic.

UNIT 3 HOUR 2 ◻ **For and against**

Argument and counter-argument

Objectives

NLS
T16: To identify the features of balanced written arguments which, eg summarise different sides of an argument.
S5: To use reading to: investigate conditionals, eg using *if... then, might, could, would*, and their uses, eg in deduction, speculation, supposition.

What you need
● Photocopiable page 104
● the children's notes from Hour 1.

Shared text-level work
● Remind the children that they have learned how to present an argument by supporting a point of view with reasons. Explain that today they will learn how to expand each reason into a paragraph.
● Display photocopiable page 104 and revise what an argument is, how it is supported by reasons and linked with connectives.
● Draw attention to the second and third rows. Explain that these give suggestions for expanding the reasons into paragraphs. Demonstrate how to do this using the first reason:

An internet ban for under 11s would be a good thing because the internet can be a very dangerous place. Young people enjoy visiting chat room sites where they can meet new friends, but if they are not careful, their new 'friend' could turn out to be a dangerous adult.

Ask the children to suggest ideas to expand the second paragraph beginning: *Another reason is that the internet can be addictive...*
● Use the third row to repeat the process with the counter-argument.

Shared sentence-level work
● Explain that a conditional sentence is one in which one thing depends upon another. Conditional sentences often contain the conjunction *if*.
● Ask the children if they can find an example in the demonstration paragraph (*if they are not careful, their new 'friend'...*).
● Ask the children to generate new sentences in the same pattern:

Connective	Condition	Consequence
If	they play online games late at night	they will be too tired for school

Guided and independent work
● In the same groups of four as Hour 1, ask the children to expand the argument and counter-argument of their preferred topic in discussion.
● The next step is to subdivide into pairs, and to write either expanded arguments or counter-arguments.
● Ask one group to write on an OHT for use in plenary (one pair writes expanded arguments, the other expanded counter-arguments).

Less able
● Ask pairs of children to concentrate on expanding one argument.

More able
● Encourage more able pairs to expanded their argument and counter-argument with at least three paragraphs.

Plenary
● Choose a good example from the group writing on OHTs for display and discussion. Explain that this is, in effect, the middle part of a balanced written argument. Show the structure like this:

Argument	Counter-argument
● Point of view	● Opposite point of view
● Reason	● Reason
● Example(s)	● Example(s)

Objectives

NLS

T16: To identify the features of balanced written arguments which, eg summarise different sides of an argument; clarify the strengths and weaknesses of different positions; signal personal opinion clearly.

S5: To use reading to: investigate conditionals, eg using *if... then*, *might*, *could*, *would*, and their uses, eg in deduction, speculation, supposition.

S&L

63 Group discussion and interaction: To consider examples of conflict and resolution, exploring language used.

What you need

● Photocopiable page 104
● the children's arguments and counter-arguments from Hour 2.

Differentiation

Less able
● Ask children to follow closely the templates for the introduction and conclusion.

More able
● Encourage children to find alternative phraseology to that used in the template.

Introduction and conclusion

Shared text-level work

● Remind the children that writing a balanced argument is a different task to writing a persuasive argument. Balance means that both sides of an argument are considered, both opposing points of view are presented. The time to come down on one side or the other (or sit on the fence) is in the conclusion to the argument, which they will be writing in this lesson.

● Display photocopiable page 104 and explain that the first row of boxes provides a template for the introduction to a balanced written argument.

● Now read the last set of boxes on photocopiable page 104 and do the same with the conclusion.

● Explain to the children that, in the final sentence(s) of their argument texts they should suggest a solution, state their group's opinion, come down on one side of the argument or the other, or sit on the fence (stay neutral).

Shared sentence-level work

● Now look at the whole of photocopiable page 104, and discuss alternative wording for each of the boxes in the introduction and conclusion, particularly *Introduction*, box four, and *Conclusion*, box one. For example: *To sum up...*
When all the facts are taken into consideration...
So, we see that...
This will help to encourage the children to write in their own words.

Guided and independent work

● Ask the groups to discuss ideas for introductions and conclusions to their written arguments, in particular, what opinion they wish to express in their conclusion. Allow them some time to discuss and agree on this as a group, and encourage them to do so in quite a formal manner to make sure everyone's voice is heard and the discussion progresses fairly. (This is good practice for the class debate later in the unit.)

● Ask the children to write introductions and conclusions for their preferred topic as demonstrated in shared work.

● When they have done this, ask them to redraft the whole argument where necessary, so that it reads well and flows smoothly from one section to another.

Plenary

● Share an example of a complete balanced written argument.
● Display the structure (see Hour 2 plenary) with the addition of *Introduction* and *Conclusion* and ask the children to compare the structure to the example argument as you read.

95

Objectives

T19: To write a balanced report of a controversial issue: summarising fairly the competing views; analysing strengths and weaknesses of different positions.
S5: To use reading to: investigate conditionals, eg using *if... then, might, could, would,* and their uses, eg in deduction, speculation, supposition.

What you need
● Photocopiable page 105
● the children's work from Hours 1 to 3.

A persuasive article

Shared text-level work
● Remind the children of what they have done so far in this unit – built up a balanced written argument bit by bit. Explain that, in the real world, arguments are written for specific audiences and purposes. Today they are going to read a balanced argument written as an article for a newsletter aimed at the parents of young children, and that, although it is balanced, it reflects a certain point of view.
● Display photocopiable page 105 and read it to the children.
● Re-read the article and ask the children the following questions. Use their answers as a basis for annotating the article.

> ● Can you identify the structural parts? Find the introduction, paragraphs on one side of the argument, paragraphs on the other side of the argument, and the conclusion.
> ● How do the introduction and conclusion differ from the models used earlier in the week? (The introduction does more than just 'introduce' the topic. It sets out to grab readers' attention by trying to shock them. The conclusion is more than a 'summing up'; it offers an eye-catching solution in the form of a list of tips.)
> ● Analyse each argument, that is, find the point of view and the reasons given to support it. What types of persuasive devices are used as examples? (Paragraph three argues that these dangers mentioned in the previous paragraph are common and uses statistics as a persuasive device to support the argument.)
> ● What is the effect of the bullet points in the conclusion? (They catch the reader's attention and make him or her think seriously about what can be done.)

Shared word- and sentence-level work
● Ask the children to find examples of connectives in the text, for example, *but, thus, so,* and emotive language, such as, *abuse, horrors, lurking, dark.*
● Discuss the effect of this emotive language.

Guided and independent work
● Ask the children, working collaboratively in their groups, to develop their preferred topic from Hours 1 to 3 into the first draft of a newspaper or magazine article similar to the one read in shared work. Ask them to focus particularly on:

> ● a specific audience (they should discuss this as a group and choose one that best suits their topic)
> ● an attention-grabbing introduction and title
> ● a range of persuasive examples
> ● a conclusion – to include bullet points if appropriate.

Differentiation

Less able
● Tell children to focus on their introduction and conclusion.

More able
● Ask children to include an example of each of the following persuasive devices: appeal to emotions, expert opinion, facts and statistics, emotive language.

Plenary
● Ask for some draft articles to be read out, and ask the rest of the class to evaluate them by listening for the features listed in Guided and independent work.

Objectives

NLS
Term 1 T18: To use IT to plan, revise, edit writing to improve accuracy and conciseness and to bring it to publication standard, eg through compiling a class newspaper, paying attention to accuracy, layout and presentation.
W1: To identify misspelt words in own writing; to keep individual lists (eg spelling logs); to learn to spell them.

What you need
● Photocopiable page 105.
● the children's articles from Hour 4
● dictionaries
● computers with word-processing or DTP software (optional).

Redrafting and presenting the article

Shared text-level work
● Tell the children that they are going to redraft and bring to publication standard the articles they wrote in Hour 4.
● Display photocopiable page 105 and begin by considering the effect of the different layout features: picture, caption, subheadings/standfirsts and so on. (For example, they make the page appealing to look at, they pick out key points to catch the reader's attention.) Tell the children to consider how some of these features may work for their own articles.
● Next, ask the children what they will need to do to bring their article to publication standard. Write down suitable points as they are suggested. These may include:

> ● Correct spelling, punctuation and sentence construction.
> ● Read the article to a partner and see if anything could be expressed more clearly, or more effectively.
> ● Consider the appropriateness of the language and style for the intended audience.
> ● Plan how to present the article using a captioned picture, subheadings, boxed text and so on.
> ● Adjust the length of the text to fit the space available.

Shared word-level work
● Encourage the children to check the spelling of any words they are not sure of, in a dictionary or portable spell-checker.
● Ask them to double-check words that have given them problems recently by going through them in their individual spelling lists.

Guided and independent work
● Ask the children, helping each other in their groups, to redraft and bring to publication standard the persuasive article that they began in Hour 4.
● Ideally, this should be done on computers using appropriate word-processing or desktop-publishing software. If this is not possible, ask the children to present their finished article on A3 paper as an A4 double-page spread.
● Encourage them to experiment with layout features by physically moving features around, and to ensure that everyone in the group is involved.
● Provide help where necessary to edit an overlong text to a specified number of words.

Plenary
● Display and admire the finished products, ideally using IT.
● Tell the children that you will be making a more permanent display of the articles and asking them to evaluate each one for impact and for accuracy. (Make time for this in the following week.)

Differentiation

Less able
● Place children in a group with a more able child acting as editor. S/he should be in role to help with the redrafting process.

More able
● Let children take it in turns to spend ten minutes each in the role of editor to less able groups, so that there is still time to work on their own articles.

UNIT 3 HOUR 6 For and against

A debate speech

Objectives

NLS

T18: To construct effective arguments: developing a point logically and effectively; supporting and illustrating points persuasively; anticipating possible objections; harnessing the known views, interests and feelings of the audience; tailoring the writing to formal presentation where appropriate.

What you need

● Photocopiable page 106
● the children's work so far.

Shared text-level work

● Remind the children that in Hour 5, they learned how to present a balanced argument in the form of a newspaper or magazine article. Tell them that, in this lesson, they are going to learn how to present an argument in the form of a debate speech.
● Display photocopiable page 106. The boxed text shows notes for the speech and below it is the sample speech.
● Read through the speech and talk about the structure and the aims of the different parts. For example:

● introducing oneself
● informal style compared with a written article
● humour
● involving the audience
● appealing to the emotions
● rhetorical questions
● attacking the opposition's main argument
● conclusion with thanks to the audience.

● To consolidate this part of the lesson, ask: How is this speech different from a written article? The two most important differences are the requirements of oral presentation (see above) and that, in a debate speech, only one side of the argument is presented or stressed. Ask the children to say what the argument on photocopiable page 106 is, and if they are persuaded.

Shared word- and sentence-level work

● Ask the children to find connectives in the text, for example, *in particular*, *but first*, and to brainstorm other useful connectives.
● Ask them to brainstorm other useful words and phrases, such as:

● There are both advantages and disadvantages in...
● In discussing whether or not...
● The basic question is, however...
● On balance, it seems that...

● Ask the class to note these and add to their lists during the week.

Guided and independent work

● Subdivide the groups of four into pairs, one pair for, and one pair against, their topic. Each pair should write a debate speech on the topic.
● Explain that they should work together to share ideas, but produce individual speeches.

Differentiation

Less able
● Ask children to write in pairs.

More able
● Ask one of a pair to produce a main speech and the other a supporting speech.

Plenary

● Display photocopiable page 106 again, and focus on the speech notes. Ask why it is important not to read out a speech. (It sounds 'wooden' and less direct, it is inflexible.)
● Ask the children to prepare for a debate in the next lesson by writing notes for their speeches for homework.

Mini debate

Objectives
S&L

55 Speaking: To present a spoken argument, sequencing points logically, defending views with evidence and making use of persuasive language.

What you need
● The children's speech notes.

Shared work
● Re-organise the groups of four so that in each group there are two different topics, each with one speaker for and another speaker against. Then explain the procedure for the mini debate:

1. The first pair (for and against) give their speeches while the second pair act as the audience.

2. After each speech, the audience should be allowed to ask questions of the speaker.

3. At the end (after the second speech and follow-up questions), the audience votes for the best speech. (Allow split votes, but stress that, whatever the outcome, the audience members must be able to give reasons for their choice.)

4. The pairs change over and the procedure is repeated.

5. Finally, the topic is voted on in terms of for and against. Has anyone changed their view? Are certain views more strongly held and more powerfully argued?

Guided and independent work
● Ask the children to begin their mini debate following the procedure outlined above. Remind them to use only their notes when speaking. Insist that any copies of the full version of the speech are put away.

● Tell them that you will be going round and listening to how well they speak from notes.

● In addition, as you circulate, listen to which topics are the most thoroughly presented or most successfully adopted as you may want to recommend these later in the week when groups choose new topics for a full debate.

Plenary
● Discuss how easy or difficult it was to speak from notes. Ask the children: Were your notes helpful? How would you change them to make them more helpful next time?

Differentiation

Less able
● These may be different to children who are less good readers or writers. Watch out particularly for shy or unpopular children. Try to put them in groups where they feel comfortable.

More able
● Put more able children together so that they can challenge each other.

Fallacies

Objectives

NLS
T18: To construct effective arguments: developing a point logically and effectively; supporting and illustrating points persuasively; anticipating possible objections; harnessing the known views, interests and feelings of the audience; tailoring the writing to formal presentation where appropriate.

What you need

● Photocopiable pages 107 and 108.

Shared text-level work
● Tell the children that they are going to begin preparation for a full-scale debate that will include rebuttal speeches. Explain to the class that rebuttal speeches attack the opponent's speech, whereas supporting speeches add more arguments to the main speech and sum up the case.
● Explain that they are going to begin by examining some common fallacies. Explain that fallacies are false arguments. Knowledge of some common fallacies will help them to write better debate speeches and give them ammunition to attack an opponent's speech.
● Display photocopiable page 107, which is based on a speech written against the first topic on photocopiable page 103, *Dogs make better pets than cats.*
● Read and discuss each extract from the speech in column one, then the explanation of the fallacy in the example in column two, and finally, ideas about how to respond to this kind of fallacy in column three.
● Explain that the last fallacy is the only one that can improve a speech rather than weaken it, because, of course, you don't want to tell the opposition about the weak points of your argument – it is for them to find them out!

Shared sentence-level work
● Ask the children to look for distributive terms (words that show how many of a thing – *one, most, all*) and for the number of examples implied by a statement, for example, *my cat is the gentlest creature you ever saw* (one cat).
● Explain that statements in which only one example is used to prove a point are probably generalisations. Similarly, statements claiming about all of something should be examined carefully to see if the statement is true.

Guided and independent work
● Work with one group to write a complete debate speech, free from fallacies, on their chosen topic.
● Ask the rest of the children to work in pairs to try to find the fallacies in the speech on photocopiable page 108. (There is a generalisation, a distorted argument, a red herring and an emotional argument.)

Differentiation

Less able

● Concentrate on finding the fallacies in the first half of the speech as these are more obvious.

More able

● Give particular attention to the second half where the fallacies are harder to detect.

Plenary
● Ask the children to point out the fallacies in the text. Annotate them as they are pointed out.
● Ask the class what other false arguments they found (false interpretation of historical evidence, anecdotal evidence of alien abductions).
● Finally, recap on the key features of a debate speech, for example introducing oneself; the more informal style when compared with a written article; involving the audience; giving a conclusion with thanks to the audience for their attention.

Debate preparation

Objectives

NLS
T15: To recognise how arguments are constructed to be effective.
T18: To construct effective arguments.
S&L
58 Speaking: To use a range of oral techniques to present persuasive argument.

What you need

● Photocopiable pages 103 and 108.

Shared text-level work

● Explain to the children they are going to prepare for a class debate.
● Organise the debate teams. The best way to do this is to split into four groups. The optimal number in each group is six. Groups of four or five can be created by omitting the supporting speaker. Every child should have something to prepare!
● The next step is to allocate roles within teams of three: main speaker, rebuttal speaker, supporting speaker. Organise a chairperson to:

> ● announce the motion/statement
> ● introduce the speakers
> ● keep time
> ● choose questioners from the audience
> ● organise the voting.

● Display and talk through the following suggested procedure (intended to involve as many children as possible):

> 1. Team A main speaker speaks for the motion (three minutes).
> 2. Team B rebuttal speaker attacks weak points (one minute).
> 3. Team B main speaker speaks against the motion (three minutes).
> 4. Team A rebuttal speaker attacks weak points (one minute).
> 5. Team A supporting speaker sums up the points for (two minutes).
> 6. Team B supporting speaker sums up the points against (two minutes).
> 7. Questions from the audience (five minutes).
> 8. Vote (two to three minutes).

Guided and independent work

● Tell the children to prepare their debate speeches. Emphasise that they should work as a team, and recommend the following process:

> ● Decide on a new topic - this can be chosen from photocopiable page 103, or can be any other topic. (Choosing a good topic is one of the most important factors in the success of a debate. The topic should interest all the children in the group, create strong feeling, and divide opinion more or less evenly. Help each group to choose, recommending those topics that worked well in Hour 7.)
> ● Work as a group to brainstorm the best arguments.
> ● Decide which arguments should be presented in the main speech and which left until the summing up.
> ● Brainstorm what the opposition might say and think of rebuttal ideas.
> ● Each child writes his or her speech - this can be written out in full, but emphasise that the final product must be *notes* only.

● Help those who are preparing a rebuttal speech. Show them how to anticipate the opposition's arguments and write a response.

Plenary

● Discuss any problems that the children found in the preparation process, for example, problems in harmonising the main speech and the supporting speech, problems in preparing a rebuttal speech. Ask the children to practise their speeches for homework.

Differentiation

Less able
● Allocate the easiest role - the supporting speaker.

More able
● Allocate the most difficult roles - the role of rebuttal speaker.

The debate

Objectives

NLS
T18: To construct effective arguments.
S&L
56 Group discussion and interaction: To understand different ways to take the lead and support others in groups.
62 Speaking: To participate in a whole-class debate using the conventions and language of debate.

Shared text-level work

● Display and re-read the debate procedure (and leave it on display throughout the debate as a reminder to the groups) and quickly remind the children of the process. Talk through some comments on the following stages:

1 and 3.	The main speaker's opening speech should be straightforward. Leave some good arguments for the supporting speaker.
2 and 4.	Rebuttal speakers have the most difficult job because they have to respond quickly. Try to anticipate what might come up. Listen particularly for fallacies.
5 and 6.	Aim to plan the summing up speech in advance but be open to ideas that come up during the debate.
7.	Questions can be directed at any speaker. The Chair should allow only one question per speaker.
8.	Hold vote(s) on one or all of: the motion, best team, best speaker.

What you need

● Poster of debate procedure from Hour 9
● the children's notes from Hour 9.

Guided and independent work

● Organise the children to begin the debate, reminding them to follow the procedure. Ideally, the groups will debate in sets of two with another pair of groups acting as the audience before switching roles. Organisation will vary according to class size, but the key principle is to involve as many children as possible.

● Tell the children that you will be moving between the groups checking on how well they are following the debate procedure; listening for how well they can speak from notes and how well they put forward and rebut arguments.

● Make sure the arguments remain formal, fair and structured, and remind speakers to allow time for questions and voting at the end.

Plenary

● Gather the results of the votes, then evaluate the whole debate process and discuss what lessons can be learned for future debates. How well did the debate go? Were children able to stick to their times? Could they improvise and adapt their speeches and questions in light of points that came up during the debate? What would they do better next time? For example, better use of notes, more practise in 'live' rebuttal speeches.

Differentiation

Less able
● Allocate the easiest role – the supporting speaker.

More able
● Allocate the most difficult roles – the role of rebuttal speaker.

Argument topics

	1	2	3	4	5	6
1	Dogs make better pets than cats.	Your parents are your best teachers.	You can learn more from experience than from books.	Boys and girls should wear the same clothes.	Learning about the past has no value because we live in the present.	We are becoming too dependent on computers.
2	It should be illegal to sell junk food to children.	Happiness is more important than money.	Films with violence and bad language should never be shown on television.	Books are more satisfying than films.	Children should be required to help with household tasks.	It is cruel to keep animals in zoos.
3	Naughty children should be punished by smacking.	Everybody should go to church (or participate in a religion).	War is always wrong.	Every job should have the same salary.	All school students should wear school uniform.	Wealthy nations should share their wealth with poorer nations.
4	Space exploration is a waste of money.	Children should be allowed to wear what they like.	Britain should replace the royal family with a president.	Footballers are overpaid.	Aliens have visited Earth.	Laws should be introduced to control car ownership and use.
5	Too much television is bad for you.	Children should not be allowed to bring mobile phones to school.	Factory farming should be abolished.	Children under 11 should be in bed by 9 o'clock.	Smoking should be treated as a drug and made illegal.	Sometimes it is better not to tell the truth.
6	Under 11s should be banned from using the internet.	Homework is good for you.	Motorists should pay to drive in city centres.	The use of animals to test drugs and other products should be banned.	Girls work harder than boys.	Progress is always good.

Argument template

Topic: Under 11s should be banned from using the internet

Introduction (one paragraph)

Sentence for	Connective	Sentence against	Link
Some people believe that children under 11 should be banned from using the internet.	However,	many people, including most under 11s, believe that access to the internet can be a good thing.	I am going to examine the arguments for and against.

Argument (two paragraphs)

Point of view	Connective	Reasons	Examples
An internet ban for under 10s would be a good thing	because Another reason is that	the internet can be a very dangerous place; the internet can be addictive.	chat rooms, disturbing images, misleading information; children can spend too much time, chatting to friends or playing games.

Counter-argument (two paragraphs)

Point of view	Connective	Reasons	Examples
On the other hand, those against an internet ban argue that the internet can be a good thing	since Also,	it is, in effect, the largest library in the world; it can be counter-productive to ban access.	many kinds of educational resources and how they can help children; children will rebel and get access anyway, eg at a friend's house.

Conclusion (one paragraph)

Connective	Summary of *for*	Summary of *against*	Suggested solution
In conclusion,	the internet has dangers	but it can also be a good thing	I believe that the solution is to allow under 11s to access the internet under adult supervision.

Internet dangers and delights

If your child changes what is on the computer screen when you walk in the room, or stays up late into the night surfing the internet, how do you know what sites they are visiting or who is 'visiting' them?

Chat room horrors

Chat rooms are the greatest danger, but there are other horrors lurking in the dark corners of the internet. These include sites with pornographic images and sites that teach children to become expert hackers, or to write damaging viruses. Of course, some of these sites require credit card access – no problem! All a child has to do is dip into mum's handbag and 'borrow' a credit card for a few minutes.

But how common are these problems? Statistics show that 22% of children have

been contacted by strangers in chat rooms, and that 60% have stumbled accidentally across disturbing images. 12% have hacked into another computer, and 9% gamble regularly.

Educational benefits

But before all this shocks you into an outright internet ban, consider the other side of the picture. The internet has enormous educational benefits, and its use in schools has been encouraged by educational experts and government bodies. It is, in effect, the biggest library in the word containing everything your child needs to know about any subject from kindergarten to degree level. But it is even better than a library because it is interactive: your child can take a test online and get the results straight away, translate a sentence into a foreign language, and even talk directly to an expert via video-conferencing.

So how can parents help their children to take advantage of the educational delights of the internet while keeping them safe from its dangers? Like anything else to do with children, it's a balancing act, and these Top Tips will help you to keep that balance:

- Set up the family computer in a public place, for example, a hallway, where it can be easily supervised.

- Install an internet content filter and a PopUp blocker.

- Tell your children never to give important information online such as address, phone number, or credit card details.

- Above all, insist that they never arrange a meeting with anyone who contacts them through a chat room.

Debate speech

Notes

Introduce myself

State point of view – I am going to make a case for censorship laws to protect internet users.

Why?

Pop-ups

Advertisements

Pornography

Gambling

Hate sites

Hacking

Chat rooms

Compare with TV and newspapers

Attack the opposition's freedom of speech argument

Solution – government to make ISP obey same laws as other media

Conclusion – thank the listeners

Speech

May I have your attention please! Thank you. My name is Marianne. I am going to talk to you about the dangers of the internet. In particular, I am going to make a case for censorship laws to protect internet users, particularly children.

But first, why do we need to censor the internet? Well, you have only got to spend an hour or so online to see the problems for yourself. You can be busily researching your next homework when a pop-up – pops up! I'm sure it's happened to everyone in this room. Most of the time they are just irritating advertisements, but some contain obscene images, or invitations to gamble.

And that's when you're not even looking for trouble – when you start looking actively it gets much worse – hate sites, hacking sites – and most dangerous of all for children, chat rooms. It is a frightening thought that if a child visits a chatroom, he or she could be in more danger than walking through the park at night!

So I'm sure you'll agree with me that the internet can be a very nasty place, and this leads me to my main point which is that we don't put up with this on television or in our newspapers, so why should we put up with it on the internet?

True, some people have argued that we need to protect freedom of speech – but I think there is a big difference between being free to express a political point of view, and being free to rip people off or corrupt them.

All that is needed is for our government to compel the Internet Service Providers to obey the same law that applies to all other media. Then we could all benefit from the internet without fear of being offended or harmed.

I hope you will support my point of view. Thank you for listening.

Fallacies

Extracts from a debate speech against the topic 'Dogs make better pets than cats'.

Extract/fallacy	Explanation of fallacy	How to respond
The reason I prefer cats is that dogs are descended from wolves. Do you want to end up like Little Red Riding Hood – attacked by a creature you thought was your friend?	Distorted argument. Reminding people that dogs are descended from wolves makes it easy to criticise them as pets, but isn't necessarily relevant.	Point out the distortion: *It is true that dogs are descended from wolves, but domestication has completely changed their nature.*
On the other hand, my cat is the gentlest creature you ever saw. She never kills mice or does anything cruel. What better proof that cats are less vicious than dogs?	Generalisation. Just because one cat is gentle, doesn't prove that all cats are.	Make a joke out of the claim: *Your cat may well be kind, but I'm sure mice would tell you that she's an exception!*
The whole world is divided into cat people and dog people. Cat people are usually intelligent and kind, but most dog people seem to be moronic and servile – just like their pets!	Emotional argument (and generalisation). This argument appeals to feelings and prejudices, or makes a personal attack on the people involved.	Expose the emotion or prejudice: *I'm sure that dog lovers here will feel as insulted as I do, especially as your insult has nothing to do with cats or dogs.*
Actually, if you really want my true opinion, I think that tarantulas make great pets. Mine is very hairy and very cute.	Red herring. The speaker has gone off the subject. The topic has nothing to do with other pets – only cats and dogs.	Use the red herring: *If you prefer tarantulas, your cat can't be a very satisfying pet – so perhaps dogs make better pets after all.*
(What I didn't say is that lions and tigers are also part of the cat family, most cats hunt small animals, and that cats tend to be proud and independent.)	Hidden evidence. The speaker deliberately omits evidence that would undermine his/her case.	Pointing out what the speaker has deliberately left out is one of the most powerful attacks.

Aliens have visited Earth

Mr Chairman, ladies and gentlemen. I am going to argue the case that aliens have visited Earth. By 'aliens' I mean intelligent life from other planets.

My first argument is that there are billions of planets in the universe, so surely there must be at least one that, like Earth, is a cradle for life.

Secondly, there is evidence that aliens have been visiting Earth for centuries. This can be seen in old drawings and carvings which show men in space suits. Some say that aliens built the pyramids and Stonehenge. This may seem a strange idea at first, but how could primitive people move such enormous stone blocks?

Since the 1940s there has been photographic and film evidence. Some of the photographs show alien spaceships called flying saucers. One film I have seen shows an unidentified flying object moving at incredible speed.

Thousands of Americans claim to have been abducted by aliens. Their descriptions of aliens are remarkably consistent; they have small bodies, large heads and large eyes.

One of the most interesting pieces of evidence that aliens have visited Earth is the Roswell Incident. In 1948 a flying saucer was said to have crashed in Roswell, New Mexico. The US military quickly removed the wreckage – which was said to include bodies of aliens – to a nearby airbase. It is true that the official report stated that the wreckage was that of a weather balloon – but this is obviously a cover up because the military did not wish to frighten the American people.

Perhaps the best evidence is from a meteorite of Martian rock found in 1996. When NASA scientists examined it they found that it contained fossils that could be bacteria-like life.

It would be a terribly sad thing for humans if we were alone in the universe. That is why so much time and money has been poured into the search for extra-terrestrial life. I believe that, very soon, we will find that we are not alone.

I hope you found these arguments convincing and that you will support my case for the motion. Thank you.

UNIT 4

Narrative 2

This unit explores genre with examples from science fiction, Western, fantasy and crime. The children have already studied examples of a classic in Term 1 (*A Christmas Carol*) and the horror genre earlier this term. In addition, they will be studying animal stories in Term 3. Hour 5 can be used in two ways. It can focus on the development and redrafting of responses to genre written throughout the week, or can be expanded into a further week's work in which the children study one genre in depth and produce an extended piece of writing.

Hour	Shared text-level work	Shared word-/ sentence-level work	Guided and independent work	Plenary
1 Science fiction	Talking about genres, introducing science fiction.	Examining author's style features.	Speculating on what will happen next; inventing own sci-fi creatures.	Looking at new creatures; revising genre features.
2 Westerns	Introducing Westerns and their typical features.	Investigating Western slang.	Storyboarding the poem.	Discussing choices in storyboards; reinforcing knowledge of genre features.
3 Fantasy	Introducing the fantasy genre and typical features; thinking up school syllabus ideas.		Writing school syllabuses for a fantasy story.	Sharing syllabuses and discussing what stories could come from them; revising genre features.
4 Crime	Introducing the crime genre and typical features.		Reading aloud, attempting to solve the crime.	Solving the crime.
5 Writing	Talking about revision and editing.	Combining seteneces in various ways for interest, emphasis and meaning.	Developing work from earlier in the week.	Revising genre; collating children's work.

Key assessment opportunities
● Do the children understand the concept of genre and know the main categories?
● Have they read examples of different genres?
● Can they write and edit a piece of work in a specific genre?

UNIT 4 HOUR 1 Narrative 2

Science fiction

Objectives

NLS
T10: To use different genres as models to write, eg short extracts, sequels, additional episodes, alternative endings, using appropriate conventions, language.
S3: To revise work on complex sentences: appropriate use of punctuation.

What you need
● Photocopiable page 115.

Shared text-level work
● Discuss genre and elicit that the term refers to different types/ styles/topics of book, such as the fiction genres adventure, romance, science fiction, fantasy. Explain that these genres encompass other fiction forms such as films, television programmes, comics.
● Ask: What other genres can you think of? How does classification by genre help the reader/viewer? Also ask the children to tell you about their favourite books. Do they read lots from one particular genre?
● Encourage the children to name books or films they know from the science fiction genre. Discuss typical characters, settings, objects and plots, such as aliens, other planets, spaceships, the future, alien invasion of Earth.
● Display and read photocopiable page 115.
● Ask the children to identify elements typical of science fiction, particularly the description of the alien being, and his spaceship. Those who know the story will know that the aliens are invading Earth – a common science fiction plot.

Shared word- and sentence-level work
● Go through the extract again, and ask the children to pick out words and phrases that describe the alien, such as, *thing, lipless brim, dropped saliva, pulsated*.
● Explain that Wells has used several similes and metaphors to make his description more powerful. Ask the children to find examples, like *the Gorgon groups of tentacles*.
● Revise work on complex sentences and the author's use of punctuation. Ask the children to find an example of a sentence expressing more than one idea. Then ask them how grammatical techniques and punctuation have been used to combine the ideas, for example, *A big greyish rounded bulk, the size, perhaps, of a bear, was rising slowly and painfully out of the cylinder.*

Guided and independent work
● Ask the children to discuss in groups of four what they think will happen next in the story. Tell them to be prepared to report back in the plenary session. (Any answer that fits the extract should be accepted.)
● Then ask the children to work on their own to sketch the creature from the description.
● Finally, ask them to invent and describe their own alien creatures, including sketches if they wish.

Differentiation

Less able
● Ask children to make sure they include lots of descriptive details in their description.

More able
● Encourage children to write in a similar style to HG Wells, with complex sentences and detailed descriptions, using a wide range of vocabulary.

Plenary
● Share the sketches and ideas about what happens next in the story.
● Evaluate the sketches by checking that as many details as possible have been correctly included.
● Share some of the children's alien descriptions.
● Identify key features of the genre in the story continuations and the descriptions.

Westerns

NLS
T10: To use different genres as models to write, eg short extracts, sequels, additional episodes, alternative endings, using appropriate conventions, language.
T8: To analyse the success of texts and writers in evoking particular responses in the reader, eg where suspense is well-built.
Term 3 S2: To conduct detailed language investigations through interviews, research and reading, eg of proverbs, language change over time, dialect, study of headlines.

What you need
● Photocopiable page 116.

Shared text-level work

● Introduce the genre of Westerns as the focus of this lesson; the name coming from the consistently used setting of the west of the United States of America.

● Discuss the typical characters, settings, objects and plots that we would expect to find in this genre. For example, the cowboy, the gunfighter, the sheriff, American Indians; the frontier town, the cattle ranch, the saloon; the Colt revolver, the ten gallon hat, spurs, horses, wagons; the shoot out in the high street, the train robbery. Encourage the children to relate these to the Western films they have seen.

● Display and read photocopiable page 116.

● Ask the children to identify the characters, settings, objects and plots that are typical of Westerns in this extract, and annotate them as they point them out: the saloon, the honky-tonk piano, the card game, the 'dangerous' gunman and so on.

● Ask the children to point out the places where Robert Service evokes particular responses in the reader, for example, how he builds up suspense and how he makes the reader feel about Lou at the end of the poem.

● Annotate similes and metaphors that the children identify, used to make the description more powerful. This line, for instance, contains both a simile and a metaphor:
He looked like a man with a foot in the grave and scarcely the strength of a louse.

Shared sentence-level work

● Ask the children to investigate the slang used in the 'Wild West' by collecting examples from the poem, and where necessary, trying to work out the meaning from the context. For example, *whooping it up* (having fun); *music-box* (piano); *poke of dust* (bag of gold dust), *pumped full of lead* (shot several times).

Guided and independent work

● Visual and kinaesthetic learning: ask the children to work in pairs to storyboard this incident. (See page 42 in Unit 3 for guidance on how to draw up a storyboard.) Tell the children to use eight frames, two per stanza.

● Ask one pair to work on OHT for display and discussion in the plenary session.

Plenary

● Display and discuss the examples written on OHT.
● Encourage the pair(s) to explain their frames and choices.
● Use their ideas to reinforce knowledge of the typical features of the Western genre.

Differentiation

Less able
● Advise children to imagine that they are watching a film of this incident before sketching the key scenes.

More able
● Ask children to write a screenplay based on this incident. (See page 42 for guidance on how to do this.)

UNIT 4 HOUR 3 📖 Narrative 2

Fantasy

Objectives

NLS
T10: To use different genres as models to write, eg short extracts, sequels, additional episodes, alternative endings, using appropriate conventions, language.
T2: To analyse how individual paragraphs are structured in writing, eg comments sequenced to follow the shifting thoughts of a character, examples listed to justify a point and reiterated to give it force.

What you need

● Photocopiable page 117.

Shared text-level work

● Introduce the fantasy genre and discuss typical characters, settings, objects and plots, inviting the children to contribute.
● Then display photocopiable page 117. Ask the children for their reaction to the title. Explain that it is from *A Wizard of Earthsea* by Ursula K Le Guin.
● Ask the children to identify typical fantasy characters, settings, objects and plots, such as, a wizard, magic ring, quest to find something.
● Then ask the children to find typical fantasy features in this extract, and annotate them as they point them out, for example, a mage (a wizard), magic, dragon, magical tree.
● Use the extract to revise the conventions of paragraphing in fiction, particularly the way that dialogue is set out.
● Tell the children they will be designing their own curriculum for a fantasy school in the independent activity. Ask if they can remember all the subjects they study at school. Write them on the board.
● Write up this example of a curriculum from another fantasy novel, *Alice in Wonderland*. This is what the Mock Turtle learned. Ask the children if they can guess what the real-world equivalents are (the first two are given as an example):

Mock Turtle's curriculum	Real world equivalent
Reeling and writhing Ambition, distraction and uglification Mystery Seaography Drawling, stretching and fainting in coils Laughing and grief	Reading and writing

● Finally, brainstorm ideas about school curricula for the following:

● Dragon slayers
● Witches
● Giants
● Gnomes
● Princesses.

Guided and independent work

● Ask the children to work in pairs to write a syllabus for their own fantasy school. Emphasise that if it is a school for witches or wizards, and that it must be original.

Plenary

● Share the school syllabuses and discuss what kinds of stories could be built around them.
● Conclude by recapping on the key features of the fantasy genre.

Differentiation

Less able
● Ask children to start by jotting down what they learn in school, then think how this would be different in a fantasy story. Science might be replaced by alchemy and astrology.

More able
● Explain that in Earthsea, magical power is wielded by calling a thing by its name in the Old Speech. Ask children, in addition, to make up their own magic words.

Crime

Objectives

NLS
T9: To increase familiarity with significant writers of the past.
T10: To use different genres as models to write, eg short extracts, sequels, additional episodes, alternative endings, using appropriate conventions, language.

What you need

● Display version of photocopiable page 118 (more able children should have copies with the clue logos removed).

Shared text-level work

● Tell the children that today they are going to look at a story in the crime genre. Discuss the typical characteristics of crime or detective stories, in particular these plot features:

Motive – the reason for committing a crime
Clues – pieces of evidence, sometimes very small (careful observation is often needed to find them, and careful thought to work out what they mean)
Red herring – something that distracts attention from the villain
Deduction – the process of using logic to solve a crime.

● Suggest that most crime stories are built around a detective with strong characteristics and idiosyncratic methods of working. Encourage the children to talk about some examples of such figures, and end with a detailed discussion of Sherlock Holmes.
● NB: text analysis is left until the plenary session to avoid giving away the solution, which children are asked to solve.

Guided and independent work

● Ask the children to read the scene in pairs (the person reading Watson should also read Amberley).
● Then challenge them to solve the crime. Encourage discussion and tell the children that they must be able to explain the motive, the clues, the red herring, what Holmes deduced and what the final proof was.

Plenary

● Discuss the solution to the crime:

Josiah Amberley was so jealous (*motive*) of his wife's affair with Dr Ernest that he decided to murder them. He locked them in a specially prepared strong room (*clue*), broke the lamp off the gas pipe (*clue*) and turned on the gas. Then, to draw attention away from himself, he pretended to be the *victim* of a crime and went to Sherlock Holmes (*red herring*). Holmes *deduced* that Amberley could have gassed his victims and then used paint to cover up the smell. To test his deduction he asked: 'What did you do with the bodies?' Amberley showed his guilt by trying to escape. The bodies were later found in a well behind the house.

● Finally, work with the children to annotate the text for the meanings of the clues and typical stylistic features of the crime genre.

Differentiation

Less able
● Advise them to look for the clue logos in the extract and to think carefully about each one.

More able
● Give them an extract with the clue logos deleted.

Objectives

NLS

T12: To study in depth one genre and produce an extended piece of similar writing, eg for inclusion in a class anthology; to plan, revise, redraft this and bring to presentational standard, eg layout, paragraphing, accuracy of punctuation and spelling, handwriting/printing.

S3: To revise work on complex sentences: identifying main clauses; ways of connecting clauses; constructing complex sentences; appropriate use of punctuation.

What you need

● The children's written work from the week.

Writing

Shared text-level work

● Tell the children that they are going to develop one of the pieces of work they did earlier in the week. Encourage them to approach this flexibly. For example, they could rewrite the Sherlock Holmes play as a story, or write a new Sherlock Holmes story or play, or write a story with a new detective.

● Outline a procedure for editing, once they have written a first draft:

  ● Read the work to a friend and discuss how it could be improved.
  ● Check sentence structure and spelling.
  ● Check correct use of conventions – indented paragraphs and correct punctuation of dialogue for stories, correct layout for plays and so on.

● Extended lesson: tell the children to choose a genre, research it, and produce an extended piece of writing which will be redrafted using the procedure outlined earlier.

Shared sentence-level work

● Remind the children how to write interesting sentences by using different ways of connecting clauses. Ask them how many different ways they can combine the statements *It was raining* and *I got wet*.

> ● Because it was raining, I got wet.
> ● I got wet because it was raining.
> ● It was raining, so I got wet.
> ● When it was raining, I got wet.
> ● It was raining and I got wet.

● Finally, discuss the subtle differences in emphasis and meaning in the different sentences.

Guided and independent work

● Ask the children to develop and edit one of their ideas from earlier in the week.

● Help those who have chosen the story form to achieve an interesting variety of sentence structures.

● Extended lesson: ask the children, working as pairs within groups of four, to choose a genre and research it in the library. Tell them to try to find some stories and poems and to make notes on films in their chosen genre. The next step is to use their research to write an extended narrative. This could be written and edited collaboratively in pairs.

Plenary

● Ask the children what they have learned about genre. Can they give examples of different types of genre? How does classification by genre help the reader?

● Collect the children's work into a class book; make multiple copies if necessary and encourage the children in the class, and in other classes, to read it.

Differentiation

Less able

● Advise children with their choices of work to develop.

More able

● Ask a group as part of developing one of their pieces to change it into a different genre.

The War of the Worlds

A big greyish rounded bulk, the size, perhaps, of a bear, was rising slowly and painfully out of the cylinder. As it bulged up and caught the light, it glistened like wet leather.

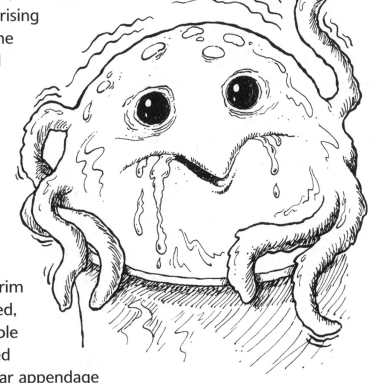

Two large dark-coloured eyes were regarding me steadfastly. The mass that framed them, the head of the thing, was rounded, and had, one might say, a face. There was a mouth under the eyes, the lipless brim of which quivered and panted, and dropped saliva. The whole creature heaved and pulsated convulsively. A lank tentacular appendage gripped the edge of the cylinder, another swayed in the air.

Those who have never seen a living Martian can scarcely imagine the strange horror of its appearance. The peculiar V-shaped mouth with its pointed upper lip, the absence of brow ridges, the absence of a chin beneath the wedgelike lower lip, the incessant quivering of this mouth, the Gorgon groups of tentacles, the tumultuous breathing of the lungs in a strange atmosphere, the evident heaviness and painfulness of movement due to the greater gravitational energy of the earth – above all, the extraordinary intensity of the immense eyes – were at once vital, intense, inhuman, crippled and monstrous. There was something fungoid in the oily brown skin, something in the clumsy deliberation of the tedious movements unspeakably nasty. Even at this first encounter, this first glimpse, I was overcome with disgust and dread.

Suddenly the monster vanished. It had toppled over the brim of the cylinder and fallen into the pit, with a thud like the fall of a great mass of leather. I heard it give a peculiar thick cry, and forthwith another of these creatures appeared darkly in the deep shadow of the aperture.

I turned and, running madly, made for the first group of trees, perhaps a hundred yards away; but I ran slantingly and stumbling, for I could not avert my face from these things.

HG Wells

The Shooting of Dan McGrew

A bunch of the boys were whooping it up in the Malamute saloon;

The kid that handles the music-box was hitting a jag-time tune;

Back of the bar, in a solo game, sat Dangerous Dan McGrew,

And watching his luck was his light-o'-love, the lady that's known as Lou.

When out of the night, which was fifty below, and into the din and the glare,

There stumbled a miner fresh from the creeks, dog-dirty, and loaded for bear.

He looked like a man with a foot in the grave and scarcely the strength of a louse,

Yet he tilted a poke of dust on the bar, and he called for drinks for the house.

There was none could place the stranger's face, though we searched ourselves for a clue;

But we drank his health, and the last to drink was Dangerous Dan McGrew.

...

And the stranger turned, and his eyes they burned in a most peculiar way;

In a buckskin shirt that was glazed with dirt he sat, and I saw him sway;

Then his lips went in in a kind of grin, and he spoke, and his voice was calm;

And "Boys," says he, "you don't know me, and none of you care a damn;

But I want to state, and my words are straight, and I'll bet my poke they're true,

That one of you is a hound of hell... and that one is Dan McGrew."

Then I ducked my head and the lights went out, and two guns blazed in the dark;

And a woman screamed, and the lights went up, and two men lay stiff and stark

Pitched on his head, and pumped full of lead, was Dangerous Dan McGrew,

While the man from the creeks lay clutched to the breast of the lady that's known as Lou.

These are the simple facts of the case, and I guess I ought to know:

They say that the stranger was crazed with 'hooch', and I'm not denying it's so.

I'm not so wise as the lawyer guys, but strictly between us two –

The woman that kissed him – and pinched his poke – was the lady that's known as Lou.

Robert Service (an extract from the poem 'The Shooting of Dan McGrew')

▲ SCHOLASTIC

The School for Wizards

In the great building, near one corner, there was a mean little door of wood. Ged went to this and knocked loud. To the old man who opened the door he said, 'I bear a letter from the Mage Ogion of Gont to the Warder of the School on this island. I want to find the Warder, but I will not hear more riddles and scoffing!'

'This is the School,' the old man said mildly. 'I am the doorkeeper. Enter if you can.'

Ged stepped forward. It seemed to him that he had passed through the doorway: yet he stood outside on the pavement where he had stood before.

Once more he stepped forward, and once more he remained standing outside the door. The doorkeeper, inside, watched him with mild eyes.

Ged was not so much baffled as angry, for this seemed like a further mockery to him. With voice and hand he made the Opening spell which his aunt had taught him long ago; it was the prize among all her stocks of spells, and he wove it well now. But it was only a witch's charm, and the power that held this doorway was not moved at all.

When that failed Ged stood a long while there on the pavement. At last he looked at the old man who waited inside. 'I cannot enter,' he said unwillingly, 'unless you help me.'

The doorkeeper answered, 'Say your name.'

Then again Ged stood still a while; for a man never speaks his own name aloud, until more than his life's safety is at stake.

'I am Ged,' he said aloud. Stepping forward then he entered the open doorway. Yet it seemed to him that though the light was behind him, a shadow followed him in at his heels.

He saw also as he turned that the doorway through which he had come was not plain wood as he had thought, but ivory without joint or seam; it was cut, as he knew later, from a tooth of the Great Dragon. The door that the old man closed behind him was of polished horn, through which the daylight shone dimly, and on its inner face was carved the Thousand-Leaved Tree.

Ursula K Le Guin

Sherlock Holmes and the Green Paint

Sherlock Holmes is sitting thoughtfully in his apartment at 221B Baker Street smoking a large pipe. Dr Watson enters.

Watson: Who was that sad old fellow who just left?

Holmes: Josiah Amberley – his case is interesting. He retired in 1896 with a large sum. In 1897 he married a beautiful woman twenty years younger than himself. One of his friends was a young doctor – Dr Ray Ernest – who often visited the house. [CLUE] It seems that Dr Ernest and Mrs Amberley fell in love. Last week they ran off with all his money. He wanted to know: Can we find the lady? Can we save the money?

Watson: What will you do?

Holmes: Dear Watson, you know I am very busy at the moment. Would you go out to Lewisham and see the man?

Watson sighs, turns and leaves. Curtain close. After a short pause, curtain opens to reveal Holmes still in the same chair, still smoking. It is later and gas lamps are lit. Watson enters. There is a splash of green paint on his jacket.

Watson: I've found out as much as I could, Holmes. Amberley's house is an untidy place, but at least he is trying to do something about it. He had a large tin of green paint and was painting the woodwork. The house was full of the smell of paint. There was another smell – gas, I think – but it was hard to be sure because of the paint. [CLUE]

Holmes: (touches the paint splash and sniffs his fingers) Mmm, so I see.

Watson: (looking with annoyance at the paint splash, which he had not noticed) He showed me his strong room. It really is a strong room with a close-fitting iron door and shutter – strange! Only a bank would need such a large place. [CLUE] Oh, and there was a gas lamp on the wall, but the lamp was missing and the end of the pipe was open. [CLUE]

Holmes: You have done well, Watson!

The bell rings and Mr Amberley is shown in.

Amberley: Have you found out anything yet?

Holmes: Yes, I believe so. I have just one question to ask you.

Amberley: What is it Mr Holmes?

Holmes: Only this: what did you do with the bodies?

Amberley looks shocked. He turns and makes a run for it, but is stopped at the door by Inspector Barker from Scotland Yard, who has been waiting for him.

UNIT 5

Formal

The unit begins with an example of official language in the form of the guarantee terms and conditions for an electronic product. The difference between informal and formal language is explored in Hours 2 and 3, and in Hour 4 the work of the Plain English Campaign is introduced. Children use an extract from a guide to Plain English written by the Plain English Campaign to distinguish between helpful formal official language, and language that is unnecessarily verbose and thus deserving of the epithet gobbledegook. The unit can be extended by providing the children with other official texts to analyse and rewrite using the Plain English Campaign guidelines.

Hour	Shared text-level work	Shared word-/sentence-level work	Guided and independent work	Plenary
1 Guarantee	Reading a product guarantee; picking out typical formal language and document features.	Revising conditionals; finding formal language.	Imagining problems with the product and assessing the guarantee.	Checking interpretations of terms and conditions.
2 Emails	Reading formal and informal emails.	Listing formal, official language.	Role-playing customers and help desk staff, writing emails.	Recapping language features; seeing if problems were resolved.
3 Letter of complaint	Writing a letter of complaint.	Checking punctuation.	Writing letters of complaint about another problem.	Sharing letters; suggesting how to solve problems.
4 Plain English	Introducing the Plain English Campaign and identifying gobbledegook.	Adding to the list of formal words and phrases.	Rewriting a guarantee in plain English.	Shared rewriting of the guarantee.
5 Fun with gobbledegook	Reading more examples of gobbledegook.	Recapping formal vocabulary.	Playing a game to generate gobbledegook sentences.	Enjoying the sentences and 'translating' them.

Key assessment opportunities
● Do the children recognise key features of official language?
● Do they understand the difference between formal and informal writing?
● Can they rewrite unnecessarily verbose documents in plain English?

Guarantee

Shared text- and sentence-level work

● Display page one of the KB 2-in-1 owner's manual. Ask the children to look at the contents and give examples of what each chapter might contain.

● Now display page 16 of the manual and read the guarantee. Discuss whether the terms and conditions seem fair. Ask the children what is meant by the following phrase:

...does not does not affect your statutory rights.

(Whatever the guarantee says or does not say, it cannot change your basic legal rights as a consumer.)

● Ask if the children have seen guarantees like the one on photocopiable 125 before when they have bought electronic products in real life.

● Use the second clause to revise conditional sentences and the use of *if*.

● Ask the children to identify the features of official documents noticeable in this text, for example, impersonal tone, no contracted forms, no slang or colloquial expressions, extensive use of the passive voice. Annotate appropriate suggestions.

● Consider the layout features of the document, such as clauses as a bulleted list, use of upper-case letters for emphasis, the footnote/'small print'.

● Ask the children to pick out examples of formal, official, technical language. Tell them that this is sometimes called officialese or, if it is badly written and confusing, gobbledegook. Make a table with explanations in everyday language:

Official language	Everyday language
rendered	made
invalid	worthless
unauthorised	done without permission

Guided and independent work

● Ask the children to discuss in pairs the terms and conditions of the guarantee. Suggest that one child thinks up a problem that could occur with the product, and the other child says whether or not it is covered by the guarantee. For example:

> Child 1: I've spilt orange juice on my 2-in-1 and it won't work. Can I claim?
> Child 2: No, because the third clause says that the guarantee does not apply to spillage of liquids.

Plenary

● Select pairs of children to re-run their questions and answers in front of the whole class. Ask the rest of the class to check that the interpretation of the terms and conditions is correct.

● Discuss the use of officialese or gobbledegook. Which role-plays were funny and which were complex?

Emails

Objectives

NLS
S2: To understand features of formal official language through, eg collecting and analysing examples, discussing when and why they are used; noting the conventions of the language, eg use of the impersonal voice, imperative verbs, formal vocabulary; collecting typical words and expressions, eg *those wishing to...*, *hereby...*, *forms may be obtained...*
S&L
66 Group discussion and interaction: To identify the ways spoken language varies according to differences in context and purpose of use.

What you need
● Photocopiable pages 125 and 126.

Shared text-level work

● Tell the children that they are going to read a series of emails about the KB 2-in-1. Explain that two of the emails are informal, one is formal, and one is formal and official.

● Introduce the emails on photocopiable page 126 and ask the children to identify which is which as you read them out.

● Note that the style of the last email on page 126 is more typical of a (posted) letter than emails.

● Go over the texts again and work with the children to identify features of informal and formal language as appropriate. For example:

Formal	Informal
impersonal tone	personal tone
no contracted forms	use of contracted forms
no slang or colloquial expressions	use of slang and colloquial expressions
extensive use of the passive voice	written mainly in the active voice
formal, official language	everyday language

Shared sentence-level work

● Add new examples of formal, official language to the table begun in Hour 1, for example, *direct*, *attention*, *clause*, *in any case*.

● Another type of language that makes the fourth email particularly difficult to understand is the technical language. Ask the children to make a separate list of these terms, such as *mini-DIN plug* and *MIDI interface*.

Guided and independent work

● Divide the class in half. Tell one half that they are going to play the roles of the staff at the KB helpdesk, and the other that they are going to play customers.

● Explain that each customer should write an email describing a problem with their 2-in-1. These can be based on the oral work in Hour 1 or can be new problems, perhaps one of the notes on the keyboard is not working.

● Ask the customers to give their emails to the Helpdesk staff who should write appropriate formal replies like the example on photocopiable page 126.

● If possible, the children could do this on computers and send the emails 'live' via the intranet. Alternatively, give some children from both groups OHTs to write on for sharing in the plenary.

Differentiation

Less able
● Allocate the role of customer.

More able
● Allocate the role of Helpdesk staff.

Plenary

● Display the emails or OHTs and use them to recap on features of formal and informal language.

● Also discuss whether the problems were satisfactorily resolved. Any that were not can be used in the next lesson.

Letter of complaint

Objectives

NLS

S2: To understand features of formal official language through, eg collecting and analysing examples, discussing when and why they are used; noting the conventions of the language, eg use of the impersonal voice, imperative verbs, formal vocabulary; collecting typical words and expressions, eg *those wishing to..., hereby..., forms may be obtained...*

What you need

● Photocopiable page 125.

Shared text-level work

● Display page one of photocopiable page 125 and ask the children to think of something that could go wrong with the 2-in-1 that is not the owner's fault, but is not covered by the guarantee. For example, you plug the 2-in-1 into your computer and your computer blows up; you get an electric shock from the 2-in-1. Add any good ideas about problems from the last lesson.

● Choose one of the ideas and tell the class that you are going to write a letter of complaint about it. Begin by explaining why you are writing to complain, and that you have already tried phoning and emailing and aren't satisfied with the responses so far. Demonstrate how to set out and write a formal letter. Discuss:

● where to place the sender's address and the company's address
● the salutation, such as *Dear Sir, Dear [name of customer services representative or manager]*
● a paragraph explaining the problem
● a paragraph or a few continuing lines explaining what contact and attempts to resolve the situation you have made
● a paragraph stating what you want – a repair or refund
● a paragraph stating what action you will take if you are not satisfied, such as contacting the local Citizen's Advice Bureau
● closure – *Yours faithfully, Yours sincerely*, as appropriate.

Shared sentence level work

● Go through your model text again, asking the children to check the necessary layout and punctuation.

Guided and independent work

● Ask the children, working in pairs to help each other, but producing their own letters, to write a similar letter of complaint, but about a different topic. For example, one of the other problems with the KB 2-in-1 discussed earlier.

● Encourage the children to write in a simple but formal style: simply and clearly but without using contractions, slang or colloquialisms. Discuss how the wording should help the tone of the letter to sound stern and firm but polite and expectant.

Differentiation

Less able
● Allow children to write about the same problem as was demonstrated in the shared session (removing the display first!).

More able
● Ask children to look at the contents page on photocopiable page 125 and think of a complaint that could arise from the contents of the chapters.

Plenary

● Ask some children to read out their letters of complaint while the rest of the class listen carefully to check that they have followed the recommended structure.

● Ask some to suggest how the problem could be resolved.

Plain English

Objectives

NLS
T17: To read and understand examples of official language and its characteristic features.
T20: To discuss the way standard English varies in different contexts, eg why legal language is necessarily highly formalised.
S2: To understand features of formal official language through, eg collecting and analysing examples; noting the conventions of the language; collecting typical words and expressions.

What you need

● Photocopiable pages 125–127.
● internet access and data-projector.

Shared text-level work

● Remind the children that official texts are sometimes so badly written or use such obscure, esoteric terminology or phraseology that it is difficult to understand. Remind them that language of this kind is often called gobbledegook. Discuss the appropriateness of this word – gobbledegook sounds like a nonsense word.

● It is important to emphasise that some formal language is necessarily technical and specific, compared with texts that are just badly written, use high-flown language merely to sound important or deliberately restrict access/understanding to certain readers.

● Explain that the Plain English Campaign is an independent pressure group fighting for public information to be written in understandable English. This is important because unclear language excludes people in important situations. The Plain English website contains a gobbledegook generator (**www.plainenglish.co.uk/generator**), which is a fun way of demonstrating the problem. Generate some gobbledegook phrases and try to translate them into plain English.

● Display photocopiable page 127 and tell the children that it is a summary of the campaign's guide to writing plain English for anyone who has an official document to write. Read and discuss the guide. Which of the points do you think will be most helpful in producing plain English? Which could you learn from? Why do you think some officials use the difficult words instead of everyday alternatives?

● Re-read photocopiable page 125 and demonstrate how to use the guide to check how well written the guarantee is. Go through each point at a time and the vocabulary list. This is by no means a bad example of official language, but the children will note the following:

● some sentences are more than 20 words long
● there are several passive sentences
● several long words and formal, official phrases could have been replaced by shorter words, for example *in accordance with, commences, purchaser.*

Shared sentence-level work

● Add new examples of formal, official language from the list on photocopiable page 127 to the table begun in Hour 1.

Guided and independent work

● Ask the children, working in pairs and using photocopiable page 127 as a guide, to rewrite the guarantee on photocopiable page 125 in plain English.

● Encourage them to read their new guarantees to their partners to see how successfully they have simplified them, but still covering all the necessary points.

Plenary

● Ask the children to help you to write a plain English version of the guarantee on the board. Ask for suggestions for the best way to simplify each sentence, and discuss why you think they are effective.

Differentiation

Less able
● Help children to get started by giving them this opening paragraph: *Everything made by KB Electronics UK Ltd* is guaranteed for 12 months from the date you buy it. These are the conditions of the guarantee...*

More able
● In addition, challenge children to rewrite the formal email on photocopiable page 126.

Fun with gobbledegook

Objectives

NLS
T17: To read and understand examples of official language and its characteristic features.
S2: To understand features of formal official language through, eg collecting and analysing examples; noting the conventions of the language.
W8: To build a bank of useful words and phrases for argument.
S&L
66 Listening: To listen for language variation in formal and informal contexts.

What you need

● Sets of 12 word cards with one of the formal, official words collected throughout the week on one side, and a 'translation' into simple English on the other (include differentiated sets)
● internet access and data-projector (optional).

Shared text- and sentence-level work

● Tell the children that they are going to have some fun writing gobbledegook. Begin by giving them some examples from the Plain English Campaign website (**www.plainenglish.co.uk/examples**). Alternatively, write these examples on the board:

Before: High-quality learning environments are a necessary precondition for facilitation and enhancement of the ongoing learning process.
After: Children need good schools if they are to learn properly. (Although the 'Before' paragraph does not mention it, the situation does involve schoolchildren.)
Before: If there are any points on which you require explanation or further particulars we shall be glad to furnish such additional details as may be required by telephone.
After: If you have any questions, please ring.

● Next, demonstrate the task for the independent work. Select a word card at random, for example, *commence*, and use it as the basis of a gobbledegook sentence, which may contain several other gobbledegook words: *Please commence writing immediately and do not terminate your efforts until I advise you to do so. (Please start writing immediately and do not stop until I tell you.)*

Shared word-level work

● Display the words you have selected for the cards and recap meanings.

Guided and independent work

● Kinaesthetic learning: organise the children into groups of four with one set of word cards and a set of blank cards for each group, to play the gobbledegook game:

Round 1

1. Shuffle the cards and place them in the middle of the table.
2. Each child takes a card from the top of the pack.
3. Each child writes a gobbledegook sentence on another card using that word (with a 'translation' on the back).
4. The best gobbledegook sentence (agreed as a group) is the winner.

Round 2

1. Swap gobbledegook sentence cards with another group, shuffle and place them in the middle of the table (gobbledegook side up).
2. Each child takes a card from the top of the pack (but must *not* look at the translation side).
3. S/he has to work out orally the meaning of the gobbledegook sentence.
4. The one who guesses the most sentences is the winner.

Differentiation

Less able
● Use the word cards containing the easier words.

More able
● Use the word cards containing the most difficult words.
● Encourage long, wordy, complex sentences!

Plenary

● Share the most interesting and amusing gobbledegook sentences and work to try to translate them.
● Ask the children to look out for examples of gobbledegook over the next few days, and build up a display of the examples they find.

16

KB 2-in-1

The all-in-one computer music solution

GUARANTEE TERMS AND CONDITIONS

All products manufactured by KB Electronics UK Ltd* are guaranteed for a period of 12 months from the original date of purchase, in accordance with the following terms and conditions:

● The guarantee commences on the date shown on the receipt and only applies to the original purchaser.

● The guarantee will be rendered invalid if unauthorised modifications are made to the product, or if non-standard components are used, or if the serial number is removed or defaced, or if the seal to the maintenance panel is broken.

● This guarantee applies only to normal use of the product. In the event of damage caused by inappropriate use, spillage of liquids, incorrect installation, or accidental breakage, the guarantee will be null and void.

Failure to comply with the licence agreement relating to the software for the product will invalidate this guarantee. The guarantee does not affect your statutory rights.

YOU ARE ADVISED TO RETAIN YOUR RECEIPT TO ENSURE PROOF OF PURCHASE.

In all cases of difficulty contact our helpline at: customerservices@kb.co.uk.

* Any claims made in respect of this guarantee must be forwarded to the dealer from whom the product was purchased. The dealer may require a receipt as evidence of the date of purchase.

Emails

Hey Jake

Your keyboard sounds great! But, if I were you, I wouldn't mess about with it – if you do, you might as well tear up the guarantee. Why don't you email the manufacturers and see what they have to say?

Cheers

Darren

Hi Darren

Why don't we get together to play at the school concert? You can play guitar, and I'll play my new 2-in-1 keyboard – it's great! The top half is a computer keyboard and the bottom half is a music keyboard – you can play a tune on the music keys and chords or bass notes on the computer keys. Only trouble is I don't fancy bringing my whole computer along. I'm gonna ask my dad if he can wire up a speaker to the keyboard.

See ya,

Jake

Customer Query Number: 638495

Dear Mr Davies

I direct your attention to clause b) in the Guarantee Terms and Conditions which explains that you will invalidate the guarantee if you make any unauthorised modifications.

The engineering department have informed me that such a modification is, in any case, not possible, as the keyboard accesses the sound card and loudspeakers in your computer via the mini-DIN plug and the built-in MIDI interface.

However, we also manufacture the 2-in-1 Companion which is a self-contained MIDI-compatible sound module designed to be used for just this purpose. Details can be found on page 13 of the KB 2-in-1 Owner's manual.

I trust that this information has been of assistance.

Yours sincerely

David Cartwright

Customer Services

Dear Helpline,

I want to use my 2-in-1 keyboard at a concert, but don't want to take my computer along. Is it possible to wire up an extension speaker to the keyboard so that I can use it by itself?

Yours faithfully

Jake Davies

How to write in plain English

● **Stop and think** before you start writing. Make a note of the points you want to make in a logical order.

● **Prefer short words.** Long words will not impress your customers or help your writing style.

● **Use everyday English** whenever possible. Avoid jargon and legalistic words, and explain any technical terms you have to use.

● **Keep your sentence length down** to an average of 15 to 20 words. Try to stick to one main idea in a sentence.

● **Use active verbs as much as possible.** Say 'we will do it' rather than 'it will be done by us'.

● **Be concise.**

● **Imagine you are talking to your reader.** Write sincerely, personally, in a style that is suitable and with the right tone of voice.

● **And always check that your writing is clear, helpful, human and polite.**

Words to avoid

Try to use the alternatives we suggest in brackets.

additional (extra)	in the event of (if)
advise (tell)	on receipt (when we/you get)
applicant (you)	on request (if you ask)
commence (start)	particulars (details)
complete (fill in)	per annum (a year)
comply with (keep to)	persons (people)
consequently (so)	prior to (before)
ensure (make sure)	purchase (buy)
forward (send)	regarding (about)
in accordance with (under, keeping to)	should you wish (if you wish)
in excess of (more than)	terminate (end)
in respect of (for)	whilst (while)

Plain
English
Campaign

See **www.plainenglish.co.uk** for a more detailed version of this guide.

UNIT 1

Reading and writing narrative

This unit prepares for reading and writing narrative in the Key Stage 2 tests. It takes children through a reading task and a writing task similar to those set in the tests, but here children are allowed to help each other and ask questions at every stage of the process. In addition to providing practice, the unit helps to familiarise children with the Key Stage 2 test marking schemes so that they know what the examiners are looking for. When this, and its companion units on poetry and non-fiction (units 2 and 3) have been completed, the children will be ready for more formal test practice in test conditions.

Hour	Shared text-level work	Shared word-/ sentence-level work	Guided and independent work	Plenary
1 Future School	Practising reading skills using short story.	Revise figures of speech and story language.	Asking and answering comprehension questions; responding personally to a text.	Discussing issues raised in text.
2 Reading test practice	Introducing and advising on test practice.		Holding reading test practice on narrative.	Going over the 'test' papers.
3 A short, boring story	Exploring why a story is boring.	Looking at tips for constructing and linking sentences and writing dialogue.	Experimenting with connectives; improving the story.	Evaluating each other's work.
4 Writing test practice	Introducing and advising on test practice.		Holding writing test practice.	Talking about how the 'test' went; sharing ideas.
5 Bart's story	Analysing an improved story.		Analysing and annotating each other's work.	Sharing ideas about paragraphs and punctuation.

Key assessment opportunities
● Do the children understand test formats and procedures?
● Do they know how to improve their test technique?
● Do they know which narrative reading and writing skills they need to work on?

Future School

Objectives

NLS
T7: To annotate passages in detail in response to specific questions.
T18: To secure the skills of skimming, scanning and efficient reading.
S1: To revise the language conventions and grammatical features of the different types of text such as: narrative.

What you need
● Photocopiable page 134.

Shared text-level work

● Tell the children that they are going to practise reading skills for the forthcoming tests. Write the following skills (summarised from QCA documentation) on the board:

> ● Finding information
> ● Deduction and interpretation
> ● Commenting on structure and organisation
> ● Explaining use of language including literary features
> ● Commenting on purpose and viewpoint.

● Display and read photocopiable page 134 to the children. Then test information retrieval. For example, *What happened to Chloe's old school? What mark did she get in the test? Who was top of the class?*
● Ask several questions that require inference or interpretation: *How did the electronic hat help Chloe? What mark did Zoe get in the fractions test? Why were the teachers unemployed?*
● Go through the story again and ask the children to label each part of the story structure: *Opening, Build-up, Dilemma, Events, Ending.* Allow them a few minutes to discuss this in pairs.
● Ask the children if the text is written in the first or third person, who the narrator is and from whose viewpoint we see the story. Annotate the personal pronouns that help to establish this viewpoint.

Shared sentence-level work

● Revise key figures of speech and story language features, particularly similes, and ask children to find and annotate examples in the story.

Guided and independent work

● Work with two small groups to generate more comprehension questions at two levels: simple questions about information in the text; more difficult questions where the answer has to be worked out from the information given (questions requiring inference and deduction).
● Ask the groups to scan the text to answer each other's questions.
● Tell the other children that some questions in the reading test will ask them to write what they think about the story or its ideas. In this session, they are going to write what they think about Future School.
● Write the following question on the board, and ask the children to work in pairs to share ideas and write about ten lines: *Would you like to go to Future School? Explain what you would like about it. Are there any disadvantages to Future School?*

Differentiation

Less able
● Tell children to go through the story step by step to see what Chloe liked, and then to say whether they would like that too.

More able
● Challenge children to look below the surface of the story and see the disadvantages.

Plenary

● Share some of the responses. What they would like is relatively easy; the disadvantages more difficult. Discuss the following issues:

> ● Will Chloe still be able to learn things when she doesn't have an electronic hat?
> ● Will she still like healthy food when she can't take a taste-zapper tablet?
> ● Won't the children miss something by not being able to talk to a teacher?

Objective
To practise reading narrative.

What you need
● Photocopiable pages 134 and 135.

Reading test practice

Shared work

● Tell the children that they are going to do some test practice. Explain that they will be given a test paper that is similar to, though not exactly the same as, a section in the Key Stage 2 test reading booklet. Make sure that you emphasise, however, that this is *not* a test. Stress they are allowed to, and should, help each other and discuss responses. Give them the following advice:

On reading
● Re-read the story and make annotations.
● Underline any interesting or important points.
● Use skimming and scanning skills when re-reading.

On answering the questions
● Read the instructions carefully.
● Look at the number of marks for each question. This will give you an indication of how much to write. For example, if there are two marks, you probably have to give two pieces of information.
● Check your answers.

Guided and independent work

● Hand out the story (photocopiable page 134) the answer paper (photocopiable page 135) and a sheet of writing paper to each child.
● Remind the children that this is not a test – just practice – so they are allowed to talk and ask each other questions, but should still keep an eye on the time.
● Allow five minutes reading time and 15 minutes for the test. (This should be ample as it is less than a quarter of the length of a full SAT reading test.) Write these times on the board.

Plenary

● Go over all the questions (except questions 10 and 11) and ask the children to mark their own 'test' papers. Give a full and detailed explanation of each answer, and consider alternative answers that may also be worth a full or half mark. Explain that questions 10 and 11 can only be marked later by you.
● Notes on marking: give the children a mark out of 20, but emphasise that it is not their mark that is important here, but what they have learned about the process.
● Note that a National Curriculum level cannot be given because the children were allowed to help each other, and because this 'test' only represents a part of what is assessed in the actual Key Stage 2 reading test.

Differentiation

Less able
● Differentiation by outcome.

More able
● Differentiation by outcome.

A short, boring story

Objectives

NLS
S1: To revise the language conventions and grammatical features of the different types of text such as: narrative.
S4: To secure control of complex sentences, understanding how clauses can be manipulated to achieve different effects.

What you need
● Photocopiable page 136.

Shared text-level work

● Tell the children that they are now going to improve a short story to practise writing skills. They have already revised *text structure and organisation* and are going to focus on *composition and effect* and *sentence structure and punctuation*.
● Display and read photocopiable page 136 (with column two covered), and ask the children to evaluate how well it fulfils the above criteria. (It is dull, because characters and settings are not brought to life.)
● Discuss how the story could be improved and annotate the text as appropriate.

Shared sentence-level work

● Reproduce the following table of tips on the board.

Sentence structure	How to do it
Complex sentences	Write sentences saying two or more things.
Expanded noun phrases	Include one (or two) adjectives before key nouns.
Adverbial phrases or clauses	Say where, when, how or why something was done.
Conjunctions/connectives	Use a wide range of joining words – not just *and*, *but* and *so*.

● Now reveal column two, and tell the children that the prompts will help them to improve the composition and effect and the sentence structure and punctuation. Demonstrate how to improve the first paragraph and explain what you are doing. For example, *Billy had seen the large, round box under the Christmas tree on Christmas Eve and he couldn't wait to open it. He tore off the paper with trembling fingers...*
● Now model how to write one of the passages of dialogue, giving particular attention to punctuation and developing the reporting clause.

Guided and independent work

● Help one group to experiment with using different conjunctions and connectives to combine statements in different ways.
● Give the other children photocopiable page 136 and tell them that they can help each other in pairs, but must produce individual work. Give the following advice:

> ● Use ideas from shared work and the prompts in column two as a guide to improving the story.
> ● Use complex sentences. (The prompts should help them to do this.)
> ● Punctuate the dialogue correctly and write interesting reporting clauses.
> ● Demonstrate your best handwriting for at least four lines.

Differentiation

Less able
● Help children to write complex sentences.

More able
● Ask children to change the viewpoint of the story, for example, to first person.

Plenary

● Tell the children that they are going to play at being the test examiner. Display some of the children's work on OHT and ask the class to evaluate how well each example meets the criteria for composition and effect and sentence structure and punctuation.

Writing test practice

Shared work
● Tell the children that they are going to do some more test practice, this time in writing. Again, explain that they will be given a test paper that is similar to, though not exactly the same as, a Key Stage 2 test paper, but emphasise that this it is *not* a test. They are allowed to help each other and ask each other questions. Give them the following writing advice:

Planning – some prompts are given to help you. Give particular attention to describing characters and thinking of a good ending.
Writing – describe everything fully. This will help you to write complex sentences. Take care with punctuation, especially dialogue.
Checking – when you have finished, read through your story and check for correctness in grammar, punctuation and spelling; also that it reads well.

Guided and independent work
● Give out the task paper (photocopiable page 137) and two sheets of writing paper to each child, explaining that one sheet is for drafting and planning, the other for the story writing.
● Remind the children that this is just practice and encourage them to help each other and discuss ideas.
● Allow 10 minutes planning time and 35 minutes writing time. Write these times on the board and make sure the children are aware of them.

Plenary
● When time is up, collect in the papers, and talk about how the practice went. What did the children find easy or difficult? Did they all manage to finish? What ideas did they have for the ending the story?
● Notes on marking: give the children a mark out of 20 using the writing marking scheme strands as a guide (allowing three marks for their four best lines of handwriting).
● Note that a National Curriculum level cannot be given because the children were encouraged to help each other, and because this 'test' only represents a part of what is tested in the Key Stage 2 writing test.

Bart's story

Objectives

NLS

T12: To compare texts in writing.

T21: To divide whole texts into paragraphs, paying attention to the sequence of paragraphs and to the links between one paragraph and the next.

What you need

● Sample answer/story (see Shared text-level work).

Shared text-level work

● Prepare for display a sample answer to the writing test from Hour 4. Include good points that you want to reinforce, such as the use of complex sentences, and bad points that you want to demonstrate how to improve, such as missing punctuation. For example:

Bart's story	Analysis
As soon as he opened his eyes, Jim saw the chocolate Father Christmas on his bedside cabinet. 'It's Christmas,' he whooped happily.	Subordinate clause introduced by conjunction *as*. Comma to mark the clause. Correct use of inverted commas. Missing exclamation mark after Christmas. Effective reporting clause with a synonym of said and an adverb. (Appropriate paragraph analysis too.)

● Explain to the children that they are going to look in detail at one child's writing test. (An imaginary child of course! Let's call him Bart.) Display Bart's story. Read it, then analyse and annotate it in discussion with the children using the strands in the writing marking scheme:

● Sentence structure and punctuation (Vary sentences for clarity and effect; write with technical accuracy in phrases, clauses and sentences.)

● Text structure and organisation (Organise and present texts effectively, sequencing and structuring information, ideas and events; construct and link paragraphs cohesively.)

● Composition and effect (Write imaginative, interesting and thoughtful texts.)

● Tell the children, in simple language, what you are looking for under each heading (see the Band details in the writing test marking scheme), with particular reference to the good and bad points that you have included as teaching points.

Guided and independent work

● Ask the children to work in pairs to analyse and annotate each other's work in the way that was demonstrated in the shared session, and then to try to improve on the weak points, for example by rewriting a passage of dialogue. Encourage them to help each other during the correction phase.

Differentiation

Less able

● Suggest just one or two areas for children to try to improve.

More able

● Tell children to ensure that they are not letting themselves down by basic mistakes in areas such as punctuation, paragraphing or grammatical agreement.

Plenary

● Ask the children to share ideas with the rest of the class, giving specific examples from their own story.

● What have they learned from this lesson? For example, how to write a story in paragraphs, how to punctuate dialogue correctly and so on.

Future School

It was my first day at Future School. In the Summer holidays, our old school had been knocked down so that a new one could be built, and the new one was bang up-to-date!

There were no classrooms. Instead, it was like a cineplex, with a different cinema for each class. A robot showed me to my seat, and gave me a special hat to put on. I was sitting next to Chloe, my best friend.

"What do you think?" I asked.

"Sssshhh!"

The lights went down and the film started. At first I was disappointed because the film showed a teacher standing in front of a blackboard explaining how to do fractions. It was just like old school, except it was a film. Then I noticed something strange. I could understand the explanations – which I never could before. I looked up and tried to see my hat. I caught a glimpse of LEDs winking on and off. I suppose it was the electronic hat that helped me to understand.

When the film finished, a little table, like those on aeroplanes, came down from the seat in front and a test paper came out of the slot. The test paper was on fractions. I felt a moment of panic because I am hopeless at tests. I wanted to run home, but I didn't want everybody staring at me. I took a deep breath, and made a start on the test. What a surprise! It was easier than a game of noughts and crosses! I put the test paper back in the slot, the lights went down, and the teacher appeared on the screen again.

"Well done, children," she said. "I'm very pleased with your test. Everybody got 100 out of 100, so everybody is top of the class!"

At lunchtime, the robot gave us a healthy-eating menu. It looked as dull as ditchwater and probably tasted worse. "Don't look so glum!" said the robot. "Just take this taste-zapper tablet."

I swallowed the tablet and my lentil burger tasted just like cheeseburger and fries, and my carrot juice tasted like cola! "You see, Zoe," the robot lectured. "Healthy eating can be fun!"

The day ended with storytime, but this was no boring old teacher reading a boring old book. It was a movie on a big screen with surround sound – a perfect ending to a fun day.

Chloe and I said goodbye to our robot, and walked through the door feeling tired but happy. We were looking forward to another day in Future School.

Only one thing spoiled it – the beggars hanging around the school gates. One of them had a sign near his begging bowl that said, UNEMPLOYED TEACHER. PLEASE GIVE GENEROUSLY.

Questions about 'Future School'

Name _____

◖ Put a ring around the correct answer.

1. The story is written in
the first person / the third person
I mark

2. The narrator of the story is Zoe / the teacher / the author / Chloe
I mark

3. The first surprise is
there is a robot / the classroom is like a cinema / she has to wear a special hat / the lesson is on film
I mark

4. The narrator understood the lesson on fractions because
it was easy / she is good at maths / the electronic hat helped her / Chloe helped her
I mark

5. "dull as ditchwater" is
a sentence / a simile / a metaphor / an adjective
I mark

◖ Write one or two sentences to answer questions 6 to 9 on a separate sheet of paper.

6. Why was the narrator disappointed when the film started?
I mark

7. Why did she panic when the test paper on fractions came out of the slot?
I mark

8. "A boring old book". Give two reasons why a book can be more enjoyable than a film.
2 marks

9. What is the unpleasant surprise at the end of the story? Do you think this is a good ending? Give a reason for your answer.
2 marks

◖ Write several sentences to answer questions 10 and 11 on a separate sheet of paper.

10. Write a different ending (of about the same length) to the story.
3 marks

11. Why do Chloe and Zoe like their new school? Give as many reasons as you can find.
6 marks

Total: 20 marks

TERM 3

A short, boring story

How to make a short, boring story...	...into a story the examiner will love
Billy got a cowboy hat for Christmas	Describe Billy; add an adjective to describe the hat; describe his excitement when he got the hat.
he took it to school	Use a temporal connective to introduce the next paragraph, eg 'After the Christmas holidays...'
the teacher said cowboy hats are not allowed in school	Punctuate the dialogue and develop the conversation; use an adverb in the reporting clause, eg 'the teacher said angrily'.
he felt upset	Describe his feelings in detail (perhaps with a simile), eg 'It felt like the end of the world.'
he threw the hat away	Add an adverbial phrase/clause explaining how he threw the hat away: 'He threw it away as if it was a piece of old rubbish.'
his family moved to Texas	Use another temporal connective to signal a big step forward in the story. Describe the move, his first impressions of Texas (with adjectives), his first impressions of his new school (with adjectives).
the teacher said you are not allowed to come to school without a cowboy hat	Develop the conversation; add a phrase of description to the reporting clause, eg 'the teacher said in a Texan drawl'.
Billy said...	Describe Billy's reaction and think of a good way to round off the story.

■ SCHOLASTIC

A guitar

◀ Here is a storyboard about a boy who gets a guitar for Christmas. Look at the pictures, make a plan using the planning notes, and write a story. Make up your own ending for the story.

◀ Jot down some useful words and phrases about these things in the story:

    characters

    when the boy gets his guitar

    music lessons

    making a new friend

    when they see the poster

    how the story ends.

Poetry

The purpose of this unit is to prepare the children for reading poetry – a task that may be included in the reading booklet in the Key Stage 2 tests. A narrative poem has been chosen for this unit as, in addition to providing practice in responding to key features of poetry, it provides further practice in responding to narrative. As there is no requirement to *write* poetry in the tests, the latter part of the week has been used to practise spelling, for which a text related to the main text, 'Haunted Hide and Seek', has been chosen.

Hour	Shared text-level work	Shared word-/ sentence-level work	Guided and independent work	Plenary
1 Play the poem	Reading a poem and noting poetic features.		Reading a mystery/game poem and discussing results.	Summarising the story in the poem to check understanding.
2 Personal response	Discussing events and characters in the poem.	Brainstorming useful words and phrases for writing opinions and making points.	Describing new settings.	Discussing ideas and how they were presented.
3 Poetry reading test practice	Advice on reading poetry in the tests.		Holding a practice test.	Going over the answers to the 'test'.
4 Spelling first aid		Learning some spelling rules and tips.	Testing each other's spelling.	Noting any patterns in mis-spellings; noting words to learn for homework.
5 Fridge boy found		Discussing spelling test procedures.	Holding a spelling test practice.	Marking each other's papers; noting own mis-spelt words; comparing test text with poem from first lesson.

Key assessment opportunities
● Do the children understand test formats and procedures?
● Can they improve their test technique?
● Do they know which poetry reading skills they need to work on?
● Do they know which spelling rules they need to work on?

Play the poem

Objective

NLS
T4: To comment critically on the overall impact of a poem, showing how language and themes have been developed.

What you need
● Photocopiable pages 144 and 145.

Guided and independent work

● Explain to the children that the usual procedure for the Literacy Hour has to be turned around in this lesson because if the poem were displayed and discussed first it would 'give away' the solution to the puzzle on which the poem is based.

● So, give out copies of the poem, covered with sheets of paper. Note that the poem is like an adventure game and is played in pairs as follows:

> 1. Cover the poem with blank paper.
> 2. Reveal and read just the prologue and the introduction to Part 1.
> 3. Choose a place to hide. (It is more fun if each player chooses a different place.)
> 4. Reveal the rest of Part 1. Each player reads the stanza about the hiding place s/he chose.
> 5. Continue with Part 2 in a similar way.

● When the children have played the game, ask them how it went. Did they end up in Hong Kong? Did they save the bride, or did they find her skeleton many years later in the old oak chest? Discuss why any differences arose.

Shared text-level work

● Display photocopiable pages 144 and 145 and read through the whole poem. Tell the children that they are going to analyse and annotate the poem to prepare for a practice test. Explain that they will use similar skills to those used in reading narrative: finding information, deduction and interpretation. They will also need the ability to recognise and comment on the unique features of poetry:

> ● verse form (rhyme schemes and stress patterns)
> ● figures of speech (especially similes and metaphors)
> ● alliteration (words beginning with the same sound)
> ● onomatopoeia (words with sounds which suggest their meaning, such as *buzz*)
> ● diction (well-chosen words).

Plenary

● Pull the lesson together by making sure that the children have grasped the story on which the poem is based (the adventure game format means that some children will have 'saved' Lucy). Re-read the introductory text, the prologue, interlude and epilogue as these give an outline of the story.

● Alternatively, read 'The Mistletoe Bough' by Thomas Haynes Bayley, a different poem on the same subject. (It can be found in *100 Literacy Homework Activities Year 5*.)

Differentiation

Less able
● Differentiation by outcome.

More able
● Differentiation by outcome.

Personal response

Objectives

NLS
T4: To comment critically on the overall impact of a poem, showing how language and themes have been developed.
S1: To revise the language conventions and grammatical features of different types of text such as: narrative, discursive texts.

What you need
● Photocopiable pages 144 and 145.

Shared text-level work
● Display the poem and re-read the prologue. Ask the children to suggest a place for Lovell to hide not mentioned in the poem and to say what happens when he hides there.
● Read the interlude and do the same for Lucy.
● Read the Epilogue.
● Discuss the story. *Do you think this story really happened – or is it just a story?* (It is a bit far-fetched, and the fact that similar stories are linked with other old houses suggests that it is a sort of antique urban legend). *Can you match the stages of the poem to the stages of story structure?* (Opening, Build-up, Dilemma, Events, Ending.) Jot notes on the board.
● Next, discuss the characters. *Was Lucy foolish, or just unlucky?* (Foolish because she didn't listen to the warnings.) *Should Lovell have been more assertive when he wanted her to stop playing the game?* (Yes. He knew the dangers of the house better than anybody.)
● Finally, discuss how the story was told. *What is unusual about it?* (The reader is the hero, and can make choices – a bit like real life.) *Was this method of telling the story successful? Did you enjoy it, or would you have preferred the story to be told in a more traditional way?*

Shared word- and sentence-level work
● Ask the children to brainstorm useful words and phrases to help them in writing their ideas. Talk about how to express personal opinions about the poem in writing. Add their suggestions to the following table:

To begin a point	To add other points
I think that... In my opinion...	Also... On the other hand...

Guided work
● Ask the children to discuss and agree on two new places for Part 1 and two new places for Part 2. Advise them that some of the places should be safe and others dangerous. Ask them to write descriptions of the places in paragraphs of about 50 to 60 words each.

Independent work
● Ask the children, helping each other in pairs and using the notes on the board as a starting point, to write a personal response of three paragraphs. Ask them to write about the events in the story, the characters and the way the story was told (as in the shared discussion).

Differentiation

Less able
● Give children three questions to answer for their three paragraphs.

More able
● In addition, ask children to write a paragraph about the setting, how it is described, and why it is essential to the story.

Plenary
● Display some of the personal responses on OHT. Comment on the use of paragraphs and the language used to introduce and develop each point. Discuss the ideas expressed and how far the rest of the class agree or disagree with them.

Objective
To practise reading poetry.

What you need
● Photocopiable pages 144-146.

Poetry reading test practice

Shared text-level work

● Tell the children that they are going to do some test *practice*. Emphasise that this activity is not a test itself. Advise them that they are allowed to discuss the activity and ask each other questions. Give them the following advice for how to approach the practice:

On reading
● Re-read the poem and make annotations.
● Underline any interesting or important points.

On answering the questions
● Read the instructions carefully.
● Look at the number of marks for each question. This will suggest how much to write. For example, if there are 2 marks, you probably have to give two pieces of information.
● Check your answers.

Guided and independent work

● Give out the poem (photocopiable pages 144 and 145), the question paper (photocopiable page 146) and a sheet of writing paper to each child.
● Remind the children that this is preparation for a test, but not a test itself. Encourage them to work together if they want to.
● Allow 10 minutes reading time and 20 minutes for completing the 'test'. Write these times on the board.

Plenary

● Go over all of the questions (except question 6) and ask the children to mark their own tests. Give a full and detailed explanation of each answer, encouraging the children to give you prompts and ideas. Consider alternative answers, which may also be worth a full or half mark. Explain that question 6 cannot be self-marked now, but marked by you later on.

Notes on marking

● Give the children a mark out of 15, but emphasise that their mark is not necessarily important here, but what they have learned about the process is. Note that a National Curriculum level cannot be given because the children were allowed to help each other, and because this 'test' only represents a part of what is assessed in the Key Stage 2 reading test.

Differentiation

Less able
● Differentiation by outcome.

More able
● Differentiation by outcome.

Spelling first aid

Shared word-level work
● Tell the children that, after working through hundreds of spelling objectives in their junior school years, there is not a great percentage that can be covered in one revision lesson! Nevertheless, a bit of spelling first aid might help.

> **Talk through the following rules and tips:**
> 1. Write *i* before *e* except after *c* when the sound is *ee*. Examples include *believe, thief, ceiling, perceive*. Exceptions include *seize, weird, weir*.
> 2. Words ending in *y* (sounded as *i* in *pit*) have plural ending *ies*, such as *parties, laboratories*.
> 3. Words ending in *f* change to *ves* in the plural. Examples include *shelves, leaves, knives*. Exceptions include *roofs, chiefs, chefs*.
> 4. Words ending in *e* drop the *e* when adding *ing*, such as *staring*. Words with a short vowel before the final letter double the final letter, for example *slimming*.
> 5. When trying to spell a long word, break it down into smaller units that you know. For example, *government*, and *acknowledging* - begin with *know* or *knowledge*, add the prefix *ack*, then apply the previous rule to the *ing* ending.
> 6. Beacuse many English words are not spelled as they sound, it often helps to learn to say a word as it is spelled. For example, when learning *criticised*, say *critic-ised*. This may help you to remember that the middle *s* sound is written with a *c*.
> 7. Invent or learn mnemonics like *There's a rat in separate*.
> 8. Learn problem words with silent letters like *answer, biscuit, February, island, pneumonia, queue, rhubarb, solemn, Wednesday*.
> 9. Learn irregular plurals like *children, deer, oxen, stimuli*.

● Draw particular attention to the spelling tips in numbers 5 to 8 by giving the children several words to practise for each tip.
● Also explore some homophones that are frequently confused such as *their, there* and *they're*. Say the words in sentences and ask volunteers to spell the problem word each time.

Guided and independent work
● Ask the children to work in pairs to test each other using the word cards.
● When they have finished, ask them to look for patterns in their mistakes, for example -*ies* plurals.

Plenary
● Ask the children to discuss the diagnostic aspect of the paired test, that is, the patterns revealed by their mistakes.
● Tell the children to make a list of all the words they got wrong, and even more important, any spelling rules that they don't understand, and study them for homework. Tell them that there will be a spelling test tomorrow!

TERM 3

...ntify mis-spelt ...wn writing; to keep individual lists; to learn to spell them.
W4: To revise and consolidate work from previous five terms with particular emphasis on: learning and inventing spelling rules; inventing and using mnemonics for irregular or difficult spellings; unstressed vowel spellings in polysyllabic words.

What you need
● The example words in italic opposite on cards or slips of paper.

Differentiation
Less able
● Ask children to test each other on the first 20 words in rules 1 to 4.

More able
● Ask children to add additional five polysyllabic words to challenge their partner. The words must be challenging but in common use (no trick dictionary words).

UNIT 2 HOUR 5 📄 Poetry

Fridge boy found

Shared word-level work

● Tell the children that they are going to do some spelling test practice. Explain that they will be given a test paper that is similar to a Key Stage 2 spelling test paper.

● Tell them that, on this occasion, unlike earlier practice lessons, they must complete the test individually and are not allowed to talk to each other or ask for help.

● Explain the procedure to the children; that you will read the text, then you will read it again, pausing while they fill in each gap with the correctly spelt word.

Independent work

● Start the test on photocopiable page 147, following the above procedure. It should take about ten minutes, allowing for a longer plenary than usual.

Plenary

● Display photocopiable page 147, with correct spellings in place.

● Ask the children to swap papers with a partner and mark the test from the display.

● When the children get their papers back, ask them to make a list of the words that they have spelt incorrectly and to add it to the list of words they are working on (see Hour 4).

● Ask the children to practise the spellings they got wrong (either in the test, or from their spelling lists) using the word diagram method (see tip 8, in Hour 4).

● Collect all of the papers for checking and use them to identify needs for future teaching.

● Finally, discuss the similarities between this text and 'Haunted Hide and Seek'. Begin by asking the children to draw up two columns like the example below, and to make notes (the headings *Form, Person, Setting* and so on can be given as prompts), then share ideas in a whole class discussion.

Haunted Hide and Seek	Fridge Boy Found
Form: Poetry. Person: Second. Setting: Marwell Hall, a haunted house. Characters: Young adults. Story: Begins with a game of hide and seek. Adventure-game format. Climax: Depends on the reader's choice. Ending: Depends on the reader's choice. Note: In the story that the poem is based on, Lucy hides in an old oak chest and dies because no one opens the chest to find her.	Form: News report. Person: Third Setting: Illegal rubbish dump. Characters: Young children and a dog. Story: Begins with a game of hide and seek. Climax: Trevor hides in an old fridge. Ending: Pip barking shows the police where Trevor is trapped.

Haunted Hide and Seek (1)

■ This poem recreates a tragic incident that happened about 100 years ago at Marwell Hall, near Owslebury in Hampshire. The scene is a wedding feast. You play the part of Lovell, who has just married Lucy.

Prologue
The wedding feast is finished, but your
   bride,
Hoping to continue with the fun,
Says: "I know! Let's play a game of hide
And seek, before the guests go home."
She tells you that, as host, you are first
   'on'.
In vain you try to warn your wayward
   spouse
That hide and seek is dangerous in a
   haunted house.

Part 1
The game of hide and seek begins with
your turn to hide. Choose one of the
following three places: The Suit of
Armour, The Huge Holdall or The Secret
Panel. All you have to do is survive. If
you are lucky enough to do this, read the
Interlude and move on...

Part 2
1. The Suit of Armour
You spot a likely-looking suit of armour
And hide yourself inside as best you
may,
Hoping that you haven't left an arm or
Leg exposed to give the game away,
But it has been a cold and windy day,
And freezing armour is no laughing
matter:
Your shivering makes it rattle, tap and
clatter!

2. The Huge Holdall
Upstairs you come across a huge
   holdall,
And, opening it, you find that you are
   able

To squeeze inside by curling up as small
As Ali-Baba in the children's fable;
But what a shame you didn't read the
   label,
You're finding out the hard way what
   went wrong:
The holdall has been posted to Hong
   Kong!

3. The Secret Panel
There is a secret panel in this room
If you can find the lever – here it is:
The panel slides and then into the
   gloom
You grope, grinning – they'll never think
   of this –
Or will they? What's that? Something is
   amiss:
Strange, skeleton-like fingers jab you,
The panel closes, then the creatures
   grab you!

Interlude
You've had your fun and found it quite
   nerve-racking:
The house seems creepier than a
   catacomb.
You whisper to your bride, "I'm all for
   packing
In: I sense a strong foreshadowing of
   doom."
But she replies, as she skips from the
   room:
"I won't allow your foolish fears to bind
   me;
I'm going to hide – now see if you can
   find me!"

Haunted Hide and Seek (2)

◼ Now it is your bride's turn to hide. You can look for her in any one of the following places: The Wardrobe, The Old Oak Chest, The Cellar. If you fail to find her, read the Epilogue.

Part 2
1. The Wardrobe

This wardrobe from a castle in Bavaria
Looks like a cottage on a mountain side:
Prettily painted, with almost as much
    area!
'Twould make a perfect place for her to
    hide;
And so you turn the key and step inside.
She's there! – or is she? – it turns out to
    be
Only her empty clothes – so where is
    she?

2. The Old Oak Chest

Half-hidden in a gloomy passageway
There is an ancient, worm-eaten oak
    chest.
Though, doubtful anyone would go that
    way,
You think you ought to check it like the
    rest.
It's just as well you did, for there,
    distressed,
Her eyes bedewed with tears, lies your
    bride:
The lock had sprung, and she was
trapped inside.

3. The Cellar

You didn't want this game; you tried to
    tell her
That games and haunted houses do not
    mix,
But conscience says you ought to check
    the cellar
In case she's got herself into a fix:
Is that her? – No, the light is playing
    tricks!
It's something much more gruesome,
    gross and grim
That gibbers while it rips you limb from
    limb!

Epilogue

That game of hide and seek became a
    search,
But nowhere could they find your
    new-wed lover:
"Perhaps," they said, "she's left you in
    the lurch."
Whatever the cause, you never did
    recover.
Then, years flown by, when you were
    looking over
Your house for the last time, you
    found the chest
And trapped inside, her skeleton in
    bridal clothes still dressed.

About the poem

◼ Draw a ring round the correct answer.

1. Where is the most dangerous place for Lovell to hide?

The Suit of Armour	The Huge Holdall	The Secret Panel

1 mark

2. Where is the safest place for Lucy to hide?

The Wardrobe	The Old Oak Chest	The Cellar

1 mark

3. Draw lines to match each extract from the poem to the best explanation.

Extracts:

This wardrobe from a castle in Bavaria
Looks like a cottage on a mountain side...

You're finding out the hard way what went wrong:
The holdall has been posted to Hong Kong!

Is that her? – No, the light is playing tricks!
It's something much more gruesome, gross and grim...

You spot a ...suit of armour/And hide yourself inside...
Your shivering makes it rattle, tap and clatter!

Explanations:

These lines rhyme
There is a simile in these lines
There is onomatopoeia in these lines
There is alliteration in these lines

4 marks

◼ Write one or two sentences to answer questions 4 and 5 on a separate sheet of paper.

4. The bride ignored two warnings. What were these warnings and when were they given?

2 marks

5. Write down six words which help to build up the atmosphere of horror.

2 marks

◼ Write 10 to 15 lines to answer question 6 on a separate sheet of paper.

6. Imagine that a family with young children is coming to live at Marwell Hall. Explain in detail what you would do to make it safe.

5 marks

Total: 15 marks

Fridge boy found

Missing schoolboy Trevor Trubb, was found by _____ *police* _____ this

morning. After a search that began at 5pm the _____ *previous* _____ day,

they found him trapped in an old _____ *refrigerator* _____ that had been

dumped illegally. His _____ *friend* _____ Simon _____ *explained* _____

what happened. "We were playing hide and seek. I found the others easily, but

we _____ *couldn't* _____ find Trev _____ *anywhere* _____ ."

"The boys came here at about 2 _____ *o'clock* _____ ," said Mrs Trubb,

"and said they'd lost Trevor. I got some of the _____*neighbours* _____ and

we searched for hours. In the end, we called the police."

PC Smith said that they started the search _____ *straight* _____ away.

"You can't be too _____*careful* _____ , these days," he said. By this time Mrs

Trubb was frantic. Mr Trubb, who had just got back from work, joined the

search party.

I asked Constable Smith how he had _____ *managed* _____ to find the

boy.

"Well, it was the dog actually," he said. "We'd passed that fridge _____

several _____ times and never _____ *thought* _____ to look in it, but this

morning, Pip was barking at the fridge door. We ripped the door open, and

there was Trevor, _____ *unconscious* _____ . An _____*ambulance* _____

was called, and the paramedics _____ *brought* _____ him round with _____

oxygen _____ .

I asked Trevor how he felt. "Scared," he said. "I shouted for help, but nobody

could hear my _____ *cries* _____ . Still, it could have been worse _____ if it

had been _____ *plugged* _____ in I'd have been freezing!"

Pip _____ *the real hero of the day* _____ barked in agreement.

UNIT 3

Reading and writing non-fiction

This unit begins preparing the children for non-fiction in the Key Stage 2 tests. It takes the children through reading and writing tasks that are similar to those set in the tests, but here, children are allowed to help each other and ask questions at every stage of the process. In addition to providing practice, the unit helps to familiarise the children with the test marking schemes so that they know what the examiners are looking for.

Hour	Shared text-level work	Shared word-/sentence-level work	Guided and independent work	Plenary
1 SMS	Revising reports and explanation texts.	Experimenting with active and passive sentences.	Writing history in text message form; writing a report on text message uses.	Revising key features of reports.
2 For and against texting	Revising persuasive and discursive texts.	Investigating uses of connectives.	Using connectives to construct a paragraph.	Sharing best connectives; noting differences between persuasive text and balanced argument.
3 The two shorter texts	Revising features of instructions and recounts.	Revising imperatives.	Writing instructions; sharing anecdotes for summarising.	Giving reports on summaries and time words used.
4 Non-fiction reading practice	Tips on reading test skills.		Holding practice reading test.	Going over 'test' paper.
5 Writing test practice	Tips on writing test skills.		Holding practice writing test.	Going over 'test' paper.

Key assessment opportunities
● Do the children understand test formats and procedures?
● Do they know how to improve their test technique?
● Do they know which non-fiction reading skills to work on?
● Do they know which skills for the shorter writing task to work on?

SMS

Objectives

NLS
T15: To secure understanding of the features of explanatory texts from Year 5 Term 2.
S1: To revise the language conventions and grammatical features of the different types of text such as: reports (eg factual writing, description); explanatory texts (how and why).
S3: To revise formal styles of writing: the impersonal voice; the use of the passive; management of complex sentences.

What you need
- Photocopiable page 154.

Shared text-level work
- Tell the children that they are going to continue with their practice for the forthcoming English tests, and that this week they are going to revise all the different types of non-fiction texts they have studied, beginning with reports and explanations.
- Brainstorm with the children the key features of report texts and jot appropriate ideas on the board. (For example, reports use formal language and an impersonal tone. They often include data such as facts and figures, sometimes in the form of diagrams or tables. The passive voice is often used to keep the tone impersonal. Reports are non-chronological in organisation.)
- Display photocopiable page 154, keeping 'How to use predictive text' covered. Read 'SMS'.
- Then ask the children to re-read the text and identify the key features of reports that you have jotted on the board.
- Allow a few minutes for discussion in pairs or groups before asking the children to contribute their ideas. Then annotate the text as appropriate.

Shared sentence-level work
- Ask the children to identify the passive clause in the text (*50 million messages were sent*) and to try to make it active (People sent 50 million messages).
- Now reverse the process by taking an active sentence from the text and working with the children to make it passive. For example, *Children are even using them in schools when they should be listening to the teacher.* (They are even being used by teenagers in school...)

Guided and independent work
- Work with one group to discuss significant historical moments and continue the history essay written in text message-speak for another four or five lines.
- Organise the other children into groups of four to discuss the different uses of text messaging, for example to arrange a meeting, to tell parents when you're going to be late, to send an instant private message to a friend. Then ask the groups to write a brief report entitled 'The uses of text messaging'.
- Remind the children to write their report in an appropriate style (see key features of reports worked through in the shared session). Ask some of the children to write on OHTs for use in the plenary session.

Differentiation

Less able
- Tell children to make a note of every use of text messaging referred to in the discussion.

More able
- Ask children to add to their discussion and include in their report an extra paragraph on the emoticons and abbreviations most commonly used by members of their group.

Plenary
- Display and read the reports written on OHT and ask the rest of the children to identify and comment on the key features of reports included.
- Encourage children to update you on any new text emoticons or abbreviations.

For and against texting

Objectives

NLS

T19: To review a range of non-fiction text types and their characteristics, discussing when a writer might choose to write in a given style and form.
S1: To revise the language conventions and grammatical features of the different types of text such as: persuasive texts (eg opinions, promotional literature); discursive texts (eg balanced arguments).

What you need
● Photocopiable page 155.

Shared text-level work
● Tell the children that in this lesson they are going to focus on persuasive texts (for example presentations of opinions, promotional literature) and discursive texts (such as balanced arguments).
● Ask the children to brainstorm the key features of persuasive and discursive texts and jot appropriate ideas on the board. (Persuasive texts, for example, aim to persuade the reader by using a series of arguments, that is, points supported by evidence. Connectives are used to link and modify the arguments. Discursive texts often present balanced arguments, that is both sides of the argument plus a conclusion).
● Display photocopiable page 155 (keeping 'Mobile life-saver' covered) and read 'For and against texting'.
● Explain that the two halves of the text (contrasting sets of statements by Gemma and Stephen) are persuasive texts, but read as a whole, they become a discursive text because they present both sides of the argument.
● Ask the children to re-read the text and identify the key features of persuasive and discursive texts that you have jotted on the board. Encourage them to discuss their ideas before presenting them to the class. Annotate the text as appropriate.

Shared sentence level work
● Note that the arguments in the text are separated by bullet points. Discuss that if Gemma and Stephen's statements had been written as paragraphs connectives would have been needed to link the points together.
● Brainstorm a list of connectives suitable for these texts, for example, *also, furthermore, after all, first of all, finally, therefore, as a result.*
● Now work with the children to join up some of Gemma's points using connectives. For example:

The rate for sending a text message is much lower than the rate for making a phone call. Also, you don't have to wait for someone to answer your email or voicemail. Another point is that...

Differentiation

Less able
● Ask children to work on Gemma's points (following on from your demonstration).

More able
● Ask children to choose two points by Gemma and two by Stephen and to link them using suitable connectives. Give particular attention to the connective linking the opposing arguments, *such as however, nevertheless, on the other hand.*

Guided and independent work
● Organise the children into pairs and ask them to use suitable connectives to link Stephen's points into a continuous paragraph.
● Remind them that they may need to change surrounding words or sentences to make the paragraph cohesive.

Plenary
● Share ideas about the best connectives to link the points made by Gemma and Stephen. Explain that the resulting paragraphs are short persuasive texts.
● Ask the more able group to show how they linked all the points and explain that the resulting paragraph is a short balanced argument.

The two shorter texts

Objectives

NLS

T19: To review a range of non-fiction text types and their characteristics, discussing when a writer might choose to write in a given style and form.
S1: To revise the language conventions and grammatical features of the different types of text such as: recounts (eg anecdotes, accounts of observations, experiences); instructional texts (eg instructions and directions).

What you need

● Photocopiable pages 154 and 155.

Differentiation

Less able
● Give children a list of appropriate imperatives to start them off.

More able
● Encourage children to organise the group work and read out the summaries for group approval before they are presented to the class.

Shared text-level work

● Discuss when instructions texts are used and ask the children to brainstorm the key features of texts that give instructions and jot appropriate ideas on the board. (Instructions are written in clear sentences that use imperative verbs to tell the reader what to do. They are written in the present tense and contain prepositions to tell the reader where components or ingredients are placed or arranged. They are often presented as a set of bulleted or numbered points, sometimes with diagrams.)
● Read 'How to use predictive text' on photocopiable page 154.
● Then ask the children to re-read the text and identify the key genre features as noted on the board. Allow a few minutes for paired or group discussion before asking the children to contribute their ideas to the class. Annotate the text as appropriate.
● Now discuss instances of recounts and brainstorm the key features of recounts. Note these on the board. (Recounts, often telling of an event or experience, are written in the past tense and use temporal connectives to link different parts of the text. They may be written in formal or informal language.)
● Read 'Mobile life-saver' on photocopiable page 155.
● Then ask the children to re-read the text and spend some time discussing and identifying examples of the key genre features listed on the board. Annotate the text accordingly.

Shared sentence-level work

● Look again at 'How to use predictive text' and revise the imperative verb form. Ask the children to find the imperative verbs in the text.
● Note that only the first instruction begins with the imperative verb. All the other instructions begin with an introductory phrase before the verb.

Guided and independent work

● Work with a group to write a set of instructions for someone who has never used a mobile phone, explaining how to write and send a text message.
● Organise the rest of the children into mixed ability groups of four and ask them to share oral recounts of an interesting event to do with telephones (mobile or landline).
● As the children listen to each other, ask them to compile a list of the words and phrases about time that are used.
● Then tell the groups to spend a few minutes working together to prepare a report for the plenary session, giving brief summaries of the recounts to highlight the time words.

Plenary

● Ask each group to give one summary and report. Jot down the time words and phrases they refer to. Go over the list, and use it to emphasise the chronological nature of recounts.

Non-fiction reading practice

Objective
To practise reading non-fiction.

What you need
● Photocopiable pages 154-157. (Remove the last section of photocopiable page 157 for use in Hour 5.)

Shared work

● Tell the children that they are going to do some more test practice. Explain that they will be given a test paper that is similar to the non-fiction part of a Key Stage 2 reading test paper. It will be helpful to tell them that the actual reading test papers are presented like a magazine that contains both fiction and non-fiction.

● Before starting the practice test, give the following advice to the children:

On reading
● Read the texts, then re-read them and make annotations.
● Keep going back to the text to check information - don't try to remember it all.
● Use skimming and scanning skills to find key points.

On answering the questions
● Look carefully at the instructions - watch particularly for words in bold print. There are several types of question: short questions that require a word or phrase for the answer; questions that require ticking boxes, circling words, or drawing lines; and longer questions that require a sentence or longer text for the answer. The number of marks for each question often indicates how much to write.
● Base your answers on the text, not on your own knowledge or opinions (unless you are asked to do so).
● Check your answers. If you find a mistake, rub it out or cross it out neatly. Make sure the correction is clear.

Guided and independent work

● Give out the question paper (photocopiable pages 156 and 157) and two sheets of writing paper to each child, explaining that one sheet is for planning, the other for writing. Remind the children that they can help each other and ask you questions. Allow 10 minutes reading time and 40 minutes answering time.

Plenary

● When time is up, collect in the papers, and talk about how the practice went. What did the children find easy or difficult? Did they all manage to finish?

● Go over the test - particularly any 'right or wrong' answers. Help the children to understand why certain answers were right. For example, Gemma did not say that one of the advantages of text messaging is that it can be used anywhere.

● Remember the tip to base ideas on the text, not on knowledge or opinions.

● Notes on marking: give the children a mark out of 25. Note that a curriculum level cannot be given because the children were allowed to help each other, and because this practice only represents part of the Key Stage 2 test.

Differentiation

Less able
● Differentiation by outcome.

More able
● Differentiation by outcome.

Writing test practice

Shared work

● Let the children know that they are going to do some final test practice on information texts. This will be in a similar form to the shorter writing task in the upcoming test paper.

● A good way to begin is to briefly revisit Unit 6 on information writing reports in Term 1. Recap on the key features of non-chronological reports (see Hour 1), planning (Hour 3), and key language features such as the use of the passive voice and writing in a formal and impersonal style (Hour 4). Ask the children to look again at the writing they did during this unit (Hours 4 and 5) and discuss what they learned from it.

● Move on to the following general advice:

> Planning – some tips are given on the test paper. Read them carefully and use them as a starting point for your plan.
>
> Writing – write in a style that is suitable for the type of text. Think about who will be reading the text and make sure that they will be able to understand it. Think carefully about layout. How many paragraphs will there be? Will it be appropriate to use bullet points or other layout features?
>
> Vocabulary – try to use an interesting variety of words, including appropriate technical terms.
>
> Checking – when you have finished, read through your work and check for correctness.

Guided and independent work

● Give out the question paper (photocopiable page 157, second half) and two sheets of writing paper to each child, explaining that one sheet is for planning, the other for writing. Remind the children that they are allowed to help each other and ask questions. Allow 20 minutes writing time (including planning time).

Plenary

● Collect in the papers, and talk about the practice. What did the children find easy or difficult? Did they all manage to finish? What ideas did they have for the text?

● Notes on marking: give the children a mark out of 10 using the mark scheme for the shorter writing task as a guide (allowing 3 marks for their four best lines of handwriting). Again, a National Curriculum level cannot be given because these were not test conditions and the practice only represents part of what is covered in the writing test.

● Additional time will be needed to go over the writing test and the teacher-marked parts of the reading test. See Unit 1, Hour 5 (Term 3) for a creative approach to this.

The text generation, part 1

SMS

SMS stands for Short Message Service. It's a way of sending short text messages by mobile phone. In 1999, when the service was introduced, 50 million messages were sent. Today the number is over a billion. Sixty per cent of 9 to 12 year olds use text messages every day, and many teenagers say they couldn't live without them. Children are even using them in schools when they should be listening to the teacher. And that's only half the problem. The 'text generation' have forgotten how to use normal English, and use 'txt-msg-speak' in their school work. Here's an example of the kind of essay that's making teachers >: -| (see the emoticons key below)!

> I tnk dat D gr8st DzastA n hx wz D Battle of Hastings coz...

What many adults don't realise is how skilful you have to be to write a text message. In addition to manipulating the tiny keys, you also have to learn a new language of shorthand, emoticons and abbreviations. Here's a quick guide:

<table>
<tr><td>

Top 10 emoticons
Happy
:-) : Happy
:-D : Grinning
:-7 : Smirk
Sad
:-(: Sad
:'-(: Crying
%-(: Confused
>:-| : Cross
Love and friendship
:-x : Kiss
<3 : Love heart
@--^----- : Rose

</td><td>

Top 10 abbreviations
CU 2MORO : See you tomorrow
CUL8R : See you (or call you) later
GR8 : Great
EZ : Easy
H&K : Hug and kiss
LOL : Laughed out loud / Lots of luck/
      Lots of love
SOHF : Sense of humour failure
THX or TX : Thanks
TTFN : Ta ta for now
YYSSW: Yeah, yeah, sure, sure,
      whatever

</td></tr>
</table>

How to use predictive text

Predictive text makes writing text messages quicker. Here's how to use it:

◼ Type the letters as usual. Your phone will suggest the word you want.

◼ To type a new letter, just hit another key. If the next letter that you need is on the same key, use the <RIGHT> or <DOWN> arrow to move to the next letter.

◼ To type a space, press <0> or use the <RIGHT> or <DOWN> arrow key. A suggested word will appear. Press <OK> if you want to accept it and move on to a new word.

◼ To type a special character, try using the <OPTION>, or <MENU> buttons: the phone will then let you select the character you want.

The text generation, part 2

For and against texting

Gemma, 11, is a pupil at Meadow Grange School. She thinks text messaging is GR8! Here's why:

● Sending a text message is much cheaper than making a call.
● You don't have to wait for someone to answer your email or voicemail.
● Everybody can hear your business when you talk into your phone, but nobody knows your secrets when you send a text, although I once sent a secret message to my mum!
● Texting can help if you're too nervous to ask somebody something. I asked a new friend to come round to my house – she replied CUL8R :-). It was easy!

Stephen is a teacher at Meadow Grange School. He is worried about some of the problems of text messaging:

● It can ruin spelling. Children in my class often write *U* instead of *you*, *B* instead of *be*, *C* instead of *see*, *4* instead of *for*, and put an *8* in any word with *ate* in it.
● It can be addictive. One of the pupils at the comprehensive school had to seek counselling to help him kick his habit – he was sending over 100 text messages a day!
● The other day I saw somebody trying to write a text message when he was driving! It's against the law and he could so easily cause an accident!
● It's anti-social. People sometimes read or send text messages when you're trying to talk to them.

Mobile–life saver
Amanda Tilsey remembers how her mobile saved her and her sister's life.

Two years ago we were on holiday near some rocky cliffs called Flamborough Head. We were playing in a small inlet when we noticed the tide coming in fast. We tried to go back, but the sea had reached the cliffs on either side and we were trapped! I could see that, in a few minutes, the water would come right up to us. I panicked, but Suki said, "Use your mobile!" So I dialled 999 and about 10 minutes later, we saw a lifeboat coming to save us. It was only just in time – the water was up to our knees!

TERM 3

About the texts (1) Name _____

◼ These questions are about the texts in 'The text generation, part 1'. Draw a ring round the correct answer.

1. SMS means

GR8!	Short Message Service	Voicemail	Secret Mobile Service

1 mark

2. Who are 'the text generation'?

9 to 12 year olds	9 to 19 year olds	everybody since 1999	the older generation

1 mark

◼ Write the answers to questions 3 to 5 on a separate sheet of paper.

3. What two problems are text messages causing in schools?

2 marks

4. What are the two skills required to write a text message?

2 marks

5. What three things is text message language made up of? Give an example from the text of each one.

3 marks

6. Draw lines to match these text messages to everyday language:

I <3 U H&K	Are you angry?
IM %-(	See you tomorrow.
TTFN	I'm confused.
RU >:-|?	I love you. Hug and Kiss.
CU 2MORO	Goodbye.

4 marks

7. In your own words, explain what predictive text is.

1 mark

8. How does predictive text make writing text messages quicker

1 mark

Total: 15 marks

◼ SCHOLASTIC

About the texts (2)

◼ These questions are about 'The text generation, part 2'.

9. Gemma gave four reasons why texting is 'GR8'. In the table below they are mixed up with four other reasons. Place a G against Gemma's reasons and an O against the other reasons.

it can be used anywhere	
it helps if you're shy	
it's cheap	
it's easy	
it's fashionable	
it's fun	
it's private	
it's quick	

4 marks

◼ Write the answers to questions 8 to 10 on a separate piece of paper.

10. Gemma talks about two things that actually happened to her. What are they?

2 marks

11. Stephen talks about two problems that text messaging is causing in school. What are they?

2 marks

12. How did Amanda and Suki get trapped?

1 mark

13. How did they escape?

1 mark

14. In about 6 to 10 lines, recount an interesting experience that you have had with mobile phones, ordinary telephones or email.

5 marks

Shorter writing task

◼ Write about 20 lines on the following topic on a separate sheet of paper. Begin by making a plan of the points you wish to include.

10 marks

'Text messaging – what it is and how to use it' – a short information leaflet to be given away free with every mobile phone.

Some tips to help you:

◼ Use ideas from all the texts as well as your own ideas.

◼ The first part should explain what text messaging is

◼ The second part should give advice on using text message, for example as a list of dos and don'ts.

Total: 25 marks

UNIT 4

Poetry

These simple and moving poems are an ideal introduction to the work of William Wordworth as well as providing the opportunity to study subject, theme, verse form and figures of speech. Children are encouraged to experiment with these aspects of poetry by exploring their personal responses to Wordsworth's ideas and writing their own short poems. In Hour 4, the children analyse the poems to find out as much as they can about the enigmatic Lucy. In Hour 5, they begin to bring together all of the objectives in the unit. This will need at least another two hours to complete. During the rest of the follow-up week, children should write their own sequence of poems.

Hour	Shared text-level work	Shared word-/ sentence-level work	Guided and independent work	Plenary
1 Subject and themes	Reading the first Lucy poem, discussing themes.		Paraphrasing the poem; discussing theme of love and writing short poems.	Identifying how theme is expressed in children's poems.
2 Form and language	Reading second Lucy poem, analysing form and style.		Comparing Wordsworth with Lyttelton; continuing discussion on love and writing a ballad.	Using children's poems to recap features of ballad form.
3 Figures of speech	Reading another Lucy poem, analysing verse form.	Revising figures of speech, annotating poem.	Discussing beliefs expressed in 'Lucy IV'; using figures of speech in a poem.	Using children's poems to recap metaphor, simile and personification.
4 Who was Lucy?	Reading last Lucy poem; discussing the series of poems.	Revising use of colons and semicolons (complex sentences).	Speculating on identity of Lucy for presentation.	Giving presentations.
5 Wordsworth's style	Going through writing frame for response to Lucy poems.		Group discussion and work allocation for essay.	Discussing points raised in group work.

Key assessment opportunities
● Can the children see how linked poems relate to one another?
● Can they describe the style of an individual poet?
● Can they write their own poems, or sequence of poems?

Objectives

NLS
T2: To discuss how linked poems relate to one another by themes, format and repetition, eg cycle of poems about the seasons.
W6: To practise and extend vocabulary.

What you need
● Wordsworth booklets (see opposite).

Subject and themes

Shared text- and word-level work

● Make a little booklet of the four poems on photocopiable pages 164–166, one for each pair of children. The booklet could also include a biography of Wordsworth and a writing frame for the work on the Lucy poems (see Hour 5).

● Tell the children that they are going to study a sequence of poems by William Wordsworth about a girl called Lucy. Give them some brief biographical information to put the poems and the poet in context.

● Begin with the first Lucy poem, to focus particularly on subject and theme.

● Elicit that the subject is what the poem is about at a basic level, the 'story' told in the poem; the themes are the ideas and wider concepts expressed by the poem.

● Read the first Lucy poem while the children follow in their booklets.

● Go through the poem again and help the children to understand any words they are unsure about.

● Ask the children to discuss in pairs the subject and themes of the poem. What is the poem about? (Remind the children of work on paraphrasing a poem from Term 2, Unit 1.) What are the themes in the poem? What ideas are expressed?

● Share ideas with the whole class. For example:
Subject: the poem describes a strange feeling that Wordsworth had (a premonition). He begins by recalling how he used to visit Lucy. Then he describes a dream in which, as he came near to Lucy's cottage, the moon seemed to drop, and it made him think that Lucy might be dead.
Themes: One is his love for Lucy, and the other is how people sometimes have premonitions.

Guided and independent work

● Work with a group to paraphrase the poem. (See Term 2, Unit 1 for more guidance on this.)

● In groups of four, ask the other children to discuss love of all kinds, including romantic love, love for pets, teddies, family, even football teams, and premonitions, such as when you thought the phone was going to ring and a moment later it did.

● Then working individually, ask the children to write short poems (which don't have to rhyme) about one of these experiences.

Plenary

● Share some of the poems, and discuss how the subjects are used to express the themes: a poem about a teddy (subject) could be used to express a serious idea about the importance of love (theme).

Differentiation

Less able
● Recommend that children write four lines with four to eight words in each line.

More able
● Encourage children to write a rhyming poem.

Form and language

Objectives

NLS
T4: To comment critically on the overall impact of a poem, showing how language and themes have been developed.
W6: To practise and extend vocabulary.

What you need
● Lucy poem booklets.

Shared text- and word-level work
● Read the second Lucy poem, to focus on form and language, while the children follow it in their booklets.
● Go through the poem again to help with difficult words such as *melancholy, cherished, bowers.*
● Discuss the children's impression of this language. They will probably say that it is old fashioned and contains difficult words. Explain that in the 18th century, this language would have been simple and commonplace, and that a feature of Wordsworth's style was to use simple verse forms and everyday language.
● Discuss the subject and themes of the poem. For example, travel and coming home; love of country, and love for another person.
● Analyse the verse form by establishing the rhyme scheme (ABAB) and counting the stressed syllables in each line (4, 3, 4, 3 in the first verse).
● In pairs, ask the children to analyse the second verse in the same way. If they do it correctly, they should see the pattern is the same.
● Remind the children that this is a ballad form and is very common in English poetry. It is one of the simplest forms and is often used to tell stories.

Guided and independent work
● With a group of more able children, explore the simplicity of Wordsworth's poetry compared with this extract from a work by George Lyttelton - a poet of the previous generation.

Once, by the muse alone inspired	But Venus now, to punish me
I sung my amorous strains:	For having feigned too well,
No serious love my bosom fired;	Has made my heart so fond of thee,
Yet every tender maid, deceived,	That not the whole Aonian choir
The idly-mournful tale believed	Can accents soft enough inspire,
And wept my fancied pains.	Its real flame to tell.

● The children will notice that Lyttleton uses a more complex verse form and more complex language, which includes references to classical literature.
● In the same groups of four as Hour 1, ask the other children to discuss love of country (patriotism). Do they feel the same love for their country as Wordsworth? Is patriotism an old-fashioned idea? Continue the discussion about human love.
● Ask the children to write a short poem about love of country or love of a person using ballad form. One stanza is enough, though some children may like to try longer poems.

Plenary
● Share and enjoy some of the children's poems (ideally on OHT or interactive whiteboard). Use them to recap on the key features of ballad form.

Differentiation

Less able
● Advise children to use the simpler version of ballad rhyme scheme (ABCB).

More able
● Encourage children to write a poem of at least three stanzas.

Figures of speech

Objectives

NLS
T3: To describe and evaluate the style of an individual poet.
S2: To conduct language investigations, eg of proverbs, language change over time, dialect.
W7: To experiment with language, eg creating new similes and metaphors.

What you need
● Lucy poem booklets.

Shared text-level work
● Tell the children that they are going to read the fourth and longest of Wordsworth's Lucy poems, focusing particularly on figures of speech.
● Read 'Three Years She Grew'.
● Discuss the subject of the poem and the themes raised. The poem describes how Lucy only lived for three years. Wordsworth believes that she was taken by nature, which is personified. It goes on to describe how Lucy will be part of nature, in the landscape, the animals, the clouds, the weather, the stars. Wordsworth thinks she will be happy like this, and he feels that he is with her when he looks at the scenery around him. Two of Wordsworth's strongest themes are brought together in this poem: his love of nature and his love of Lucy.
● Ask the children to analyse the verse form using the same technique as Hour 2 (the first and third lines are extended into couplets).

Shared word- and sentence-level work
● Revise the key figures – speech of simile, metaphor, personification and ask the children to work in pairs to find examples of these in the poem.
● Share their findings in a class discussion, and ask them to annotate their texts. In particular, ensure that they have grasped the personification of nature, presented as a human-like spirit who speaks most of the poem.

Guided and independent work
● Ask the groups to discuss their personal responses to the themes in the poem. For example, do they think it is possible that, when people die, they become part of nature? Be careful here with regard to children's religious beliefs, but help the children to recognise that this was Wordsworth's belief, expressed in this poem.
● Next, ask them to discuss if personifying nature is an effective way to express this belief.
● Ask the children to write a short poem in which they use figures of speech to express their ideas along these lines. One good simile, metaphor or example of personification may be enough. Tell the children that they can use free verse if it will help them to concentrate on the figures of speech.

Plenary
● Read out some of the children's work, and reinforce understanding of simile, metaphor and personification.

Differentiation

Less able
● Advise children to write similes using the comparison words *like* or *as*. Use the line '*She shall be sportive as the fawn*' as an example.

More able
● Challenge children to extend the use of metaphor or personification. (In line 2, Lucy is compared to a flower, and this is linked to line 3 and the word *sown*.)

UNIT 4 HOUR 4 ⬛ Poetry

Who was Lucy?

Objectives

NLS

T2: To discuss how linked poems relate to one another by themes, format and repetition (in this unit, subject matter).
T3: To describe and evaluate the style of an individual poet.
T7: To annotate passages in detail in response to specific questions.
S4: To secure control of complex sentences.

S&L
65 Speaking: To use techniques of dialogic talk to explore ideas, topics or issues.

What you need
● Lucy poem booklets.

Shared text-level work

● Explain to the children that the identity of Lucy is a mystery. Ever since the poems were first published, people have tried to match her to a real person in Wordsworth's life, but even those who knew Wordsworth were unable to do this. In this lesson, they are going to find out as much as they can about Lucy by analysing the evidence in the poems.

● First, read 'A Slumber Did My Spirit Seal' while the children follow it in their booklets.

● Discuss the poem by relating it to what you have read so far. The poem is written in ballad form and simple language (for the time). The subject is a dream (compare with the first Lucy poem) in which Wordsworth sees Lucy as part of nature (compare with 'Three Years She Grew'). In this poem 'Sleep' is personified.

● Discuss the Lucy poems as a whole sequence, and the children's responses to it. Ask: What did you think and feel as you read the poems? What was particularly effective?

Shared sentence-level work

● Briefly revise the use of colon and semicolon using the examples in the poem. The colon shows the break of ideas in the poem. After the colon, Wordsworth is talking about Lucy, not his sleep.

Guided and independent work

● Ask the groups to re-read all the Lucy poems and to highlight and discuss anything that gives us information about Lucy, however small the detail may be.

● Help them to put their notes together as an oral presentation.

Plenary

● Ask selected groups to give their presentations. Do they agree on the main points? Clarify or add information as necessary:

> Lucy lived until she was three (IV). She lived in a cottage, so she was probably part of a working family (I). Even though she was only three, she worked at a spinning wheel, probably to help her mother earn a little more money (II). She was a beautiful child (IV). She liked to play in the fields and woods near her house (II). Wordsworth loved her very much and had a premonition of her death (I). He believes that she is now a part of nature (III, IV).

● Conclude with the following information:
Literary critics suggest that Lucy was not a real person, but a combination of several girls that Wordsworth knew: Annette Vallon, a girl he loved in France; Anne Caroline, his daughter; and Dorothy, his sister. Suggest that Wordsworth may have made up the character of Lucy, and described her dying and becoming part of nature, so that he could express through poetry his deeply held beliefs of the spiritual qualities in nature.

Differentiation

Less able
● Tell children to find five facts about Lucy and to put them in the most logical order.

More able
● Encourage children to use deduction in their analysis and to work through these with the rest of their group.

Wordsworth's style

Objectives

NLS
T3: To describe and evaluate the style of an individual poet.

S&L
63 Group discussion and interaction: To consider examples of conflict and resolution, exploring language used.
65 Speaking: To use techniques of dialogic talk to explore ideas, topics or issues.

What you need
● An essay writing frame (see Guided and independent work)
● Lucy poem booklets.

Shared text-level work
● Tell the children that they are going to pull together everything they have learned about Wordsworth and his Lucy poems by writing an extended essay over a number of Literacy Hours.
● Display the writing frame for the essay and talk about each section, referring back to other lessons during the week and giving suggestions and advice:

Introduction: a short biography of Wordsworth (this could be a summary of the biography in the Lucy poems booklet).
Paragraph 2: an explanation of the Lucy poems (What are they about? How are they linked?).
Paragraph 3: a discussion of Wordsworth's favourite themes (love, nature) referring to some examples in the poems and giving a personal response.
Paragraph 4: an explanation of Wordsworth's style (simple verse forms and simple language; use of figures of speech).
Paragraph 5: an exploration of ideas about who Lucy was (using work from Hour 4).
Conclusion: a personal response to the sequence of poems. (What did you think and feel as you read the poems? What was particularly effective?)
● Briefly revise the key skills of essay writing. Remind the children how to set out their work in paragraphs, and how to use connectives to link key points, by modelling how to write one of the paragraphs.

Guided and independent work
● Tell the children that you want them to collaborate in groups of four to write the essay.
● Each child should write his or her own introduction and conclusion and one other paragraph.
● The focus of this lesson will be for the group to discuss in detail what they will write about in paragraphs 2 to 5, and to allocate the paragraphs to specific writers. Advise the children that you will be listening to how well their group discussions proceed.
● Go around the groups and listen in to the discussions in order to pick up problems, or interesting points, to discuss in the plenary. Give particular attention to agreement on work allocation and to personal responses.

Differentiation

Less able
● Ask children to write a shorter essay based on the Introduction, paragraphs 2 and 5 and the conclusion. Each child in the group should be responsible for one of these, but ask them to discuss all sections.

More able
● Ask children to produce individual versions of the whole essay. However, they should still begin their work with group discussion.

Plenary
● Discuss points that have come up from the discussions, and encourage the children to share their personal responses.
● Tell the children that they are to continue to work on this essay for two hours next week, and that this work will then be followed by writing their own sequence of poems.

Lucy Strange Fits of Passion I Have Known

STRANGE fits of passion have I known:
    And I will dare to tell,
But in the lover's ear alone,
    What once to me befell.   *happened*

When she I loved looked every day
    Fresh as a rose in June,
I to her cottage bent my way,
    Beneath an evening moon.

Upon the moon I fixed my eye,
    All over the wide lea;   *grassland*
With quickening pace my horse drew nigh
    Those paths so dear to me.

And now we reached the orchard-plot;
    And, as we climbed the hill,
The sinking moon to Lucy's cot   *cottage*
    Came near and nearer still.

In one of those sweet dreams I slept,
    Kind Nature's gentlest boon!   *gift*
And all the while my eyes I kept
    On the descending moon.

My horse moved on; hoof after hoof
    He raised, and never stopped:
When down behind the cottage roof,
    At once, the bright moon dropped.

What fond and wayward thoughts will slide
    Into a lover's head!
'O mercy!' to myself I cried,
    'If Lucy should be dead!'

William Wordsworth

I travelled among unknown men

I TRAVELLED among unknown men,
   In lands beyond the sea;
Nor, England! did I know till then
   What love I bore to thee.

'Tis past, that melancholy dream!
   Nor will I quit thy shore
A second time; for still I seem
   To love thee more and more.

Among thy mountains did I feel
   The joy of my desire;
And she I cherished turned her wheel
   Beside an English fire.

Thy mornings showed, thy nights concealed,
   The bowers where Lucy played;
And thine too is the last green field
   That Lucy's eyes surveyed.

felt for

sad

leave

spinning wheel

hid

sheltered places among trees

saw

A Slumber Did My Spirit Seal

A SLUMBER did my spirit seal;
   I had no human fears:
She seemed a thing that could not feel
   The touch of earthly years.

No motion has she now, no force;
   She neither hears nor sees;
Rolled round in earth's diurnal course,
   With rocks, and stones, and trees.

William Wordsworth

sleep

daily

Three Years She Grew

THREE years she grew in sun and shower;
Then Nature said, 'A lovelier flower
On earth was never sown;
This child I to myself will take;
She shall be mine, and I will make
A Lady of my own.

'Myself will to my darling be
Both law and impulse: and with me
The Girl, in rock and plain,
In earth and heaven, in glade and bower,
Shall feel an overseeing power
To kindle or restrain.

*clearing,
sheltered place*

hold back

'She shall be sportive as the fawn
That wild with glee across the lawn
Or up the mountain springs;
And hers shall be the breathing balm,
And hers the silence and the calm
Of mute insensate things.

soothing breath

*silent, unable to
feel (inanimate)*

'The floating clouds their state shall lend
To her; for her the willow bend;
Nor shall she fail to see
Even in the motions of the Storm
Grace that shall mould the Maiden's form
By silent sympathy.

'The stars of midnight shall be dear
To her; and she shall lean her ear
In many a secret place
Where rivulets dance their wayward round,
And beauty born of murmuring sound
Shall pass into her face.

'And vital feelings of delight
Shall rear her form to stately height,
Her virgin bosom swell;
Such thoughts to Lucy I will give
While she and I together live
Here in this happy dell.'

valley

Thus Nature spake—The work was done—
How soon my Lucy's race was run!
She died, and left to me
This heath, this calm, and quiet scene;
The memory of what has been,
And never more will be.

spoke

William Wordsworth

UNIT 5

Authors and texts

This unit compares animal stories by different authors. Ideally, choose one animal story for reading as a shared text with the class and make others available for group reading and reading at home. Aim for a significant difference between the two stories, perhaps classic/modern, anthropomorphic/realistic. Ask the children to keep a reading journal, allocating left-hand pages to the shared text and right-hand pages to the group text. Encourage comparisons on characters, settings, plot devices and so on. Hours 1 and 2 begin the readings and introduce the reading journal. Hours 3 to 5 should be done when both stories have been read. The lessons here are based on *Mrs Frisby and the Rats of NIMH* by Robert C O'Brien (Puffin) and *Greyfriars Bobby* by Eleanor Atkinson (Penguin), but they can be readily adapted to work with other similar animal stories. Group work in Hour 4 links with Unit 54 in *Grammar for Writing*.

Hour	Shared text-level work	Shared word-/sentence-level work	Guided and independent work	Plenary
1 Reading journals	Setting up the reading journals.		Writing first journal entries.	Sharing personal responses and discussing questions raised in reading.
2 Comparisons	Reading story sections to make comparisons.	Revising active and passive sentences.	Reading another work by same author; adding to reading journals.	Sharing journal entries; continuing reading for homework.
3 Author style	Reading and annotating an extract to examine author's style.	Focusing on story language and grammar.	Annotating own choice of extract; writing up annotations as a paragraph.	Discussing style points; speculating on how themes may be developed.
4 Connections and contrasts	Comparing class text with group texts.	Focusing on story language and grammar.	Investigating dialect; comparing authors' styles.	Discussing similarities and contrasts.
5 A written comparison	Shared writing of comparisons across the two texts.	Finding connectives and considering their use in own work.	Writing extended essay.	Talking about and evaluating stories compared with each other and other animal stories.

Key assessment opportunities
● Have the children kept a reading journal and used it for further study?
● Could they summarise a story?
● Can they describe writers' styles?
● Can they compare and contrast the work of two writers?

Reading journals

Objectives

NLS
T8: To use a reading journal effectively to raise and refine personal responses to a text and prepare for discussion.
T9: To write summaries of books or parts of books, deciding on priorities relevant to purpose.

What you need

● *Mrs Frisby and the Rats of NIMH* or other animal story as shared text
● animal stories for reading at home
● standard exercise books, to become reading journals.

Shared text-level work

● Tell the children that they are going to be reading two animal books over the next few weeks, and that they will be writing a reading journal for each book. The following procedure is recommended:

> ● Ask the children to label alternate pages for the first ten pages of their exercise books with the titles of the two books.
> ● Ask them to write these headings on the first page (to be transferred to each journal entry as required): Short summary of the section, Personal response to the section, Question for discussion, Comparisons.

● Explain that sometimes a 'section' will be just one chapter and at other times it will be several chapters. Therefore, divide the reading book into five sections (ideally corresponding to the five stages of story structure: opening, build-up, dilemma, events, ending).
● Help the children to do the same with the book they are reading for homework.
● Read chapter one of *Mrs Frisby and the Rats of NIMH* (or your chosen book), then model how to write a reading journal entry for that chapter (except Comparisons), encouraging the children's contributions.
● Give particular attention to the skills of writing a personal response. Explain that it can include one or more of the following:

> ● *appreciation*, for example, I liked the scene where...
> ● *empathy*, for example, Timothy's illness reminded me of the time when I was ill...
> ● *evaluation*, for example, I thought the characters were very true to life because...

● Introduce the word anthropomorphic. Explain that it means describing animals as though they had human characteristics. Ask the children if they can think of other animal stories in which the animals speak, wear clothes or behave like people (such as Russell Hoban's *The Mouse and His Child* and the classic *Wind in the Willows* by Kenneth Grahame). How many animal stories can they think of where the animals behave 'naturally'? (One of the best examples is *Tarka the Otter* by Henry Williamson.)

Differentiation

Less able
● Ask children to focus on the appreciation and empathy aspects of personal response.

More able
● Encourage children to include some evaluation (with reasons and explanations) in the personal response.

Guided and independent work

● Ask the children to write their own journal entries based on the model (which should be removed from display). Tell them that you are particularly interested in their personal responses and their questions. (Tell them to omit *Comparisons* at this stage.)
● When the children have finished their entries, ask them to share and discuss each other's questions.

Plenary

● Share the children's personal responses and try to discuss similarities and differences in opinion.
● Ask the children to share any unanswered questions and talk about them briefly.

Comparisons

Objectives

NLS
T5: To compare and contrast the work of a single writer.
T8: To use a reading journal effectively to raise and refine personal responses to a text and prepare for discussion.
S3: To revise formal styles of writing: the use of the passive.

What you need
● The group text (such as *Greyfriars Bobby*)
● Robert C O'Brien's *Z for Zachariah* (Puffin).

Shared text-level work
● Tell the children that they are going to begin their reading journals on their group text.
● Read the beginning of *Greyfriars Bobby* (up to *…he was ready for any adventure*), then model how to write a reading journal entry for this section, again omitting the *Comparisons* section for now.
● Ask the children to compare and contrast this story with the shared text you are using. If you are using *Mrs Frisby and the Rats of NIMH*, the main contrasts are:

● Mrs Frisby and her family are like a human family and they speak. Bobby is more like a real animal. He doesn't talk, he behaves like a dog, and he has a human master.
● *Mrs Frisby and the Rats of NIMH* is set in an imaginary vegetable garden. *Greyfriars Bobby* is set in a real place – Edinburgh.

Shared sentence-level work
● Write out an example of a passive sentence from this extract, for example, *The market was closed*. Ask the children why the author put this sentence in the passive. (We don't know who closed it. Indeed, it was probably no-one in particular, but all the stallholders closing together because it was time.)
● Ask the children to make the sentence active by telling them that it was the Beadle who was responsible for such matters.

Guided and independent work
● Ask a group to read an extract from *Z for Zachariah*, and to compare it with *Mrs Frisby and the Rats of NIMH*. Is *Z for Zachariah* written for a different audience? How is this reflected in the language and style? Are there any similarities of approach between the two books? How can you tell that they are by the same author?
● Have copies of the book available for any children who would like to read the whole story.
● Ask the rest of the children to discuss in their groups the first chapter of their group text and then to write a reading journal entry for it.
● Ask them to complete the *Comparison* section of the reading journal for both books.
● Encourage them to discuss each other's questions.

Differentiation

Less able
● Ensure that the group text is well-matched to reading ability.

More able
● Ensure that the group text is suitably challenging, perhaps a classic like *The Wind in the Willows* by Kenneth Grahame, or *Tarka the Otter*.

Plenary
● Share some of the reading journal entries, and in particular discuss the comparisons with the shared text.
● Carry on reading the shared text over the next few weeks and ask the children to keep reading their group text at home. At appropriate points, ask the children to write reading journal entries for both of the books.
● Keep this work going in the background of other literacy work until both books have been read, then move on to Hour 3.

Author style

Objectives
T1: To describe and
evaluate the style of an
individual writer.
T7: To annotate passages
in detail in response to
specific questions.
S1: To revise the language
conventions and
grammatical features of
the different types of text
such as: narrative.

What you need
● *Mrs Frisby and the Rats
of NIMH.*

Shared text-level work
● Display and read an extract from your text to focus on author style
and themes. For example, you could use the scene in *Mrs Frisby and the
Rats of NIMH* in which Nicodemus explains how the rats were trained
(from *I won't go into details about the rest of our training...* to *...we seem
scarcely any older than we were then*).
● Annotate the text for features of Robert C O'Brien's style, taking
suggestions from the children. You could focus on the following points:

> ● The 'I' is Nicodemus. Most of the book is narrated in the third person, but a
> large section is narrated in the first person by Nicodemus.
> ● Simple, modern style of writing.
> ● The use of past tense and temporal connectives
> ● The use of dashes to add information and for dramatic effect.

● Demonstrate how to turn the annotations into a descriptive
paragraph, explaining that this skill will be needed in Hour 5:
Robert O'Brien uses a simple, modern style of writing. He writes in the
third person, but this section of the book is narrated by Nicodemus in
the first person. He uses dashes to suggest the excited way Nicodemus
tells his story. The author uses more formal, scientific language when Dr
Shultz speaks. His main theme is the effect of experiments on animals.

Shared sentence level work
● Go through the extract again and annotate it with a focus on story
language conventions and grammatical features of narrative (use a
different coloured pen to pick these out).

Guided and independent work
● Ask the children, working in pairs where possible, to choose another
extract from the shared text and to annotate it in the same way, for
stylistic features and presentation of themes.
● When they have finished analysing the extract, ask the children to
write up their annotations as a short paragraph. They will then have two
sources of detailed evidence as a basis for writing about the author's
style in Hour 5.

Plenary
● Discuss points of the author's style that the children have noted.
What themes could they identify? How do they think these will be
developed in the rest of the story?

Differentiation

Less able
● Check that children have
made useful annotations
before asking them to
write their paragraph.

More able
● Ask children to expand
their paragraph by
referring to examples from
elsewhere in the book.

Connections and contrasts

Objectives

NLS
T6: To look at connections and contrasts in the work of different writers.
T7: To annotate passages in detail in response to specific questions.
S2: To conduct detailed language investigations through research and reading, eg of language change over time, dialect.

What you need
● *Mrs Frisby and the Rats of NIMH*
● an extract from *Greyfriars Bobby* to show dialogue, dialect and old-fashioned vocabulary and realistic description, for example pages 106–107.

Shared text-level work
● Tell the children that they are going to compare and contrast the shared text with their group text. As several different group texts are in use, you are going to demonstrate this using *Greyfriars Bobby*. They will then be asked to apply the same approach to the text they are reading.
● Read your chosen extract to the children, and then annotate it together, focusing on the author's style and the themes of the story. For example, standard English is used for narration; Scottish dialect is used for much of the dialogue; Bobby is not an anthropomorphic animal character as he never speaks – his loyal behaviour is 'typical' and realistic of dogs.
● Now work with the children to turn the annotations into a descriptive paragraph, but make the focus of the paragraph comparisons between the two authors. For example:
Eleanor Atkinson's style is more difficult than Robert C O'Brien's style. She uses a lot of abstract and formal sentence constructions and old-fashioned vocabulary mixed with Scottish dialect. Her animal character, Bobby, is more true to real life. He does not talk and he behaves like a real dog does. Her main theme is the loyalty of dogs to their human owners.

Shared sentence-level work
● Go through the extract again to focus on story language conventions and grammatical features, such as the old-fashioned, sometimes abstract, language used in the narration, and the punctuation and layout features of dialogue. Ask the children to help you to annotate the text accordingly.

Guided and independent work
● Work with a group to investigate the Scottish dialect in *Greyfriars Bobby*. If you have the appropriate licences, photocopy an extended example of dialect from the book and ask the children to translate it into Standard English using the glossary at the back of the book.
● Ask the other children to work in pairs to choose an extract from their group text. Tell them to annotate it as demonstrated in shared work, and then turn the annotations into a paragraph comparing the style of that author with the style of the shared text.

Plenary
● Discuss the different authors' styles. What particular features have the children found?
● Are there any notable similarities across the books? What are the interesting contrasts?
● Of course, most of the groups will not have read the other books, so emphasise the point that many different styles lend variety and distinctiveness and ensure appeal to different readers. Explain that different author styles can all be equally effective if done well.

Differentiation

Less able
● Support the children to speak clearly in sentences by elaborating their words or phrases and by modelling complete sentences.

More able
● Encourage the children to use a greater range of vocabulary.

A written comparison

Objectives

NLS
T12: To compare texts in writing, drawing out: their different styles and preoccupations; their strengths and weaknesses; their different values and appeals to a reader.
S1: To revise the language conventions and grammatical features of the different types of text such as: narrative.

What you need:
● *Mrs Frisby and the Rats of NIMH*
● *Greyfriars Bobby*
● the children's reading journals and work from Hours 3 and 4.

Shared text-level work
● Explain to the children that they are going to produce a piece of extended writing in which they compare the two books they have read.
● Write the following headings on the board: *Plot, Author style, Characters, Settings, Themes, Personal response* and relate them to the books and the work done so far.
● Next, demonstrate how to write one or two sections of the 'essay'. The section on *Plot* could include three paragraphs:

> 1. Summary of the story of *Mrs Frisby and the Rats of NIMH*
> 2. Summary of the story of *Greyfriars Bobby*
> 3. Brief comparison of the two plots.

The section on *Author style* could include the same format:

> 1. Comments on Robert C O'Brien's style
> 2. Comments on Eleanor Atkinson's style
> 3. Brief comparison and evaluation of the two.

As you write, include a commentary like the following:

> Notice that I am keeping these summaries as short as possible by including only the most important events. Now that I have summarised each story, I am beginning to write a brief comparison...

Shared sentence-level work
● Point out how the subheadings and a paragraph structure are used to organise the material in the comparison on the board.

● Ask the children to identify connecting words and phrases, such as *but, later in the story, when, unfortunately...* and to consider how these will be useful in their own comparisons.

Guided and independent work
● Ask the children to write their own extended essays comparing the two animal stories they have been reading.
● Encourage them to help each other, for example by sharing out the sections of the essay amongst the group and by discussing their work as they go along.
● Remind the children to draw upon their reading journals and work done earlier in the week. For example, the section on *Author styles* uses ideas from work done in Hours 3 and 4 but is modified to include information from the rest of the book.

Differentiation

Less able
● Break down this long task into more manageable chunks, either by sharing the work out or by reducing the number of headings (omit *Characters, Settings* and *Themes*).

More able
● Ask more able children to include a final section in which they evaluate the strengths and weaknesses of each book.

Plenary
● Use the essays as the basis for a discussion of comparisons of authors.
● Ask the children what they enjoyed most in the different animal stories and what they found the most uninteresting or difficult.
● Finally, ask them how reading and analysing another story alongside the shared text helped them to appreciate both stories more fully.

UNIT 6

Extended narrative

This unit follows on from the animal stories in unit 5. It uses 'story cubes' as a fun way of inspiring children's own ideas for animal stories. Prepare sets of story cubes by pasting the squares from photocopiable pages 179-182 onto the faces of dice, or the children could make their own. If time is very limited, children could simply roll dice and refer the number to the appropriate square on the sheet. Hours 1 to 3 introduce the three main story cubes that focus on animals, settings and plot. Hour 4 offers the children another way of finding inspiration for plots. This can be omitted if time is limited, to allow more time for writing. However, in view of the requirement for the stories to be 'extended', and the NLS suggested allocation of three weeks for this unit, it would be a good idea to allow another whole week for writing and redrafting.

Hour	Shared text-level work	Shared word-/sentence-level work	Guided and independent work	Plenary
1 Animal characters	Devising a story around a randomly chosen character.	Experimenting with complex sentences.	Brainstorming animal story words; describing animal characters.	Sharing descriptions and discussing stereotypes.
2 Settings	Developing a story from a setting.	Revising the use of pronouns.	Making animal word cubes; describing settings.	Thinking of story potential from settings.
3 Plot cubes	Developing a whole story; revising storytelling techniques.	Revising story language and structures.	Making up a story and preparing it for telling to the class.	Storytelling.
4 Proverb cubes	Using proverbs in stories.	Brainstorming animal similes.	Repeating storytelling game, with proverbs.	Storytelling; discussing which cube generated best stories.
5 Extended narrative	Bringing ideas together to make a longer story.	Developing story vocabulary.	Planning stories.	Sharing ideas; writing blurbs.

Key assessment opportunities
● Can the children describe and develop characters and settings?
● Can they tell stories orally?
● Do they collaborate in producing oral and written narratives?
● Have they written an extended story?

UNIT 6 HOUR 1 ▢ Extended narrative

Animal characters

Objectives

NLS
T14: To write an extended story, worked on over time on a theme identified in reading.
S4: To secure control of complex sentences, understanding how clauses can be manipulated to achieve different effects.

What you need

● One *Animals* story cube for each group and a blank cube for the more able group.

Shared text-level work

● Show the *Animals* cube to the children and demonstrate how to use it. Roll it like a dice to select an A animal (to be the protagonist, or hero). Roll again for a B animal (the antagonist, or enemy).
● The next step is to give each animal a name and decide what it is like (male/female, young/old, brave, wise, cunning and so on).
● Finally, write a brief description of each animal. For example:
(3A Dog) Madison is a female Husky puppy. She has a white coat with streaks of grey and big grey eyes. She is very lively and strong and loves to fight with other puppies. She likes it best when it is cold, and is in heaven when it snows.

Shared sentence level work

● Examine the sentences in the example. The first is short – one clause. The three following sentences are compound, each with two clauses joined by *and*.
● Ask the children to experiment by recombining the information in different ways, for example, *Madison is a female Husky puppy who has a white coat with streaks of grey and big grey eyes...* The first and second sentences are joined into a longer complex sentence using the relative pronoun *who*.

Guided and independent work

● Work with a group to brainstorm useful words for animal stories (see examples below). Explain that they should try to devise six lists, each containing ten words. These lists will be useful for oral descriptions of the animals in the work below. (Share this work between groups here and in Hour 2.)

● Adjectives: furry, scaly.
● Movement verbs: fluttered, slithered.
● Movement adverbs: sluggishly, swiftly.
● Sound verbs: quacked, whinnied.
● Speech adverbs: gruffly, squeakily.

● Kinaesthetic learning: in groups of four, ask each of the other children to roll the cube twice to select an A animal and a B animal. They should then make up a name and a description for each animal and describe them orally to the rest of the group. Finally, each child should write a description of his or her two animals.

Differentiation

Less able
● Ask children to choose and describe an A animal only.

More able
● Give a more able group a blank cube and ask them to make up another set of animals, for example, dinosaurs, jungle creatures, minibeasts, sea creatures.

Plenary

● Share the descriptions and discuss the extent to which we stereotype animals as good, bad, cunning, wise and so on. How can we modify the game to avoid stereotyping? (One way would be to choose two animals first, and then flip a coin to decide which is to be the hero and which the enemy.)
● Discuss well-known animal poems and stories that use stereotypical traits, such as *The Hare and The Tortoise*.

UNIT 6 HOUR 2 ▢ Extended narrative

Settings

Objectives

NLS
T14: To write an extended story, worked on over time on a theme identified in reading.
S4: To secure control of complex sentences, understanding how clauses can be manipulated to achieve different effects.

What you need
● One *Settings* cube for each group and a blank cube for the more able group.

Shared text-level work
● Tell the children that, today, they are going to continue their animal stories, this time getting ideas for settings with a *Settings* cube.
● Show the *Settings* cube to the children and ask a volunteer to roll the cube once to pick an A setting (a good environment for animals) and then roll the cube again to pick a B setting (a bad place for animals to be).
● Ask the children to suggest names for particular places within the settings or for the settings themselves, and to fill in the details.
● Ask them to help you to write a brief description of the first setting. This could be something like:
(3A Hedgerow) The thorny hedgerow has stood between Farmer Oak's upper field and Farmer Boldwood's lower field for over a hundred years. It is a wonderful place for small animals to live. It provides a good safe site to build nests and gives cover for burrows and sets, as well as food such as blackberries, gooseberries and insects.
● Repeat the process with the B setting.

Shared sentence-level work
● Help the children to understand how the pronouns in the paragraph above are used to link the sentences and avoid unnecessary, awkward repetition.
● Ask the children what each pronoun replaces (it replaces hedgerow) and how the paragraph would sound with the repeated word instead of the pronoun (clumsy and repetitive).

Guided and independent work
● Continue guided work as Hour 1, making the cubes if this hasn't been done already.
● Kinaesthetic learning: ask the other children to continue in their groups of four, taking it in turns to roll the cube twice to select their settings and make up a name and a description for each setting to describe orally to the rest of the group, and relate them to the animals they wrote about in Hour 1. Finally, each child should write a description of his or her two settings.

Differentiation

Less able
● Tell children to select and describe an A setting only.

More able
● Give a more able group a blank cube and ask them to create other settings to match their animals from Hour 1, for example, Jurassic jungle, rainforest, rock garden, ocean.

Plenary
● Share the children's descriptions of their settings and discuss the plot potential of some or all of them. For example, what might happen to an old hedge dividing two fields? What hazards would a road present to animals?

UNIT 6 HOUR 3 🔲 Extended narrative

Plot cubes

Objectives

NLS
T14: To write an extended story, worked on over time on a theme identified in reading.
S1: To revise the language conventions and grammatical features of the different types of text such as: narrative.

S&L
67 Drama: To devise a performance considering how to adapt the performance for a specific audience.

What you need
● One each of *Plot*, *Animals* and *Settings* cubes for each group.

Shared text-level work
● Remind the children of the preparatory story work done in the previous lessons. Tell them that today they are going to begin putting a whole story together, thinking of story plots using the *Plot* cube, and then using all three cubes for oral storytelling.
● Introduce the *Plot* cube and explain that the A sections contain six suggested subject matters for plots and the B section contains six plot devices (ways of structuring plots). Explain that the B sections will be used later and that for now, they will be concentrating on the A sections only.
● Roll the plot cube to give a plot, for example 4A Frankenstein. Discuss what kind of animal this might involve and how the animal might change. Will the change be good or bad? What happens next? How will the story end? What will happen to the animal?
● Now that you have shown the children how to use the *Plot* cube, demonstrate how to use the full story cube set for oral storytelling. Roll the *Animals* cube, the *Settings* cube and the *Plot* cube, and work with the children to make up a short story based on the result.
● Recap on key oral storytelling skills. For example, using story language, such as temporal connectives, not just saying *and then and then*, keeping the audience's attention by using different tones of voice and even different voices if characters are speaking, giving a structure to the story.

Shared sentence-level work
● Revise the stages of story structure and encourage the children to try to use them when making up their oral stories: opening, build-up, dilemma, events, ending.

Guided and independent work
● Tell the groups to familiarise themselves with the different plot suggestions on the cube before each child rolls all three cubes and makes up an oral story.
● The next step is to prepare one of the stories for presentation to the whole class. This could be presented by one child, or by all the children working together.
● Tell the children that they will be allowed three minutes for their story presentation, and that this could be a complete short story or part of a more detailed story.

Plenary
● Ask each group to present its story to the class. Ask the rest of the children to listen for the story presentation skills discussed in the shared session. Ask for comments from the class when each presentation has finished.
● Conclude by reminding the children of the features of a good oral story.

Differentiation

Less able
● Advise children to read their plot suggestion carefully as it is almost a complete plot in itself. They only have to add details.

More able
● Ask children to roll the *Plot* cube again to suggest plot devices (B sections).

Proverb cubes

Objectives

NLS
T14: To write an extended story, worked on over time on a theme identified in reading.
W7: To experiment with language, eg creating new words, similes and metaphors.

What you need
● The story cubes from photocopiable pages 179-182.

Shared text-level work

● Tell the children that they are going to look at an alternative way of getting plot ideas. They will also explore a wider range of animals and settings.

● Show the *Proverbs* cube to the children. Talk about what proverbs are (popular wisdom expressed in short sayings). Ask the children to share any they know, for example, *A stitch in time saves nine*, which is a traditional proverb advising that if you repair something when you first notice a problem it will be much easier than if you leave it.

● Explain that each face of the *Proverbs* cube contains two animal proverbs from different parts of the world. Talk about the meaning of each proverb.

● Explain that these proverbs often suggest plot ideas and can be used as an effective way of rounding off a story. Roll the cube and read the two proverbs that come up. Ask the children to choose one of them, and explain how it could be developed into a story. For example, if you choose *4A Cross in a crowd and the crocodile won't eat you*, the proverb could be treated literally, that is, it could form the ending of a story about a group of small animals, perhaps monkeys, which are in danger of being eaten when they cross the river. They solve the problem by crossing in a crowd making lots of noise, which confuses and frightens the crocodile. However, it is probably more fun to treat the proverb metaphorically: it could be part of a story about a group of rabbits who face danger crossing a busy road, but they solve the problem when they cross in a large crowd, forcing the traffic to stop.

Shared word-level work

● Brainstorm a list of animal similes with the children: *as blind as a bat, as busy as a bee* and metaphors, such as *a fish out of water, a snake in the grass* and so on.

● Encourage the children to make up their own animal similes and metaphors and to explain them if necessary.

● Finally, discuss what story ideas can be drawn from the various similes and metaphors generated.

Guided and independent work

● Ask the children to repeat the oral storytelling game, but using the *Proverbs* cube instead of the *Plot* cube.

● Again, ask the groups to choose and prepare a story for telling to the class.

Differentiation

Less able
● Advise children to plan their story 'backwards' from the proverb-ending.

More able
● Challenge children to adapt the proverbs to suit the alternative characters and settings they are using.

Plenary

● Enjoy each group's storytelling.

● Discuss any similarities or differences between the group stories.

● Briefly discuss whether the *Plot* cube or the *Proverbs* cube inspired the best story.

Extended narrative

Objectives

NLS

T10: To write a brief synopsis of a text, eg, for a back cover blurb.

T14: To write an extended story, worked on over time on a theme identified in reading.

W6: To practise and extend vocabulary.

S&L

60 Group discussion and interaction: To understand and use a variety of ways to criticise constructively and respond to criticism.

What you need

● A full set of story cubes
● the children's descriptions from Hours 1 and 2.

Shared text- and word-level work

● Explain to the children that this lesson brings together the best ideas that they have thought of or heard during the week so that they can write an extended animal story.

● Tell them that they should work in pairs, sharing the writing of different chapters and acting as response partners during the redrafting process. Display guidance like the following and briefly explain it where necessary:

● Aim to write around 1000 words.

● Choose characters and settings drawing on work from Hours 1 and 2 if desired, or choosing completely new characters and settings.

● Develop a plot using ideas from the *Plot* cubes and/or *Proverb* cubes.

● Include one or more of the plot devices on the *Plot* cubes.

● Use the animal stories read in Unit 5 as models for writing.

● Use a range of sentence types and lengths of sentences.

● Write in paragraphs and construct chapters.

● Include dialogue between the characters and observe the conventions for punctuating and setting out dialogue.

● Make use of the word cubes made by the guided groups to enhance the vocabulary in the story.

● Redraft the story with the help of a response partner, and be a response partner yourself, providing polite and supportive criticism and suggestions for improvement.

● Present the final draft as an illustrated booklet (perhaps using images from photocopiable pages 179 and 180).

● Use the *Plot* cubes to remind the children of different plot devices and discuss how they could be applied to different story ideas. Note that the story idea and plot device are linked, though are also fully interchangeable.

Guided and independent work

● Ask the children to start planning their stories. This should include the main characters and settings, and an outline of the plot showing the opening, build-up, dilemma, events and ending. It should also include a detailed paragraph breakdown and a note about who will write each paragraph.

Differentiation

Less able
● Set pairs a lower word limit, perhaps 500 words, and help them to organise their collaboration.

More able
● Ask pairs to base their story on their alternative characters and settings and to aim for an increased word limit (perhaps 1500 words).

Plenary

● Ask each pair to share their story plans. Encourage discussion and allow children to make notes of each other's ideas that might suit their stories.

● Here, or as a follow-up exercise in an additional hour, ask the children to exchange stories with a partner and to write a blurb for the story. Remind them that a blurb should summarise at least the beginning of the plot, to make the reader want to read the story, but mustn't give away the ending.

Story cubes – animals

1A Badger

1B Bat

2A Horse

2B Crow

3A Dog

3B Fox

4A Mouse

4A Rat

5A Owl

5B Snake

6A Pig

6B Wolf

TERM 3

Story cubes – settings

1A Field

1B City

2A Forest

2B Factory

3A Hedgerow

3B Field of GM crops

4A Mountain

4A Housing estate

5A Country lane

5B Motorway

6A Riverbank

6B Nuclear power station

Story cubes – plots

1A Cruel treatment
An animal is badly treated and escapes. Will it be recaptured or find a happy new home?

1B Quest
A series of adventures leading to the fulfilment of a goal.

2A Environmental destruction
The animals' environment is destroyed. How do they survive? Where do they go? What adventures do they have? Do they find another habitat that is as good?

2B Circular
The story ends where it began, for example, if the animals in this story found a home like the one they left.

3A Best friend
An animal and a human are best friends, but something goes wrong – what is it? Does the human get a new toy, a new pet, a new friend? Does a parent send the animal away? Do they get back together? How?

3B Flashback
When the narrative jumps into the past. The human (or animal) could have flashbacks to the experience before the change.

4A Frankenstein
An animal eats GM crops and changes. Is the change good or bad? Does the animal become an evil monster, or a super-intelligent being? What happens as a result of the change? Does the animal return to normal?

4A Twist
An unexpected ending, often the opposite of what was expected. Perhaps the 'evil monster' turns out to be a force for good.

5A Metamorphosis
A human and an animal change places. What happens? What do they learn about each other's lives? How do they get back into their own bodies?

5B Parallel plot
A story with two strands, the narration switching from one to the other. For example, alternate chapters could tell the story from the human's and the animal's point of view.

6A Saved
An animal saves its owner. What is the danger that the animal saves the human from? How does it do it? What happens next?

6B Cliffhanger
A situation (usually near the climax of a story) where there is extreme suspense. The cliffhanger could be the moment just before the animal saves its owner.

TERM 3

Story cubes – proverbs

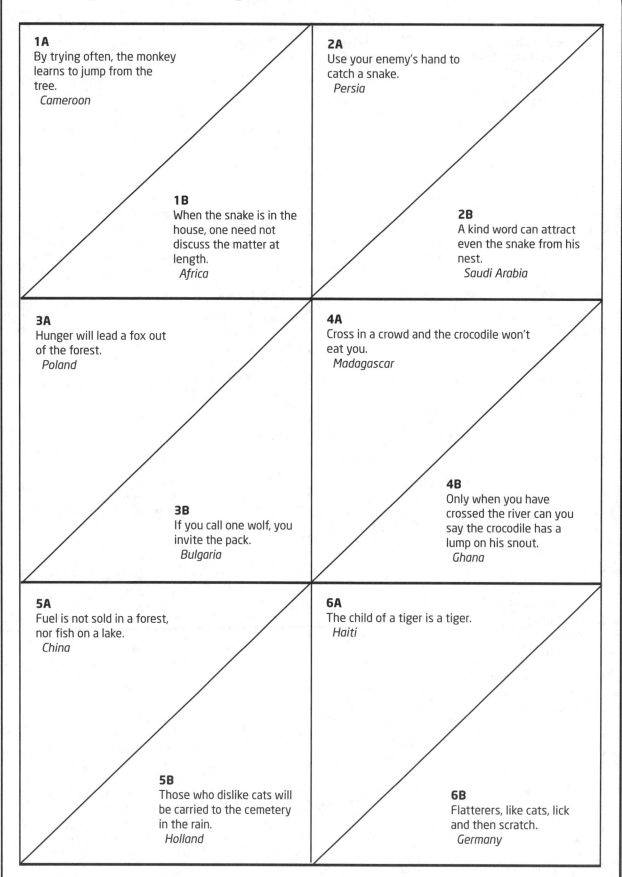

1A
By trying often, the monkey learns to jump from the tree.
Cameroon

1B
When the snake is in the house, one need not discuss the matter at length.
Africa

2A
Use your enemy's hand to catch a snake.
Persia

2B
A kind word can attract even the snake from his nest.
Saudi Arabia

3A
Hunger will lead a fox out of the forest.
Poland

3B
If you call one wolf, you invite the pack.
Bulgaria

4A
Cross in a crowd and the crocodile won't eat you.
Madagascar

4B
Only when you have crossed the river can you say the crocodile has a lump on his snout.
Ghana

5A
Fuel is not sold in a forest, nor fish on a lake.
China

5B
Those who dislike cats will be carried to the cemetery in the rain.
Holland

6A
The child of a tiger is a tiger.
Haiti

6B
Flatterers, like cats, lick and then scratch.
Germany

MSCHOLASTIC

UNIT 7

Impersonal writing

In this unit the children read and write three types of impersonal writing: explanations, reports and reviews. The subject matter is the pieces of hi-tech equipment that play such an important part in the modern world. Children are also asked to invent their own modern devices as a basis for writing reports and reviews.

Hour	Shared text-level work	Shared word-/sentence-level work	Guided reading/writing	Plenary
1 DVD	Reading explanation text and identifying genre features.	Investigating use of passive voice.	Comprehension exercise.	Going over answers to comprehension.
2 Own explanation	Revising explanation genre for own writing.	Discussing details of impersonal style.	Explaining how a hi-tech product works.	Evaluating children's explanation texts.
3 Sunglasses with a better view	Reading a non-chronological report, annotating genre features.	Picking clauses out of sentences.	Thinking of new uses for (imaginary) hi-tech product.	Sharing ideas.
4 Own report	Revising report genre.	Examining use of different tenses.	Inventing and reporting on a new product.	Reading the reports.
5 Review	Talking through features of a review.	Thinking of better name for product.	Writing product reviews for magazine readers.	Sharing reviews; voting for favourite invention; recapping on features of impersonal writing.

Key assessment opportunities
● Can the children recognise key features of different genres and retrieve information efficiently?
● Can they write with the appropriate language, style and impersonal tone?
● Do they manage complex sentences and use the passive voice to good effect?

DVD

Objectives

NLS

T16: To identify the key features of impersonal formal language, eg the present tense, the passive voice and discuss when and why they are used.
T17: To appraise a text quickly and effectively; to retrieve information from it; to find information quickly and evaluate its value.
S3: To revise formal styles of writing: the impersonal voice; the use of the passive; management of complex sentences.

What you need
● Photocopiable page 189.

Shared text-level work
● Introduce photocopiable page 189 and ask the children what key features of explanation texts they can remember. (They explain how or why something happens, in sequence. They usually contain connectives expressing cause and effect and time. The passive tense often occurs in this kind of writing.)
● Read the text, then go through it again to identify and annotate typical genre features.

Shared sentence-level work
● Investigate the use of the passive voice in the text.
● Remind the children how passive sentences are formed: the subject and object change places, and the verb changes to match, for example, *Dog bites man – Man is bitten by dog.*
● Explain that the choice of active or passive is sometimes a matter of emphasis, but often the passive is the only form that can be used if no subject is given.
● Ask the children to make the clause, *DVDs are made in the same way*, active by using the subject *they*. (*They make DVDs in the same way.*)
● Finally, find other examples of passive sentences in the text.

Guided and independent work
● Work with one group to investigate impersonal text features. (The writer is not present – he never refers to himself or expresses his opinions. The style is anonymous – any educated person could have written it. The style is formal, with many complex sentences, passive sentences and technical terms.)
● Ask the rest of the children, working in pairs, to retrieve the following information from the text and write individual responses.

● What does the abbreviation DVD stand for?
● What is the difference between a DVD and a CD?
● How is information stored on CDs and DVDs?
● What process is used to fit a full-length film onto a DVD?
● Name four different materials used in the manufacture of DVDs.

Differentiation

Less able
● Ask children to use the diagram to help to understand paragraph three.

More able
● Give this more challenging alternative to question five: Rewrite paragraph three so that the explanation can be understood by younger children.

Plenary
● Go over the information retrieval exercise. Most of the questions involve finding and restating specific information. An answer to the question for more able children might read something like:
A DVD records information as pits and bumps that are protected by layers of plastic, aluminium and gold. The information is read by a laser beam that turns the pit and bumps into information for a DVD player or a computer. DVDs are sturdy, but greasy marks or scratches can make them jump.
● Evaluate the article by discussing whether it help the children to understand how a DVD worked. Were any parts too difficult to understand? Was there anything else they wanted to know?

Own explanation

Objectives

NLS
T20: To secure control of impersonal writing, particularly the sustained use of the present tense and the passive voice.
S3: to revise formal styles of writing: the impersonal voice; the use of the passive; management of complex sentences.
W6: To practise and extend vocabulary.

What you need
● Photocopiable page 189
● a selection of up-to-date reference books and encyclopedias, and/or internet access.

Shared text-level work
● Tell the children that they are going to write their own explanation of a modern hi-tech device. Explain that their audience will be children about two years younger than themselves, so they don't need to have a great deal of technical knowledge about the product. If they are unsure about how their chosen device works, they can look it up but stress that they are not allowed to copy directly from source material.
● Display and briefly revisit photocopiable page 189 to revise the explanation genre and the type of produce to be described. Explain that their final text will have similar layout features:

● subheadings
● a logical sequence of separate paragraphs
● diagrams.

● Explain too that you want the language they use to be similar to the example, though simpler because it is for a younger audience. So, it will use:

● mainly the present tense
● a formal and impersonal tone
● the passive voice and complex sentences where appropriate
● connectives
● technical terms.

● Point out examples (or encourage the children to) of the above features in the text on photocopiable page 189 to reinforce the children's understanding.

Shared sentence-level work
● Ask the children who worked with you in Hour 1 to explain what is meant by impersonal style.

Guided and independent work
● Ask the children to work in pairs to choose an existing hi-tech device and to write a simple explanation of how it works. Suggest that they could get an idea by thinking of a favourite hobby and devices that might improve it, or of different areas of the house and how they could be automated. The next step is to try out these ideas in group discussion and choose the best. Finally, the children should think of the materials that the device is made from and how it might be manufactured. Is it a personal (small) product or something more 'domestic' and so larger?

Differentiation

Less able
● Ask children to focus on how their device is used rather than how it works.

More able
● Tell children to write for an older audience and to use a range of complex and passive sentences.

Plenary
● Ask some children to read out their explanations. Ask the rest of the class to evaluate how helpful they are. Have they got the language level right for the intended audience? Have they missed out any important information?

UNIT 7 HOUR 3 ▢ Impersonal writing

Objectives

NLS
T16: To identify the key features of impersonal formal language, eg the present tense, the passive voice and discuss when and why they are used.
S3: To revise formal styles of writing: the impersonal voice; the use of the passive; management of complex sentences.
S4: To secure control of complex sentences, understanding how clauses can be manipulated to achieve different effects.
S&L
65 Speaking: To use techniques of dialogic talk to explore ideas.

What you need
● Photocopiable page 190.

Sunglasses with a better view

Shared text-level work
● Show photocopiable page 190 to the children and explain that it is an example of a report on a new hi-tech invention.
● Ask the children what they can remember about the key features of reports. (A non-chronological text that describes or classifies. It often begins with a general classification, moving to a description of particular characteristics with a final summary. It is often written in the continuous present tense and is usually formal, impersonal and will make use of complex sentences and the passive voice.)
● Read the text to the children, then go through it together, annotating examples typical of the report genre.
● Ask the children who the intended audience of the report is and how can they tell? (It is aimed at the professional business person. Business users and business meetings are mentioned several times.)

Shared sentence-level work
● Examine the complex sentence structure of the third sentence:
Originally intended for the business user, they are designed to be plugged into a laptop computer so that sensitive data can be kept private.
Show that it consists of three clauses:
1. they were originally intended for the business user
2. they are designed to be plugged into a laptop computer
3. they keep sensitive data private (they refers to the TMF Spectacles).
● Encourage the children to experiment with different ways of ordering and joining these clauses, for example:
The TMF Spectacles, which were originally intended for the business user, keep sensitive data private because they are designed to be plugged into a laptop computer.
Discuss the results.

Guided and independent work
● Organise the children to work in groups of four. Ask them to imagine that the marketing department of ModoFi Inc has asked them to think of two new uses for the TMF Spectacles that are not mentioned in the report. Mention that these will give two new selling points and perhaps a wider base of potential customers. Specify that one of the uses should be for business and one for pleasure.
● Tell the groups to be prepared to present their ideas in the plenary session and that you will be listening for good group work and organised discussion.

Differentiation

Less able
● Tell the less able group to think of two new uses for pleasure only.

More able
● Challenge this group to think of two new devices that can be added on to the original product.

Plenary
● Ask each group to present its ideas. Where ideas are the same, give particular credit to the best realisation of the idea. Announce that the winning group will receive a free TMF Spectacles multi-pack and a free trip to New York! (Only joking!)

Own report

Objectives

NLS
T20: To secure control of impersonal writing, particularly the sustained use of the present tense and the passive voice.
S3: To revise formal styles of writing: the impersonal voice; the use of the passive; management of complex sentences.
W7: To experiment with language, eg creating new words.

What you need
● Photocopiable page 190.

Shared text-level work
● Tell the children that they are going to invent a new hi-tech device and then write a report on it.
● Display photocopiable page 190 and explain that their report will have similar layout features including a labelled diagram and structured paragraphs. Reiterate that as well as the layout, the language should be suitable for the intended audience, and the product, and include key features of report writing:

● introduction to orientate the reader
● non-chronological organisation
● mainly present tense (present simple and present continuous)
● formal and impersonal
● use of complex sentences and passive voice where appropriate.

Shared sentence-level work
● Introduce or revise the difference between the present simple and present continuous tenses and identify examples in the text.
● Practise the tenses orally by saying phrases in the present simple for the children to convert into the present continuous, for example, *I watch television – I am watching television.*
● Add time phrases to show that the present simple is mainly used to describe habit, and the present continuous is used to describe what is happening now: *I walk to the station every morning; I am watching television at the moment.*
● In addition, ask the children to identify the future tense formed with the auxiliary verb will.

Guided and independent work
● Visual learning: ask the children, sharing ideas in groups, but producing individual work, to invent a new product that makes use of the latest technological advances. Then tell them to imagine that they have seen it displayed at a trade fair and are writing a report about it. The audience for the report should be the likely user.
● Ask the children to begin by drawing a labelled diagram, then write their report.
● Tell them that the lesson will be followed up with a competition to find the most useful invention.

Differentiation

Less able
● Help less able children to plan their report in two parts: describe the device by explaining each label on the diagram, then describe its uses.
● Suggest that they choose a device for a child or teenager.

More able
● Ask children to create a device for a sophisticated adult user.

Plenary
● Choose some children to read their reports. Discuss them briefly to see if they give a good idea of the product. What do the children think of the products?
● Explain that at the end of the week all of the reports will be posted on a noticeboard and that each child will be given one coloured pin. Time will be given to browse the noticeboard and to stick the pin into the report on the most useful invention. The report with the most pins is the winner.

Review

Shared text-level work

● Tell the children that they are going to swap the reports they wrote in Hour 4 and write a review of their partner's invention.

● Display photocopiable page 191 and explain that it is a review of the TMF Spectacles that they read about in Hour 3. Read the text to the children.

● Explain that this review has most of the features of a report except that it is a little more personal and informal in style and as a result uses no passive sentences. Ask the children to identify the following features and annotate them on the text:

> ● introduction to orientate the reader
> ● non-chronological structure
> ● present tense (present simple and present continuous)
> ● complex sentences.

● Above all, point out how important it is to use the imagination when writing a review of the gadget.

● Look through the report again and find examples where the writer has used his imagination. For example, he imagined:

> ● what would be in the box, even down to the charger and guarantee
> ● what the device would look like –adding that it was larger than expected
> ● what it would be like to use
> ● what problems there might be.

Shared word-level work

● Ask the children if they can think of a better name for the TMF Spectacles. Suggest they use known roots, prefixes and suffixes to invent new words, for example, *Cyberspecs, Minicine, Spectop Theatre*.

Guided and independent work

● Ask the children to exchange their reports from Hour 4 with their partners. They should then read very carefully the report they have received and talk about it with the person who wrote it.

● The next step is to write a review, using their imagination to add interesting details as in the example on photocopiable page 191. Ask the reviewers to end with a star rating out of five. The review should be aimed at a specific audience - magazine readers who may be interested in buying the product.

Plenary

● Share some of the reviews and ask the rest of the class to evaluate how 'realistic' they are. How well have they used their imagination to give the impression that they really have tried out the device?

● Remind the children of the display where they will see which is the favourite product.

● Pull the unit together by recapping on key features of impersonal writing, particularly the sustained use of the present tense, the passive voice and complex sentences.

How DVDs work

The DVD, which was introduced in March 1997, is a development of the CD. The abbreviation DVD used to mean Digital Video Disk, but when they began to be used for other purposes, such as data storage, the name was changed to Digital Versatile Disk. 'Versatile' means that it can do lots of things, and this is a good description, as DVDs are now used for video, music and data storage, and have recently been introduced in a recordable format.

Outwardly a DVD looks just like a CD, but that's where the similarity ends. DVDs are made in the same way, but a DVD can hold seven times more information, enough to store a complete film. However, the film still has to be compressed to make it fit. This is done using MPEG-2 encoding. Basically, this 'freezes' the parts of the film that are not moving, such as the background. This is done so cleverly that it is almost impossible to tell that a film has been compressed.

A DVD records information as a series of pits and bumps that are burned into the disk – a bit like an old wind-up gramophone, only much more sophisticated. These pits and bumps are the 0s and 1s that make up digital data. A DVD is built up from several layers of polycarbonate plastic. A thin layer of aluminium is placed behind the data layer and a very thin transparent gold layer is placed above. (It is very thin, so don't try to melt it down and spend it!) The layers are then sealed together with lacquer. The data is read by a laser beam, which is reflected off the pits and bumps and converted into information that the DVD player or computer can understand. Generally, DVDs are quite sturdy, but greasy marks or scratches can confuse the laser and cause the DVD to jump or not play properly.

A generation of DVDs is being developed that can store even more data. This will make it possible to store several films on one disk, or one film in a high definition format. You will also be able to store all your computer data and your entire music collection on one DVD.

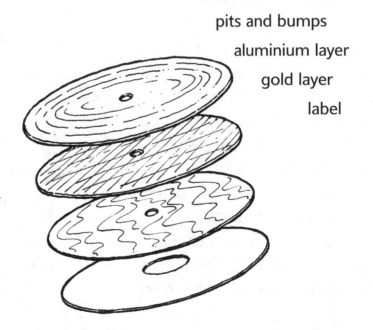

pits and bumps

aluminium layer

gold layer

label

TERM 3

Sunglasses with a better view

Next time you're bored at a business meeting, try some of these recently released ModoFi products.

ModoFi's TMF Spectacles look like ordinary sunglasses but instead of lenses, they have two tiny TMF screens. Originally intended for the business user, they are designed to be plugged into a laptop so that sensitive data can be kept private.

When the TMF specs are first used, they have to be focused. This is done by turning two small wheels at each side of the spectacles. The sound pods also have to be positioned correctly. This is done by carefully bending the stems of the pods until they are in the right position for your ears. The result is amazing. Because the TMF screens are so close to the eyes, the screen appears to be enormous – like sitting in the cinema. The sound is high-quality stereo, but with the right input, it can deliver full surround sound.

If all that sounds too good for the world of work, ModoFi has just released an add-on called the TMF Personal DVD Player. The DVD player is similar in size to a portable CD player and can be carried in a pocket or handbag. When linked to the TMF Spectacles, it allows the user to view movies in private – just the thing for long journeys, or, if your kids get hold of it – for school!

ModoFi is also working on a personal games player. This will consist of a pocket-sized games console controlled by a joypad which looks like a ballpoint pen. The company is also planning a version with wireless technology.

If you're thinking of buying one in time for your next business meeting, check your bank balance first. The TMF Spectacles alone retail at over £1000.

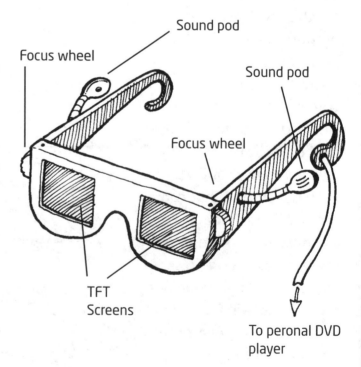

TFT Spectacles by Futuretech Inc.

The ModoFi personal DVD player

A review by Jack

This review of the ModoFi Personal DVD Player is based on a short trial that took place over a weekend. The ModoFi Personal DVD Player came in a large box containing:

- DVD player
- TMF Spectacles
- Laptop adaptor
- Recharger
- Demonstration DVD
- Instruction manuals, guarantee, etc.

The DVD player looked like any portable CD player, but I was more interested in the TMF Spectacles. At first, I was disappointed. They were bigger and heavier than I had expected. 'Goggles' would be a better word to describe them. It was certainly not possible to pretend they were ordinary glasses – so my idea of wearing them at school wouldn't work.

However, the screen did seem huge. It was just like sitting in the cinema. I tried the demonstration DVD and was very impressed by the quality. What I liked most was that whatever position you sat or lay in, the screen was always right in front of you – so you can watch a film in bed, or on the toilet, or even moving around (but be careful you don't bump into anything!).

The sound quality is excellent. It is like listening to a high-quality personal stereo. So it is possible to enjoy all those explosions, and monster roars without disturbing the rest of the family.

After using the TMF Spectacles for an hour, I began to get a headache, and I had to give my eyes a rest before carrying on with the film. My mum says it'll ruin my eyes, but then, she believes mobile phones fry your brains and microwave ovens are radioactive.

Another big disadvantage is the price: £1793.50, but, as with all brand new products, I expect the price will come right down in a year or two.

Overall, this is an excellent product. I can't wait to review their personal games player!

Verdict: ★★★★☆

In this series:

ISBN 0-439-97164-0
ISBN 978-0439-97164-5

ISBN 0-439-97165-9
ISBN 978-0439-97165-2

ISBN 0-439-97166-7
ISBN 978-0439-97166-9

ISBN 0-439-97167-5
ISBN 978-0439-97167-6

ISBN 0-439-97168-3
ISBN 978-0439-97168-3

ISBN 0-439-97169-1
ISBN 978-0439-97169-0

ISBN 0-439-97170-5
ISBN 978-0439-97170-6

To find out more, call: 0845 603 9091
or visit our website www.scholastic.co.uk